The Presidency of
MARTIN
VAN BUREN

AMERICAN PRESIDENCY SERIES

The Presidency of
MARTIN
VAN BUREN

Major L. Wilson

UNIVERSITY PRESS OF KANSAS

© 1984 by the University Press of Kansas

Published by the University Press of Kansas (Lawrence, Kansas 66045),
which was organized by the Kansas Board of Regents
and is operated and funded by Emporia State University, Fort Hays State
University, Kansas State University, Pittsburg State
University, the University of Kansas, and Wichita State University

Library of Congress Cataloging in Publication Data

Wilson, Major L.
The presidency of Martin Van Buren.

(American presidency series)
Bibliography: p.
Includes index.
1. Van Buren, Martin, 1782-1862.
2. United States—Politics and government—1837-1841.
I. Title.   II. Series.
E387.W54 1984   973.5'7'0924 [B]   83-17871
ISBN 0-7006-0238-0

Printed in the United States of America

To
Shannon and Morgan

CONTENTS

Foreword ix

Preface xi

1 A Restless Nation 1

2 The Road to the White House 21

3 The Panic of 1837 43

4 A Proposal of Divorce 61

5 The Meaning of Divorce 79

6 A Separation without Divorce 99

7 The Second Declaration of Independence 123

8 Peace with Honor 147

9 Running the Shop 171

10 The Last Step 191

Notes 213

Bibliographical Essay 233

Index 243

FOREWORD

The aim of the American Presidency Series is to present historians and the general reading public with interesting, scholarly assessments of the various presidential administrations. These interpretive surveys are intended to cover the broad ground between biographies, specialized monographs, and journalistic accounts. As such, each will be a comprehensive, synthetic work which will draw upon the best in pertinent secondary literature, yet leave room for the author's own analysis and interpretation.

Volumes in the series will present the data essential to understanding the administration under consideration. Particularly, each book will treat the then current problems facing the United States and its people and how the president and his associates felt about, thought about, and worked to cope with these problems. Attention will be given to how the office developed and operated during the president's tenure. Equally important will be consideration of the vital relationships between the president, his staff, the executive officers, Congress, foreign representatives, the judiciary, state officials, the public, political parties, the press, and influential private citizens. The series will also be concerned with how this unique American institution—the presidency—was viewed by the presidents, and with what results.

All this will be set, insofar as possible, in the context not only of contemporary politics but also of economics, international relations, law, morals, public administration, religion, and thought. Such a broad approach is necessary to understanding, for a presidential administration is more than the elected and appointed officers composing it, since its work so often reflects the major problems, anxieties, and glories of the nation. In short, the authors in the series will strive to recount and evaluate the record of each administration and to identify its distinctiveness and relationships to the past, its own time, and the future.

The General Editors

PREFACE

In a public letter accepting the nomination of the Democratic party to succeed Andrew Jackson as president, Martin Van Buren pictured himself "the honored instrument" of the administration party and vowed "to tread generally in the footsteps of President Jackson." Friends welcomed the statement as a pledge to defend the work of Jackson. Whig foes, by contrast, seized upon what they took to be the sycophantic tone of the statement and used it to furbish the image they had already cast of Van Buren as a "politician by trade," scheming for power. In mocking fashion they thus looked forward to nothing more than a "footsteps administration." When divested of partisan rhetoric, Van Buren's statement, and others of like tenor, have been taken by historians as texts for the persistent interpretation of his presidency as the "third term" of Jackson.

There is much to recommend the interpretation. Through Jackson's influence Van Buren became president, and with power came the task of defending the work of his predecessor. Unhappily for the new president, the panic of 1837 was part of the heritage, constituting in fact the central domestic event of his administration. His basic response to it, the proposal for the Independent Treasury, followed logically from Jackson's policies: Jackson had divorced the Treasury from the national bank; in Jackson's steps, Van Buren made the operations of the Treasury independent of the state banks as well. In 1840 he ran for reelection on the basis of the measure and assimilated it to all of Jackson's earlier policies in a platform, the first ever adopted by a national party.

But the concept of a third term must be qualified in several ways. As one of the principal architects of the Democratic party, on which Jackson's administration reposed, Van Buren helped to shape the heritage he was to defend. The way he formulated the policy for divorcing the Treasury from the banks, and the political tactics he used to get it passed, made it in large part his own. His avowed intention to veto any measure against slavery or in favor of a new national bank suggested the power of the presidency, which Jackson had done much to invigorate, yet his style and personality contrasted sharply with the Caesarian menace the Whigs found in Jackson. While carrying out the policy of Indian removal begun by his predecessor, Van Buren stood against most other expansionist tendencies in his party.

In this connection, Van Buren also addressed the rising sectional consciousness of the day, enlisting the support of northern party spokesmen against abolitionism and getting southern Democrats to surrender the demand for the immediate annexation of Texas. Relative success in securing sectional harmony was matched by peace with foreign nations. He soon resolved a crisis that Jackson had precipitated with Mexico, and he worked for peace with Britain at a time when the Maine boundary dispute and incidents arising from the Canadian rebellion threatened war. In the context of events, following in Jackson's steps meant taking steps of a far different kind. After the stormy administration of his predecessor, Van Buren sought a respite for the nation.

The sequel of events provides another perspective for seeing the distinctive quality of Van Buren's presidency. He suffered defeat in his bid for reelection in 1840 because of depressed economic conditions and the belief, pushed by Whig foes, that his policies abetted, if they did not actually cause, the downturn. His hopes for the nomination of his party in 1844, and thus for a chance to vindicate his defeat, were then dashed by many of the same forces he had sought to allay during his term. Central in his failure to receive the nomination was his opposition to the immediate annexation of Texas; with Jackson's blessing, the party turned, instead, to James K. Polk. Along with the call for Texas, Polk invoked the spirit of expansive nationalism to fulfill the destiny of the nation's movement westward to the Pacific. War with Mexico achieved the goal, but it also sparked a new and more fateful round of controversy over slavery, which was not resolved until the Civil War. Between the more dramatic presidencies of Jackson and Polk, that of Van Buren constituted an interim of relative order and repose.

In preparing this volume, I have acquired a number of debts. I am grateful to the editors of the American Presidency Series for assigning me the task. A summer grant from Memphis State University greatly facilitated early work, and a grant from the American Philosophical Society made possible later research trips. Librarians in the John Willard Brister Library at Memphis State University have been very supportive; and two colleagues, Gabor S. Boritt and C. Edward Skeen, gave valuable help at different stages of research and writing. The Department of History has also provided means for typing the manuscript.

Major L. Wilson

Memphis, Tennessee
May 1983

1

★ ★ ★ ★ ★

A RESTLESS NATION

In 1831 a distinguished visitor to the United States, Alexis de Tocqueville, found Americans to be a "restless people." The regnant ideal of equality at work on a relatively undeveloped continent, he supposed, had set the people in motion, generated a "spirit of enterprise," and given to their pursuits of happiness a very dynamic quality. The restless activity of its citizens meant dramatic growth for the nation and provided substance for the official credo of optimism and progress. New forms of economic, social, and political organization, evincing the principle of voluntary association, were a response to rapid change and gave order to the common life. For many at the time, President Andrew Jackson symbolized popular aspirations: his own rise from obscurity gave strength to the ideal of the self-made man; his policies removed the presumed obstacles of aristocracy and monopoloy in the way of freer development; and his claim to be the direct representative of the people lent strength to the presidency as the voice of a free and sovereign people.[1]

But the dynamic quality of the emerging order excited doubts and fears as well as hopes. By the mid 1830s, moreover, conservative misgivings about the tendencies of the day were enhanced by many particular instances of disorder. In the background was a new cycle of economic growth after 1830, which moved toward a speculative boom within five years and seemed to gain momentum from the effects of Jackson's policies. A rapid rise in consumer prices was one result, which contributed to a general sense of derangement and played a part in the

1

record number of strikes among workingmen. More generally, the incidence of mob action reached a peak by the end of Jackson's presidency and, in the view of many, bore a close relationship to Jackson's political style, which cast him as an "anarchic hero" or ultimate symbol of the sovereign individual. Mobs attacked gamblers, free Negroes, and slave dealers in the West and South; immigrant Irish workers on the canals and a Catholic convent in Massachusetts; a defaulted bank in Baltimore; a post office in South Carolina; and abolitionist meetings in the North.[2] At the same time the voice of abolitionism, the nullification controversy, and rising demands for the annexation of Texas raised greatly the level of sectional consciousness. It was with hopes and fears, in sum, that a restless nation in 1836 chose Martin Van Buren to succeed Jackson as president.

The country that Jackson was about to turn over to his successor had grown dramatically since George Washington had become the first president. The acquisition of Louisiana and Florida had greatly extended the nation beyond its original boundaries on the Mississippi River and the thirty-first parallel. The number of states had doubled; three of the twenty-six states were west of the Mississippi; and many people wanted to make Texas another. The population had increased about fourfold, from 4 million to nearly 16 million. More than one-third of the people lived west of the Appalachians, and Jackson's removal of the Indians had opened the way for the numbers to increase. Immigrants added to the movement of people, as around one-half million entered the United States during the 1830s, mainly from Ireland and Germany.

Central to the growth of the country was a process of economic development which accelerated greatly after the War of 1812. More than seven out of ten Americans were still farmers in the mid 1830s, it was true, but the pursuits of many of them were becoming increasingly dynamic as the "transportation revolution" drew more areas into the market economy. In the wake of turnpike construction, a canal boom, which was highlighted by the completion of the Erie Canal in 1825, connected the Atlantic to the Old Northwest and the Great Lakes to the Ohio and Mississippi rivers, amounting by 1840 to 3,326 miles. New York State was out front in the development of empire, and its port city boasted a population of about three hundred thousand. Meanwhile, steamboats plying the western river ways dramatically reduced freight charges and doubled the amount of cargo moving down to the Gulf of Mexico in each passing decade. Starting in 1830, railroads assured their future; they equaled canals in mileage by the end of the decade. Business enterprise grew in scale with the nationalizing tendency of the economy and increasingly took on a corporate form of organization. The extension of the factory system to most areas of production lay beyond 1840, but market forces had profoundly altered the older pattern. The merchant capitalist, with his knowledge of distant markets and control of materials, was transforming the earlier relationship of master and journeyman into an adversary one of capital and labor.[3]

Enhancing the long-term forces of change was a new cycle of economic growth after 1830, led by cotton but shared in all parts of the country. On the export side, cotton became "king": its earlier dominance as the leading export grew toward a peak, rising from 36 percent in 1830 to 55 percent six years later. At home, cotton was also king or, as a recent study has called it, the "carrier" industry which stimulated economic activity in other sections.[4] The foreign demand for cotton brought expansion in the Southwest and increased the pressure on the government to remove the Indians. This expansion in turn stimulated banking, shipping, and manufacturing interests back East and further migration into the Northwest. Added impetus was given through state aid to canal construction, and about two thousand miles were completed in the decade after 1830.

On the basis of solid economic growth, forces within the country led to excess or "overaction," to use the term of the day. The normal increase in the sale of public lands for cotton and foodstuffs grew by 1835 into a feverish mania of speculation. The statistics on revenue from public land were stunning, jumping from $4.9 million in 1834 to $24.9 million two years later and making 1836 the first and only year in which land revenues exceeded tariff revenues. Statistics on banking also reflected overaction. The number of banks increased from 330 in 1830 to 788 by the end of 1836; bank loans, from $200.5 million to $525.1 million; and bank notes, from $61.3 million to $149.2 million. A sharp rise in the price of goods followed in the wake of currency inflation. From the index figure of 100 for March 1835, wholesale prices rose steadily toward a peak of 131 by February 1837; and retail prices for most basic items doubled during the same period.[5]

Informed by the "spirit of enterprise," champions of economic progress swelled the chorus in its praise. But there were others to count the costs as well as the rewards. For them, an unchecked spirit of enterprise eroded the "virtue" of the people on which the republic depended; paper money to excess was somehow dishonest and unnatural; state tax money for internal improvements was a special benefit for the privileged few; and in corporate organization lurked a monopolistic threat to equal opportunity. While these ideas ofen expressed a moral concern about the direction in which the country was moving, they also signaled, in many instances, a threat to vital interests. An increase in paper money and bank loans might open opportunity for "credit seekers" on the make, but it also hurt "note takers," who related to the economy principally as consumers.[6] Large numbers of farmers and planters apparently identified in this way, seeing themselves passed over, not yet reached, or otherwise affected adversely by market forces.

Many eastern workingmen were also hurt. Among other goals, their unions sought to restore the older relationship of master and journeyman which merchant capitalists were disrupting. Membership in unions accordingly grew to an estimated three hundred thousand by the mid 1830s, and the National Trades Council for a time gave a united voice to workingmen's interests. Inflation added to their difficulties and contributed to a record number of strikes. Wages lagged behind prices, and payment in the notes of distant banks compounded the problem. At best, these notes were at some discount from par; at worst, they were actually worthless.[7] Clearly, there were elements in the nation which were adversely affected by the course of economic events.

Socially, the mobility of Americans was the feature in the restless nation which struck Tocqueville most forcibly. Indeed, to a French aristocrat rooted in space, the commonplace change of residence and occupation by so many people was simply amazing. His sympathy for the Indians who were being driven west of the Mississippi was understandable; but it also serves to underscore that concept of freedom which Jackson supposed had attracted Europeans to America in the first place and was now driving them across the continent. Tocqueville rightly sensed, however, an ambivalence about the process. If movement expressed the hopeful side of equalitarian ideals and boundless opportunity, it also generated anxieties as traditional values, larger family ties, and older social arrangements weakened or lost their hold.[8]

The further triumph of revivalism was a basic religious response to these concerns. Stretching from the turn of the century to a new peak of enthusiasm in the decade after 1825, the second Great Awakening constituted an organizing process, which offered salvation to the individual and fashioned new bonds of community. The intensity of emotionalism in the revivals, however disorderly in appearance, reflected a basic impulse to order. Charles G. Finney, the leading revivalist of the day, outlined the elements of new order remarkably well in his *Lectures on Revival*, published in 1835. Here the claim for free will and the opportunity for all to be saved marked the great advance of democracy over older Calvinist views. Nor did revivals have to await a "shower of grace" from God; rather, they could be precipitated by the revivalist through purely natural means. Revivalism thus became a profession, and the principle of voluntary association became more firmly established.[9] New religious bodies were formed during the awakening—Cumberland Presbyterians and the Disciples of Christ among them—while Methodists and Baptists moved toward the front rank in Protestant America.

Conservatives had deep misgivings about the erosion of Calvinist views, the vulgarity of revival methods, and the anti-intellectual tendency in them to contemn an educated ministry. But many embraced the new methods and sought to tame them. They also worked for a consensus about values underlying the diversity of religious bodies, thus hoping to make America a Christian nation. For this purpose, Congregational and Presbyterian evangelicals in the East created and sustained, in the period after the War of 1812, a number of new organizations—the American Bible Society, the American Home Missionary Society, the American Sunday School Union, and the American Tract Society. Of special concern for these "benevolent" organizations was the saving of the West.[10] One measure of the success in making America a Protestant nation was the increase in tensions with Catholics.

Another distinctive feature of life in democratic America was the "ferment of reform." At no other period in the nation's history have so many proposals for improvement been set forth. "We are all a little wild here with numberless projects of social reform," Ralph Waldo Emerson thus observed. Many new organizations mounted efforts on several fronts against a myriad of evils—intemperance, imprisonment for debt, inequality of women, the martial spirit, prostitution, lack of public education, wretched treatment of the helpless and insane, carnivorous eating habits, and the like. Most fateful of all was abolitionism. With the appearance of the *Liberator* in 1831, William Lloyd Garrison parted company with the gradualist emphases in earlier antislavery thought, branded slaveholding a sin, and called for an immediate remedy. Recent studies have found in most of these reform efforts a mix of hopes and fears—an imperative to realize democratic ideals and the impulse to social control. As in religion, efforts at social reform illustrated the working of the voluntary principle and the emergence of the professional reformer.[11]

Politics was also becoming a profession, as new party organization began to provide order to political life. Whig criticism of Van Buren as a "politician by trade" at once recognized the fact and expressed conservative doubts about it, doubts that evoked the earlier fears of party as a "faction" and a preference for leadership by patrician elites to whom the people deferred. But economic and social developments began to render older deferential patterns unacceptable or, in many cases, obsolete. The movement of people eroded the social bases of patrician rule and gave added strength to equalitarian ideals. By the 1820s most states had dropped property qualifications for white male voters and had adopted the practice of choosing presidential electors by popular vote. New party organization was an institutional response: it supplied a means for mobilizing the mass of voters, choosing officials, and defining issues. As family and partnership ventures gave way to corporate forms of business organization, parties did the same thing in the political sphere. In later years, Van Buren slyly admitted that parties resembled the "soulless corporations" that his party had so often scourged.

Out front in economic development, New York also led the way in shaping the new political order. Van Buren was a central figure in the process: to use the language of a recent study, he was one of the first and greatest "inventors" of parties. By 1819 conflict had matured between his "Bucktail" faction and the patrician leader, De Witt Clinton, for control of the Republican party. Success ultimately came through the power of organization, which drew new elements into the political process and forged unity by the attraction of spoils, the use of the caucus, and an ethos of absolute loyalty to the will of the majority. Van Buren's self-image as an "honored instrument" of party, which he had fashioned by the time of his nomination for president, actually described the outlook of his whole earlier career. Van Buren and his close associates had created by 1825 the so-called Albany Regency— essentially a political board of directors—which communicated downward to county and local committees and adopted the device of holding conventions at several levels in order to harmonize party councils. The *Albany Argus* stood at the head of a growing number of party papers in support of the cause. Meanwhile, parades, rallies, and other means of mass appeal made campaigning an exciting spectacle, not unlike religious revivals. With a rhetoric of antipartyism, foes opposed the process, but increasingly they were compelled to adopt the same methods.[12]

Although development came early in New York State, it did not serve as a precise model for organization elsewhere. Personalities, local issues, and circumstances simply varied too greatly from one state to another. There was a tendency in the Middle Atlantic States and in the Northwest for political maturity to advance along with that of economic development. But parts of New England were an exception to this trend, while much of the South did not have substantial party competition until the mid 1830s. Apart from local conditions, three related forces contributed to the extension of party competition into all parts of the country: intense contests for the presidency, debate over national economic policy, and the impact of rising sectional consciousness. Emerging in the 1820s and attaining considerable clarity under Jackson, the lines of party competition reached maturity during the presidency of Van Buren. Fuller consideration of these matters will reveal much about the state of the nation that he was to govern.

In part because of opposition to the War of 1812, Federalists were discredited as a national party, and their rapid decline brought to an end the "first party system." Many at the time welcomed its end and hailed the presidency of James Monroe as an "era of good feelings" above party strife. In fact, political conflict became intramural and often very sectional. The decline of the Federalists reduced external pressures on the Republicans and greatly weakened the internal discipline that Thomas Jefferson and James Madison had forged between its basic elements—the "planters" of the South and the "plain republicans" of the North. The Missouri controversy was one result, as many northern Republicans joined with surviving Federalists to oppose for a time the admission of a new Slave State. Meanwhile, elements within the Republican party were attracted to some of the national economic policies that Alexander Hamilton had set forth during the 1790s. In 1816 President Madison accordingly approved the creation of a new national bank and a protective tariff. But for constitutional scruples, moreover, he looked with favor on expenditures by the federal government for projects of internal improvement.

Politically, the era of good feelings ended in the disputed election of 1824. Because President Monroe had dropped the practice, used by Jefferson and Madison, of designating his successor through a caucus of party members in Congress, four Republicans sought to succeed him. Secretary of the Treasury William Crawford of Georgia claimed a large following of "Radicals," who were distinguished by their opposition to the nationalizing trend in the party and sought to restore the States' rights emphasis of old Republicans in the 1790s. Although he received the vote of the congressional caucus, others boycotted it and, with a new democratic rhetoric, brought it into disrepute. John Quincy Adams, Monroe's secretary of state, expected strong support from New England and from other areas that shared his views on national economic policies. A third candidate, Speaker Henry Clay of Kentucky, identified with these views and began to call them the American System of policies. Because of early strength shown by Jackson, Secretary of War John C. Calhoun gave up his bid for president in 1824 and settled for the vice-presidency. Jackson's views on policy were not very clear at the time; but his reputation as a hero won wide popular support and ninety-nine electoral votes, more than any other candidate. Since none had received a majority, however, the election went into the House, where Adams, who had come in second with eighty-four electoral votes, was chosen president, thanks in part to the support of Speaker Clay.

When Adams announced the appointment of Clay as secretary of state shortly after the election, Jacksonians raised the charge of ''bargain and corruption'' and set the stage for the presidential contest of 1828. Adams's presidency became, as a consequence, the forum of sustained political warfare and the reappearance of party lines. Adams and his supporters aligned under the National Republican banner and, in terms of policy, embraced the American System. The national bank, in this scheme, provided a sound and uniform currency for economic development and salutary restraints on the tendency of state banks toward excess. Tariff protection, begun in 1816 and increased in 1824, fostered domestic manufacture and enlarged the home market for farm goods. Within the system, Adams placed special emphasis on policies for land and internal improvements. Considering unsold government land a great national treasure, he wanted to put land up for public auction very slowly and thereby to receive a higher price for it. Part of the accumulating revenue from the lands was to be used in constructing road and canal projects; other of the revenues could be devoted to promoting education, science, and the arts. Finally, he was in no hurry to remove the Indians beyond the Mississippi. Among other things, their presence constituted an obstacle to rapid expansion and contributed to more solid economic development.

A coalition against Adams soon began to form, generally known by the name of Democratic Republican. The Jackson men of 1824 were the first in the field, determined to avenge the corrupt bargain that they now supposed had thwarted the true will of the people. Vice-President Calhoun was the most prominent figure to join the group; and the newspaper edited by his friend Duff Green, the *United States Telegraph*, became in 1826 the official organ of the opposition. A third group was made up of Crawford's followers, who were strong in Virginia, North Carolina, Georgia, and in New York among Van Buren's Bucktails. Assuming leadership for the group in Congress, Senator Van Buren needed all of his reputed political skills to smooth the way between the Crawfordites and Calhoun, their enemy of long standing.[13]

Policy differences no less than personal enmities existed within the new coalition, particularly in regard to the tariff. Jackson himself had favored the higher tariff in 1824, while the Crawford Radicals from the South had opposed it. Elsewhere it was thought by 1828 that the hopes for Jackson in the Middle Atlantic and western states depended on taking the tariff issue away from Adams. For this purpose, Van Buren pushed through Congress a new tariff bill, which had special appeal for the interests of these states. Meanwhile, Calhoun was in the process of rapidly retreating from his earlier nationalist positions toward a radical antitariff stand. In 1828 this position found full expression in his anonymously written pamphlet *The South Carolina Exposition and Protest,* which outlined the theory of nullification.

The campaign of 1828 ended in victory for Jackson, who received 56 percent of the popular vote and 184 electoral votes to 83 for Adams. Along with the American System of policies the National Republicans pressed the issue of Jackson's incompetence for the presidency. He was condemned as a military chieftain who had little education or political experience and as a bigamist—a charge that was based on the fact that he and Rachel had been married for about two years before it became known that Rachel's divorce from her first husband had not been made final. The Jackson Committee in Nashville responded with a lengthy letter on the matter, while zealous partisans elsewhere sought to answer in kind by charging that Adams had, among other things, served as a procurer while he was minister to Russia. Clearly, the campaign was not pitched at a very high level. In other ways, Jackson's status as a military hero and his personal qualities were turned to advantage. Depicting the issue with Adams as being one of democracy versus aristocracy, partisans dramatized it with parades and rallies replete with hickory poles and huzzas to Jackson. Evasive on specific issues, they also made appeal as being the true heirs of Jefferson and promised to restore the government to its simple republican tack. Ultimately, Jackson won because of superior party organization at the state and local levels.[14]

The course of events during Jackson's presidency gave greater coherence to the party and specific policy content to its avowed Jeffersonian creed. Amos Kendall, one of Jackson's closest advisers, could thus observe later that there had been a "general shaking" which served "to separate parties on original principles" and make them "much better defined and understood than they were even in the days of Jefferson."[15] By the end of Jackson's tenure, his presidency reposed on the principle of party government and identified with a set of policies for his successor to defend.

Defections from the coalition of 1828 marked the process, with that of Calhoun being the first and most dramatic. Chosen vice-president with Jackson in 1828 and hopeful for the succession, he became alienated from the administration within two years. Personal and political matters were involved, including the role of Secretary of State Van Buren, which will be dealt with later. To his own harm, Calhoun persisted in relating to Jackson as a peer rather than as a loyal subordinate. Even worse, Jackson thought that Calhoun's wife was part of the so-called petticoat war, which was designed to socially isolate the wife of Jackson's close friend and secretary of war, John Eaton, and to drive him from the cabinet. In addition to Eaton, other enemies of Calhoun's were close to Jackson's ear; and the prediction of one of them that Van Buren would "outwit the Southron" possessed the power of self-fulfillment.[16] Among other things, these enemies brought back to Jackson's attention the fact that Calhoun, as a member of Monroe's cabinet in 1818, had favored a censure of the then General Jackson for his Florida campaign. Differences over tariff policy reinforced their personal differences. Pressed by radical antitariff forces at home, Calhoun wanted Jackson to commit himself early to substantial tariff reform. Jackson, by contrast, resisted early reform because of the higher priority he placed on retiring the national debt.

Several events signaled the closing of party ranks against Calhoun. In early 1830 Jackson's toast at the Jefferson Day Dinner—"Our Federal Union: it must be preserved"—served to rebuke the low-tariff friends of Calhoun as being nullifiers and not true Jeffersonians. Later in the year the *Washington Globe*, with Francis Blair as editor, was founded as the voice of the administration to replace the *United States Telegraph*, which retained its loyalty to Calhoun. In April 1831 the resignations of Van Buren and Eaton opened the way for Jackson to remove other members of the cabinet who were loyal to Calhoun and to appoint a new cabinet that was totally divested of his influence. The decision of the Jacksonians to hold their first national convention was also aimed in part at thwarting any effort by Calhoun to stand once more for vice-president. Used widely in a number of states during the 1820s and at the national level by Anti-Masons in 1831, the convention device enabled Jacksonians to "harmonize party councils" in behalf of his choice of Van Buren for the vice-presidency. The bitter comments of the *United States Telegraph* reflected the progress of Jackson toward party government: "Van Buren is now put up as the *party* candidate, and Mr. Calhoun and his friends are denounced because they will not support him on *party* grounds."[17] By resigning as vice-president in 1832 and by accepting election to the Senate, Calhoun openly put himself in the opposition.

In regard to policies, the "general shaking" that Kendall spoke of added up to a dismantling of the American System. While Jackson's veto of the Maysville Road bill in 1830 did not stop appropriations for many individual projects, it did end the commitment of the federal government to any system of improvements. Jackson also vetoed Clay's bill for distributing land revenues among the states for the same purpose. In the short run he wanted to retain land revenues in the Treasury for paying off the national debt and thereby realizing one of the most distinctive Jeffersonian goals. Over the long run he wanted to replace land sales by some scheme for getting land into the hands of actual settlers. Here, again, he echoed Jefferson's view that farmers were God's chosen people. Meanwhile, Congress provided authority for the government to commence removing Indians west of the Mississippi River.

Final disposition of the tariff question came during the nullification crisis. In July 1832 Jackson approved a new tariff measure which lowered or removed duties on many items but retained the principle of protection in regard to other items produced in the country. South Carolina responded in November with an ordinance of nullification, which absolved its citizens from paying tariff duties after February 1, 1833. Jackson answered in two ways: his annual message on December 4 called for a reduction in duties to the "revenue level" (the minimum to support economical government); six days later his proclamation denounced nullification as disunion and vowed to enforce the tariff laws. The popularity of the proclamation enabled Jackson to isolate South Carolina from the remainder of the South; and his call in mid January for additional powers of enforcement prompted South Carolina's leaders to postpone indefinitely the operation of the nullification ordinance. In this context, Clay, the champion of protection, joined forces with Calhoun to bring forth a compromise tariff, which provided for a gradual reduction in duties over a ten-year period to the revenue standard. Jacksonians initially favored more rapid reductions but came around to the Clay measure. Jackson did insist, however, on a party vote in Congress on his force bill. He also made a point of signing it before he signed the tariff bill.

Jackson's war on the national bank was the last important measure for undoing the American System. By vetoing Clay's bill renewing the charter of the Bank of the United States, Jackson accepted the challenge of making it the central issue in the presidential contest of 1832 against Clay. His veto message accordingly became a campaign document with great appeal: it damned the bank as being unconstitutional and warned that its monopolistic power threatened to corrupt government and to destroy republican freedom. With the victory over Clay in November, Jackson proceeded, after nullification, to another and more controversial step, that of ceasing to make further deposit of Treasury funds in the national bank and placing them on deposit with selected state banks. Finally, Congress responded to his call for a number of measures for enlarging the amount of specie in circulation: it revalued gold in relation to silver; made foreign coin legal tender; enlarged the facilities of the United States Mint; and forbade the Treasury to receive notes of less than $10 denomination or to disburse notes of less than $20 denomination. Hopefully these "hard money" measures would replace the presumed control that the national bank exercised over the currency by substituting a "natural" and more effective regulator.[18]

Jackson's policies involved the concept of a negative role for the federal government. Among other goals of the American System, Adams and Clay hoped it might provide elements of order for the developing nation; its economic policies were calculated to fashion new bonds of mutual interest and dependence. Jackson, by contrast, would "rivet the attachment" of the people by simply leaving them alone. The retirement of the national debt, in this view, gave seminal freedom to restore the government to what he supposed was its Jeffersonian simplicity. Freedom from the federal government did not preclude, however, a positive role for the states. On the contrary, two decisions by the Supreme Court in the January 1837 term underscored the role of the state governments in matters of internal improvements and banking. In the *Charles River Bridge* case, the Court upheld the right of the Massachusetts legislature to charter a new bridge across the Charles River, as opposed to the claim that the charter of the old bridge constituted a solemn contract, the obligation of which a state could not impair. The rights of private property had to yield to the good of the whole community, which would be realized, in this instance, by a new means of transportation. In *Briscoe* v. *Kentucky* the Court decided that the notes issued by state banks were not, in the language of the Constitution, "bills of credit," which states were forbidden to emit.[19] With the national bank destroyed, state banks were to play a more important role.

Contrary to Jackson's own wishes, many of his policies appeared to abet the expansive forces that were leading, by 1835, to a speculative boom. The additional specie attracted by his measures went mainly into bank vaults and provided the basis for new issues of bank notes. The rage of land speculation clearly ran counter to the professed ideal of keeping land for actual settlers and was enhanced by the policy of Indian removal. The land revenues that Clay wanted to distribute to the states began to accumulate after the retirement of the debt; placed on deposit in state banks, these revenues provided added means for new loans. To the extent that the American System exercised control over the forces of economic development, Jackson's policies lifted their restraints and added to the restiveness of the nation.

Jackson's political style, as manifested in the "bank war," had the same effect. Political foes believed that the removal policy violated the express terms of the old bank charter, which was not to expire until 1836. Moreover, the policy impinged on what they regarded to be the special relationship that Congress, under the Constitution, had with the Treasury in the collecting, keeping, and disbursing of the people's money. Adding to their sense of executive usurpation, finally, was the high-handed way in which Jackson executed the policy, moving one secretary of the Treasury to another cabinet post and firing a second one before settling on Roger B. Taney to do the job. In March 1834 Clay provided the opposition's response by pushing through the Senate a resolution censuring the president for his actions. The Senate also refused to ratify the appointment of Taney.

From another perspective, one with the "era of good feelings" in view, Jackson's actions greatly enhanced the power of the presidency. Under President Monroe, cabinet members had enjoyed both a great degree of autonomous power and, often, their own constituencies in Congress. The success of a presidential initiative thus depended on a consensus among such powerful men. In the name of a vigorous and united executive, by contrast, Jackson reduced the role of cabinet members to a more subordinate position, if not to the level of clerks, as some critics thought.[20] His frequent use of the veto was also distinctive. Earlier presidents used it more sparingly and only on matters involving the Constitution. But Jackson's vetoes, on grounds of policy as well as constitutionality, had the effect of enlarging the legislative role of the presidency.

Most of all, Jackson placed the presidency on a popular basis. In his official protest to Clay's censure resolution, he claimed to be the "direct representative" of the people, indeed the only one chosen by all the people. This gave him independent power and made the presidency, rather than Congress, the true organ of the nation's will. While Whigs called him Caesar, friends regarded him as a tribune of the people, standing up against assorted enemies of freedom—such as Nullifiers, bank monopolists, and manufacturers who were seeking special tariff privileges. The support of the people for his Proclamation against the Nullifiers was so immediate and intense, one observer supposed, precisely because it made the people "feel like men."[21] Transcending older categories of nationalism versus States' rights, of Federalist versus Republican, Jackson gave voice in a new age to the rising spirit of democratic nationalism.

But sectionalism was also at work during the period, and it rose to a new level of self-consciousness by the end of Jackson's administration. Against the background of the Missouri controversy, a growing number of southern voices in the debate over economic policy warned that the consolidation of the federal government, which they thought came with the American System, posed a threat to slavery. The power of Congress to promote internal improvements, John Randolph of Virginia warned, included the power to "emancipate every slave in the United States." Nullifiers professed to see the same danger in a protective tariff. On the other side of the question, John Quincy Adams was right in claiming that sensitivity to the slaveholding interest played a big part in the undoing of the American System. In a bitter moment, indeed, he characterized Jacksonian democracy as a combination of "the nullifiers of the South and the land robbers of the West."[22] Other events in the early 1830s—abolitionism and the Nat Turner insurrection in Virginia among them—served to make the issue of slavery more explicit and to make differences over it more extreme. If Garrison damned slavery as a "sin" to be purged at once, Calhoun began to defend it as a "positive good."

Three specific issues brought the slavery question into sharp political focus. In August 1835 a mob at the post office in Charleston, South Carolina, protested the distribution of "incendiary" abolitionist literature in the mail. Jackson's response, granting discretionary power to the Charleston postmaster in handling the materials, pleased Carolinians but provoked considerable criticism in the North. Another issue arose over the flood of abolitionist petitions to Congress, as angry southerners wanted to slam the door against them. A compromise resolution was finally adopted in May 1836 by which the petitions were admitted into the House chamber but then were laid on the table without further action. Critics condemned the resolution as being a "gag," however, and began to link free speech to the antislavery cause. Finally, the victory of Texas rebels over Mexico at San Jacinto in April 1836 was soon followed by calls for the recognition of Texas and its admission as a slaveholding state. In reaction, abolitionist Benjamin Lundy published a series of articles warning about a conspiracy of slaveholders, and Adams presented these views on the House floor.

Rising sectional consciousness was thus one of the elements, along with conflict over economic policies and presidential politics, that shaped the political life of the nation. Party realignments reflected the impact of these elements and set the stage for the election of Jackson's successor. By 1834 a coalition against Jackson began to form which was soon to be called the Whig party. Clay's National Republicans formed the largest group. Anti-Masons in most parts of the Northeast began to move toward the new coalition. Organized in the late 1820s as a third party and driven by equalitarian passions against secret societies and monopoly, they generally found themselves opposed to Jacksonians at the local level and in sympathy with Clay's concept of a positive role for the government at the national level. Calhoun also raised the Whig banner and helped to fashion the central principle of the party, suggested in its name—that of opposition to executive usurpation. It was clearly about the only principle on which Clay's Nationals and Calhoun's own Nullifiers could agree. Others were drawn to Whiggery out of personal disappointment, dislike for Van Buren as Jackson's favorite, or opposition to one or another of his policies. Southern foes of the force bill thus joined with westerners who were still in favor of internal improvements. John Bell of Tennessee, who had once been close to Jackson, openly broke with him over the bank question and managed, by 1836, to create a Whig following in the state which was strong enough to override Jackson's support for Van Buren.[23]

Although the lines of the Jacksonian party gained greater clarity during the course of his presidency, new differences within its ranks began to emerge over banking and currency. One group in the party, which now tended to drop the Republican suffix of the 1820s and call itself simply Democratic, posed as champions of enterprise. Their support for Jackson's war on the national bank looked primarily to the removal of the restraints that the bank exercised over the expansion-minded state banks. Speaking for this group, Senator Nathaniel P. Tallmadge of New York extolled the "credit system" of banking for its role in promoting the economic development of the country. With the enthusiastic support of this group the Deposit Act, passed by Congress in June 1836, made formal the connection of the Treasury with state banks and distributed the surplus in the Treasury to the states.

Senator Thomas Hart Benton of Missouri spoke for another group of Democratic members who identified with Jackson's own "hard money" inclinations. For them, the true sequel to the war on the national bank was not the connection of the Treasury with state banks; it was, rather, the measures that Jackson had pushed for increasing the amount of specie in circulation. The response of this group to the Deposit Act was the "Specie Circular," which Benton helped Jackson to draw up in July 1836. It extended the hard-money policy by requiring that specie be used in payment for all federal lands. Clearly the ambivalence among Americans that was noted earlier between "credit seekers" and "note takers" found expression within the Democratic party.[24]

By October 1835 the open split between conservative and Locofoco Democrats in New York City revealed intraparty differences most dramatically. The Locofocos gained their name from the fact that they used "locofoco" matches to light candles after the Democrats who were friendly to banks had turned out the gaslights in the meeting hall. With a platform of "equal rights against monopoly," they voiced the long-standing concerns of eastern workingmen and the more immediate threat posed by currency inflation. Particular opposition to chartered banks, which possessed the monopolistic right of issuing their own notes, was linked to support for a hard-money currency.[25]

At the national level, personal ambitions for higher office created other differences in the Democratic party. While it was generally assumed that Van Buren was Jackson's choice as a successor, the claims of others, particularly Col. Richard M. Johnson of Kentucky, could not be disregarded. He enjoyed a reputation as a military hero, having presumably slain the Indian chief Tecumseh during the War of 1812. In the Senate his voice against imprisonment for debt and against the proposed ban on the delivery of mail on Sundays had won supporters in many areas, while recent statements on banking and currency were to find favor with the Locofocos. Meanwhile, the choice of a candidate for vice-president was of special concern to Virginia. Hoping to reclaim its rightful place of power in national councils, the Old Dominion pinned its hopes on Senator William C. Rives. He had been a stalwart in Jackson's war on the national bank and had served well as minister to France.

In the hope of heading off further divisions within the party, the decision was made, with Jackson's consent, for the national convention to be held in May 1835, more than a year before the election. Acting upon Jackson's wishes, the delegates at Baltimore easily nominated Van Buren for President. The choice for vice-president was not so easy. Support for Johnson, including Jackson's, was doubtless strengthened by the desire to relieve his disappointment at not getting the presidential nomination. But Virginia would not go along. Bitter because Rives was being passed over, delegates from the state withheld the votes that Johnson needed in order to gain the required two-thirds majority. At this point, party managers resorted to a dubious expedient. Because Tennessee had sent no delegates to Baltimore, a Tennessean by the name of Edmund Rucker was brought in off the street to cast the state's fifteen votes for Johnson. While the choice of Johnson opened Democrats to the Whig charge of a "ruckerized convention," the disappointment of Rives represented a serious problem for Van Buren within the party.[26]

The new Whig coalition was not able to unite on a single candidate to oppose Van Buren. Partisans in Massachusetts nominated Daniel Webster. The Tennessee Whig delegation in Congress, led by John Bell, chose Senator Hugh L. White. Though White had at first been very close to Jackson, White's alienation was roughly parallel with and related to Van Buren's rise to favor. Anti-Masons and Whigs in Pennsylvania put forth the name of another military hero of the War of 1812, Gen. William Henry Harrison of Ohio. Because each of these candidates had a personal following, sectional identification, and freedom to appeal to narrow sectional interests, it was thought that they would greatly erode Van Buren's support and, by preventing a majority in the electoral college, throw the contest into the House. Articulated in leading party papers, this constituted the basic Whig strategy in 1836.

In support of this strategy, Whig campaigners made an issue out of party organization itself. Too disunited to hold a convention of their own, they condemned the meeting in Baltimore as being an "officeholders' convention," made up of "Caesar's" disciplined cohorts and assembled to register his will for the succession. Because of this new and alarming order of things, they appealed to the antiparty feelings of an earlier age, which assumed that the very existence of the Republic depended on the "virtue" and independent judgment of its leaders. In this context the image of Van Buren as a "politician by trade" was given wide currency and gained its crudest expression in a campaign piece ghosted under David Crockett's name. Compared even to the hated Jackson, Van Buren was "as dung is to a diamond." Bound up in corsets like a woman and dressed in fancy clothes, he gave the appearance of a crow strutting in the gutter. Epithets such as "sly fox," the "little magician," or "Talleyrand" sounded the judgment against a professional politician who had no principles, a member of the "non committal" tribe who could laugh out of one side of the mouth and cry out of the other.[27]

Disunity in the party also enabled southern Whigs to set themselves up as the special patrons of sectional interests. By viewing Van Buren's earlier career through the colored glasses of 1836, they pictured him as a man of strong antislavery sentiments if not an abolitionist proper. He had helped elect to the Senate in 1820 the *bête noire* of the Missouri controversy, Rufus King; he had approved resolutions in the New York state legislature against Missouri; and he had favored suffrage for free Negroes in the constitutional convention of 1821. With these charges, Whigs skillfully exploited the uneasy feeling among southern Democrats that Van Buren was the first candidate from the North to head the old Jeffersonian party of "planters and plain republicans." Heretofore, Jefferson, Madison, Monroe, and Jackson had been the Republican candidates for president, while "plain republicans" from New York— such as Aaron Burr, George Clinton, Daniel Tompkins, and Van Buren—had been their running mates. And in 1836 a good southern "planter" had not been nominated for vice-president. To the contrary, Johnson was peculiarly vulnerable as a candidate in the South, for he had lived with a mulatto mistress and claimed two daughters by that union.[28]

Van Buren's public role in the campaign was limited mainly to letters written by himself or close associates in response to queries about his past record and present views. In a long letter to a congressman from Kentucky, Van Buren expressed approval for the economic policies of the Jackson administration and the belief that they conformed to the Jeffersonian creed. On the specific issue of banking and currency, which had created differences within his own party, he took a middle position. On the one side, he accepted that part of the Deposit Act which connected the Treasury to the state banks and promised to give the act a "fair trial." On the other side, he agreed with the goal of Jackson's measures for diffusing "an adequate specie currency" in the general circulation. Most of all, Van Buren sought to transcend intraparty differences by recalling the glory of the "bank war," in which all had fought under Jackson, and by pledging to veto any bill for a new national bank.[29] One measure of Van Buren's moderate position was the fact that the Locofocos withheld their endorsement.

Turning from his friends to his foes, Van Buren responded in several ways to the charge of southern Whigs that he was hostile to slavery. A number of letters sought to clarify his earlier record in New York. His support for Rufus King and for the resolution in the state legislature against Missouri was aimed, not at the South, but against the designs of De Witt Clinton to exploit the issue for local political advantage. And he had not given the vote to free Negroes in the constitution of 1821: he had merely favored a continuation of the suffrage provision from the old constitution. In regard to abolitionism, he encouraged party friends in New York to hold rallies and to adopt resolutions against it. As vice-president, he cast the tie-breaking vote for Calhoun's bill granting discretionary power to local postmasters over the delivery of "incendiary" materials. He also helped to work out the compromise resolution on abolition petitions, which critics called the "gag," and his Bucktail followers in the House voted solidly for it.

Two other actions taken by Van Buren during the campaign constituted a sectional trade-off that was to define the course he would follow as president. Because of growing opposition in the North, he resisted southern pressures to speak out in favor of recognizing, to say nothing of annexing, Texas. On the other hand, northern feeling against the abolitionists enabled him to take a strong stand in opposition to congressional meddling with slavery in the District of Columbia. In a letter that was widely reprinted, he made this position clear: "I must go into the presidential chair the inflexible and uncompromising opponent of any attempt on the part of Congress to abolish slavery in the District of Columbia, against the wishes of the slaveholding states; and also with a determination *equally* strong, to resist the slightest interference with the subject in the states where it exists." For this pledge a member of the ruling junto in Richmond expressed a widely held sentiment of gratitude: "We ought not to expect stronger proofs of your favorable disposition towards this section of the country."[30] Van Buren's pledge, as a candidate in 1836, to veto any bill for a national bank or against slavery was one measure of the power that Jackson had given to the presidency. In the latter case it also revealed how explicit the slavery question had become.

The outcome of the election was much closer than had been expected. In 1832 Jackson had received 219 electoral votes to 67 for the opposition and a popular margin of about 157,000 votes. Van Buren won 170 electoral votes, with the remaining 124 being scattered among the active Whig candidates and Willie P. Mangum, who received the protest vote of South Carolina. Van Buren's popular margin was about 26,000, and a shift of 2,183 votes in Pennsylvania alone could have fulfilled the Whig strategy and thrown the election into the House.

A further comparison with the 1832 results reveals a paradox— namely, the way in which a divided Whig opposition led to the maturity of a national two-party system. Harrison, who took away about 7 percent of the vote that Jackson had received in the Northwest, carried Ohio and Indiana. In the East, Van Buren held his own in the Middle Atlantic States and did better than Jackson had done in New England, winning the states of Rhode Island and Connecticut, which had been lost to the opposition in 1832. The most stunning shift came in the slaveholding states, where Jackson's popular margin of 68 percent fell to an even split with the Whigs in 1836. Senator White won Georgia and Tennessee, which had been solid for Jackson, but lost Mississippi and Louisiana by a very narrow margin.[31] Thus, the sectional identification of candidates brought about relatively even competition in all parts of the country and defined the political framework of Van Buren's presidency.

Misgivings about party organization remained strong throughout the 1830s, which was seen by many as itself an element of disorder in the national life. In fact, the maturing party system provided basic order to the political life of the people, who were caught up in rapid growth, were devoted to equalitarian ideals, and were becoming increasingly aware of sectional differences. And no other political figure of the day had contributed more to the new order of things than President-elect Martin Van Buren.

2

THE ROAD
TO THE WHITE HOUSE

On March 4, 1837, Martin Van Buren became the eighth president of the United States. It was a beautiful early spring day, and a record number of people turned out for the inauguration. In the perception of many, however, the day belonged to the old president and not to the new one. Rising from a sick bed, Jackson insisted on escorting his successor from the White House to the Capitol in a phaeton made of timbers from the *Constitution* and presented to him by admirers in New York. At the Capitol, Jackson savored the scene as a final triumph over his foes, particularly those who had controlled the Senate earlier in his administration. Van Buren, whose nomination as minister to England had been rejected by the Senate, now took the oath of office from Chief Justice Roger B. Taney, who had been turned down as secretary of the Treasury because of his zealous support for Jackson's war on the national bank. Rounding out the old president's joy was the knowledge that Thomas Hart Benton had recently "expunged" from the Senate journal Henry Clay's resolution censuring Jackson. The people listened respectfully while Van Buren read his Inaugural Address and took the oath of office, but as the party made its way back to the carriage, they erupted into sustained cheering and applause. "For once," Benton later remembered, "the rising was eclipsed by the setting sun."[1]

Personal appearances added to the image. Whether a Caesar, as the Whigs charged, or a tribune of the people, Jackson struck many observers as the last of the Romans. Though worn by illness and scarred by many battles, he yet bore himself as erectly as his weakened condition and swollen feet would allow; and there still shone in his countenance the old spirit of defiance, pride, and stern resolve. Van Buren presented striking contrasts. He appeared to most contemporaries to be shorter than his five-foot-six frame, which had been trim in earlier years but was now growing obese. Ease and grace of movement, meticulous dress and grooming, the glow of health and good cheer—all suggested the drawing room or a caucus more than the battlefield. His head, which was large, round, and bald, was a phrenologist's dream; and his face, framed by a prominent brow and sandy red sideburns that were now mostly gray, gained its particular feature from big blue penetrating eyes and the ever-present trace of a smile. Many saw in his countenance less of defiant pride and resolution than of suavity, dignity, and self-control, with a look that was at once quick and calculating yet amiable, contented, and benign.

Three days after the inauguration, Van Buren personally escorted Jackson to the railway station for the first leg of the trip back to the Hermitage and, over Jackson's protest, ordered the surgeon general to accompany him all the way. Only then did party friends in Washington feel that a new administration had begun. Expecting nothing new, mocking Whig critics looked instead for a "footsteps administration." Along with power, in this view, Van Buren had inherited from Jackson a burden of defending the latter's work which preempted new initiatives or further steps. There is a good deal to recommend this perception, and in some form it has found its way into most historical accounts. It is a view, however, that needs to be qualified and refined. A close look at Van Buren's background, his early political career, and the role that he had played in Jackson's administration will demonstrate that he had helped to shape the heritage he vowed to defend and that an essentially conservative outlook lent character and distinctiveness to his course.

His road to the White House began on December 5, 1782, in the small town of Kinderhook, New York, where he was born into the household of Abraham and Hannah Hoes Van Buren, both of respectable if undistinguished Dutch ancestry dating back to early colonial days. The father, a somewhat shiftless farmer and tavern keeper, could not provide the son an ample start in life; but he did pass on a healthy constitution, an amiable disposition, Republican politics, and an easygoing outlook which contrasted with the Puritanism of nearby New England. The mother apparently recognized her son's abilities and sparked his ambition.

After an irregular schooling at the Kinderhook Academy ended when he was fourteen, the young Van Buren served the next five years as law clerk in the office of Francis Silvester, a leading Federalist of the area, and then completed his legal apprenticeship in New York City. Admitted to the bar in 1803, Van Buren commenced practice back in Kinderhook, building upon the reputation he had gained as a "boy lawyer" in pleading small cases as Silvester's clerk. Securely launched by 1807, he married Hannah Hoes, a childhood playmate and distant relative on his mother's side, and in the following year he moved to Hudson and to a larger circle of practice. Hannah bore four sons— Abraham, John, Martin, and Smith Thompson—and most of the burden of rearing them. After her untimely death in 1819, neighbors and kinfolk helped to care for the children as law and politics claimed more of Van Buren's time. There were later flirtations and rumors of a proposal to Ellen Randolph, a granddaughter of Thomas Jefferson, but he never married again.

In 1816 Van Buren moved to Albany and formed a partnership with Benjamin F. Butler which ended only when Van Buren retired from practice twelve years later. During a quarter century in the law he managed by hard work, chiefly for small clients, to lay a solid basis for financial independence. Thrifty habits and prudent investments enabled him to build an estate estimated at $200,000, to survive recurring panics, and to retire to the leisure of a gentleman farmer at Lindenwald after leaving the White House. Along with financial independence the law brought recognition and respect. His success was particularly impressive because Federalist gentlemen dominated the bar in his area. His strength lay less in courtroom oratory than in patient homework on the points of law and a redoubtable skill in ordering the facts of a case. An early biographer observed that others might sway the jury, but Van Buren more often won the judgment of the court. Consideration of Van Buren for appointment to the Supreme Court in the 1820s was another measure of professional recognition.

Because law was his vocation for so long, Van Buren can be considered the first lawyer-president. In lieu of a higher education, moreover, it provided the principal discipline for his mind. Ever defensive about his lack of education, Van Buren ascribed to it his "besetting infirmity," namely a "disinclination to mental efforts." Instead of sustained reading on serious subjects, he confessed, he generally read only for amusement or not at all; and he bestirred himself to consideration of "weightier matters" of law or public affairs only after "it became indispensable to grapple with them." John Randolph later observed that Van Buren knew less about a subject in debate at the beginning and more at the end than anyone else. Van Buren took the observation as both a compliment and a criticism.[2] In either case it suggested the make-up of a man who was less disposed to think critically about the world around him than to adapt himself to its demands. As a lawyer he responded to the case at hand; as a governmental official he reacted to events more than he tried to shape them.

Movement in higher social circles matched his success in the law and reflected the same conservative impulses. Though dour patricians, on one side, and demagogues, on the other, called him an opportunist, an upstart dandy, or a social climber, Van Buren accepted with little question the goodness of social arrangements at the time and sought to attain their rewards within the existing rules. An incident in his early life illustrates this lifelong pattern: the new fourteen-year-old law apprentice shed his simple Republican clothes and, on borrowed money, dressed up in the tricornered hat, knee breeches, and buckled shoes of his Federalist mentor. Along with fine clothes, Van Buren also developed a taste for good wine and social life among the elite. Here his sense of humor, his great conversational gifts, and a suavity of manners blended with irrepressible good cheer to make him an "ornament of the social circle." When he arrived in London as minister in 1831, the secretary of the legation, Washington Irving, quickly succumbed to his charms and expressed admiration at the ease with which Van Buren mingled with members of the ruling class. Back home, party workers grumbled from an early day about Van Buren's preference for Federalist companions, but the pattern continued. A campaign biography in 1835 claimed that Van Buren's humble background enabled him to share the feelings of "plebians and common people." From a social point of view, however, Van Buren was more a courtier than a companion of the people.

When he reached the White House, Van Buren discarded the more democratic and partisan style of Jackson. Guards and guest lists for most occasions reduced access to the president, while a more festive and high-toned air prevailed. With the marriage of his son and private secretary Abraham to Angelica Singleton, the White House gained a South Carolina belle who was closely related to many political figures. Adding to this tone was Van Buren's partiality for the southern aristocratic members of the cabinet. Of special note were the small Saturday-night dinner parties to which political foes as well as friends were invited. Former President John Quincy Adams paid frequent tribute to Van Buren's social prowess, and Henry Clay similarly praised his "generous and liberal hospitality." Van Buren also enjoyed the hospitality of others, as he broke with the practice of earlier presidents by attending parties given by others. One must be somewhat skeptical of his protest that his tenure in the White House was "one of toilsome and anxious probation.''[3] As was the case with Leo X and the papacy, Van Buren apparently embraced the presidency as something to enjoy.

While law brought him good fortune and entry into a larger social world, politics was his passion and the pathway to power. From an early day, Van Buren showed an instinct for choosing the winning side amid the welter of New York factions, and by 1808 he claimed his first reward, appointment as judge for his home county. In 1812 he began an eight-year tenure in the state senate on an auspicious note by serving as De Witt Clinton's floor leader in the bid for the state's electoral votes. Appointment as attorney general three years later marked his growing prominence in state politics, but the truly decisive phase in his career was reached in 1819, when the conflict matured between the Clintonians and his own ''Bucktail'' faction for control of the Republican party. Though the fortunes of this conflict shifted over the next few years, he did enjoy early and significant triumphs, winning election to the United States Senate in 1821 and gaining some of the credit for calling the constitutional convention of the same year.

Van Buren's early success was due in part to his extraordinary skill in the art of politics. As one of the first ''politicians by trade,'' he was also one of the best. His ''unrivalled knowledge of human character,'' one close associate observed, gave him an uncanny power of ''penetrating into the designs'' and ''defeating the purposes of his adversaries.''[4] Epithets such as ''little magician,'' a ''giant of artifice,'' a Talleyrand, or ''sly fox'' were a tribute to his skill, which also included the knack of relating to political enemies in a personable and civil way. Among his political friends his forte was that of resolving differences and reaching consensus. More attentive to individual motives of political behavior than to public issues in debate, he also evinced great facility in eliciting the views of others without divulging his own. In part for this reason the charge of ''non committalism'' soon arose and caused the addition of the word *vanburenish* to the political vocabulary.

Van Buren often chuckled at such charges, and mention of two examples in his autobiography suggests a certain pride in the broker's art of obfuscation. With feelings strongly divided in the tariff issue by 1827, he delivered such a masterful speech at Albany that all applauded but none could say for certain where he stood. More famous was the response he supposedly made to the question of whether the sun rose in the east: ''I presumed the fact was according to the common impression, but, as I invariably slept until after sun-rise, I could not speak from my own knowledge.''[5]

Ultimately, Van Buren's success came through the power of party organization. As one of the most important inventors of party, he realized how the discipline and order in its ranks would outmatch the older patrician style. Just as surely he saw how it could serve the interests and personal ambitions of the "new men" in politics. The spoils of office were a great attraction to party workers, along with the opportunity for them to move in a sphere of power once thought to be reserved for gentlemen. For Van Buren himself, party also served as a basis for his social aspirations. If older social arrangements tended to accord power as a right to gentlemen, it must have been easy to assume that new men of power might take on the style of gentlemen.

Along with self-interest, however, Van Buren saw in party an important means for promoting order in a society devoted to republican and equalitarian ideals. It provided a practicable way for much larger numbers to participate in the common life, in the *res publica*. From an early day, moreover, Van Buren felt that the older patrician style of leadership, which had been based on a loyal personal following and coalitions formed with other leaders, no longer worked very well. In a letter to a Clintonian in 1819, Van Buren thus observed that Governor Clinton's highly personal if not capricious appointments and his use of spoils had created a pervasive restlessness in the state. It was much more conducive to order, he assumed, when a disciplined party reached internal consensus before an election and brought a united will to the task of governing.[6]

Van Buren's views on public policy in New York also expressed an inclination toward order. The reforms he favored in the constitutional convention in 1821 were moderate in scope. Among other things he drew up short of universal suffrage for whites, wanted to retain the high property qualification for Negroes, and opposed the elective principle for judges. On policies dealing with economic development he generally came down on the restrictive side. His initial opposition to the Erie Canal was undoubtedly personal to some degree, for it was the pet project of Clinton. But when Van Buren's party was in power, it generally managed the canals and other improvements in a sound and prudent manner. As a state senator he voted against all charters for new bank corporations except one, that for aiding war-torn Buffalo, because he feared the excess of bank credit and note issues. During his brief tenure as governor in 1829, he approved a measure that devoted 3 percent of all bank capital to a safety fund for protecting holders of bank notes. This measure also provided a model for state regulation elsewhere in the form of a regulatory commission.

When Van Buren went to Washington in 1821 to claim his Senate seat, he took along the ideas of party that he had developed in New York. He accordingly saw in James Monroe's "era of good feelings" some elements of discord that were not unlike those under Clinton. The error of Monroe—for Van Buren, a grave Republican "heresy"—was the effort to efface old party distinctions and to harmonize government councils above party; new distractions, and not harmony, were the result. In this view the bitter Missouri controversy arose with the decline of the discipline that Jefferson had forged between southern "planters" and the "plain republicans" of the North. Similarly, the failure of President Monroe to designate his successor through the party caucus in Congress led to intraparty conflict, the disputed election of 1824, and the choice of John Quincy Adams, a new Federalist in Van Buren's view.

From the outset, Senator Van Buren sought by "radical reform" to end the era of good feelings and to "resuscitate old party feelings."[7] Through his influence, Bucktail members in the House switched support for Speaker from John W. Taylor, a New York Clintonian, to an old Republican from Virginia, Philip P. Barbour. On a patronage matter, Van Buren made a spirited though unsuccessful effort to stop Monroe's appointment of an old Federalist to the Albany post office. In the Senate he took a strong position against Adams's call for internal improvements and argued with Virginians in behalf of strict construction and States' rights. Identified fully by 1827 with the Democratic Republican coalition against Adams, he worked hard to bring fellow Crawfordites into the Jackson camp. With the caucus discredited as a device for uniting party councils, he began to speak out in favor of a national convention. A convention was not called or needed in 1828, but his thought about it revealed the importance he attached to some device for party unity. By harnessing the "personal popularity" of Jackson to the purposes of party, nomination by a convention would go a long way toward reviving "old party feelings." The election of Jackson as a hero above party was one thing; victory in the name of a united party would be "a far different thing."[8]

Clearly, Van Buren stood to benefit greatly from a revival of the old Jeffersonian party of planters and plain republicans. Supposing that the party would still repose on power bases in Virginia and New York, he realized how the dramatic growth of his Empire State had enhanced its weight in the Union and had strengthened the claims of its sons for preferment. Heretofore, Virginia planters had dominated the Republican alliance, with New Yorkers serving the dynasty as vice-presidents. Now Van Buren had reason to expect that a New Yorker might be elected president under the party banner.

But order as well as self-interest was a genuine concern, and Van Buren clearly understood how party constituted an invaluable bond of the Union. Without national party competition, he wrote to the editor of the influential *Richmond Enquirer*, "geographical divisions founded on local interests, or what is worse prejudices between free and slaveholding states will inevitably take their place." The Missouri controversy, coming in the midst of the era of good feelings, illustrated the point most clearly. "Party attachments," by contrast, generated "counteracting feelings," which served as "a complete antidote" to the fever of sectional feelings. The best party attachments, Van Buren thought, were still the old ones that had originally been defined in the contests between Alexander Hamilton and Jefferson.[9] Hamilton and his Federalist followers stood for vigorous central government and economic policies for consolidating the nation. The Jeffersonian Republicans, by contrast, thought that States' rights and severely limited central government best expressed the interests of the nation and defined political freedom as the opposite of encroaching government power. Focus on economic issues generated party competition along national lines, and the idea of a limited government allayed the concerns that planters had about outside meddling with the slavery interest.

By paying a visit to his "beau ideal" at Monticello in 1824, Van Buren gained a greater appreciation of party and the ideology of "republicanism." Party distinctions of Whig and Tory were inevitable in a free republic, Jefferson told Van Buren, because the one always trusted and the other always mistrusted the people. Mistrust for the people might take many forms, but it became corrupting, if not fatal, when organized into a self-interest that was powerful enough to control the government. In the United States, corruption found expression in Hamilton's fiscal policies, which were calculated to attach the powerful interests of banking and commerce to the government and to make them the controlling element. Jefferson, on the other hand, wanted the government to repose on its true republican base—the "virtue" and patriotism of a predominately agricultural people, relatively independent and equal in means and therefore capable, in their role as citizens, of transcending self-interest and of supporting policies for the general good of all. The ultimate difference between the parties was, to use the language of a recent essay, "virtue" versus "commerce." In this view, Jefferson supposed that there could be only one popular party; indeed, by its trust for the mass of the people the Republican party *was* the nation in an essential sense.[10]

The primary task of the Republican party when in power was negative, mainly to purge old elements of corruption and to serve as a sentinel or tribune in guarding freemen from new aggressions by the selfish and privileged few. In this connection the "history of parties" became a distinctive part of the party ideology by the 1820s.[11] It was a history of a very special sort, however, designed less as a full narrative of events than for the purpose of elucidating a cyclical pattern of decline and restoration. Thus, in 1776 the nation had begun its existence in a high state of republican virtue and eleven years later had taken on a more perfect constitutional form. Unhappily, the Hamiltonian policies brought corruption in the following decade as freemen relaxed their vigil; and only with the "civil revolution of 1800," as Jefferson's election to president was called, did the nation pass the crisis and regain its original purity. A new round of corruption arose after the War of 1812 with the neo-Hamiltonian program of the American System; and with the multiplying evils of the era of good feelings, it rose to a new peak under President John Quincy Adams. At this point the nation clearly stood once more in need of restoration and reform.

These ideas were not original with Van Buren. Here, as elsewhere, he showed greater facility at assimilating ideas around him than in fashioning his own. What was new and distinctive, however, was his role in fusing old ideology with the new reality of party organization. Though Jefferson recognized in theory the inevitability of party differences in a republic, he never fully accepted the need for permanent organization or, at least, for the legitimacy of an organized opposition. It was as if his own election in 1800 had restored the republican principles of the nation and had ruled out the need for further contests. In this regard he tended to identify with older patrician views of the eighteenth century, which deemed parties to be an element of disorder.

Van Buren apparently never realized the extent of his differences with Jefferson or of the newness of elements that he added in the effort to "resuscitate old party feelings." Unlike the view of the eighteenth century, he deemed parties to be a vital element in promoting social order. As a partisan leader he also saw the pragmatic value of a permanent opposition, for its external pressure excited greater zeal and discipline within his own ranks. Ideology, likewise, had great practical value. Because effective organization and sustained party activity were found mainly at the state and local level, the "history of parties" and related ideas constituted an invaluable bond for a party that was claiming to speak for the whole nation. Indeed, ideology provided corporate identity and direction to the national party. A politician by trade, he was also an ideologue of party; and he ever looked to Jefferson as the great republican father. If Van Buren had come to power in Jackson's steps, he wanted both to follow in Jefferson's steps.

As politician and ideologue, Van Buren played an important role in the campaign of 1828. We noted earlier that he had pushed through Congress a higher tariff measure in order to enhance Jackson's appeal in the Middle Atlantic and western states. In a speech in the Senate on the "history of parties," he defined the issue of the election in ideological terms as being one of republican restoration and reform. Correspondence with Jacksonians in other states helped to sustain a common strategy. Meanwhile, problems in his own state claimed most of his attention. One was Anti-Masonry in western New York, for its strong equalitarian appeal threatened to draw support from his own ranks. He wisely counseled the party's papers to cease their attacks, to disregard the third-party challenge, and to picture the election as an archetypal repeat of the "real old ninety-eight fight" between Federalists and Republicans.[12] To aid the cause, Van Buren ran for governor. Along with a personal tour of most counties he kept busy with all aspects of the campaign down to the smallest details of organization, voter canvassing, and party rallies. Victory in November was the reward: he was chosen governor, and Jackson, with a popular margin of five thousand votes, received twenty of the state's thirty-six electoral votes.

Appointed by Jackson to the State Department, Van Buren resigned as governor after less than three months and returned to the national political scene. His major achievement as secretary of state was a successful negotiation for removing longstanding barriers that Britain had posed to trade with the West Indies. In April 1831 Van Buren took a very dramatic step, resigning his position and sparking the resignation or removal of the remainder of the cabinet. This allowed Jackson to resolve the political problem that had developed in the "petticoat war." With the make-up of the new cabinet reflecting Van Buren's growing influence, he then decided to leave the country and its political battles by accepting appointment as minister to England. But another dramatic political stroke soon called him back, for in January 1832 the Senate turned down his nomination as minister by the deciding vote of Vice-President Calhoun. Sympathy for Van Buren in the wake of the Senate's action enabled Jackson to act upon his earlier inclinations and to designate the rejected minister as his running mate in 1832. Elected as vice-president for Jackson's second term, Van Buren thus passed a very big turn on the road to the White House.

Calhoun's mistakes undoubtedly contributed to Van Buren's advancement. Van Buren, in turn, had full knowledge if not direct agency in the scheme to discredit Calhoun by bringing to Jackson's attention the position that Calhoun had taken, as secretary of war under President Monroe, in favor of censuring Jackson for the Florida campaign. A Van Buren protégé, James Hamilton, worked closely with Calhoun's enemies in the matter, yet Van Buren left few traces of scheming behind. "Van Buren glides along as smoothly as oil and as silently as a cat,"

Amos Kendall observed. "If he is managing at all, it is so adroitly that nobody perceives it."[13] Evidence can also be cited in support of the longstanding charge that Van Buren was a timeserver who ministered shamelessly to Jackson's egomania. Van Buren's public statements constantly invoked Jackson's name and heroic virtues, while a tone of flattery sounded in some of the private correspondence.

But there was much more in the relationship—namely, a degree of mutual respect and reciprocal influence—which did great credit to both men and helps to explain the favor that Jackson showed for Van Buren. In this regard the later assessment made by Van Buren must be given due weight: at once "political and personal," he wrote, it was a relationship "the confidential nature of which can never have been surpassed among public men." On one side, as a perceptive study has shown, Van Buren admired many of Jackson's qualities in which he felt himself to be deficient. Jackson was no "politician"; he hated all concealments; he acted from disinterested motives with unflinching courage; and he always knew that his power lay with the people. While this recital of virtues might have been Van Buren's way of masking his own vices, it also pointed to more positive influences. His deference to the overriding judgment of Jackson was not always that of a timeserver; for all Van Buren's caution and prudence, he seemed at times genuinely to have admired Jackson's power of making swift decisions and his intuitive sense of public opinion. The way people supported the vetoes, the Nullification Proclamation, and the death knell of the national bank struck him with the force of new discovery. Campaigning in 1832, he thus found that the bank veto was "popular beyond my most sanguine expectations."[14] Reflecting later upon the mainspring of political popularity, he found Jackson's popularity to lie in the unquestioned trust that people placed in his motives.

Meanwhile, many of Van Buren's qualities served Jackson well. Companionable and cheerful, sensitive to Jackson's moods and solicitous for his health, Van Buren provided invaluable personal support; and in this context their regular horseback rides became a welcomed diversion for both. To an old friend, Jackson was soon praising Van Buren's efforts to "render my situation, *personally*, as pleasant and comfortable as the nature of my public duties will admit." On matters of state, Van Buren's counsel mingled caution and tact with consistency and candor. After decisions were made, moreover, he remained absolutely loyal. His pledge of "immoveable constancy," given on the eve of the struggle against the national bank, was matched by another equally strong: "I go with you agt. the world."[15] If this sounded like the opportunism of a timeserver, it also manifested the political ethic of his

31

entire career—namely, that of subordinating private judgment at some point to the will of the party. An "instrument" of party could do nothing less. Two examples illustrate how other of Van Buren's qualities—caution and prudence—served as a makeweight to Jackson's more impulsive tendency. He was able to tone down a saber-rattling response that Jackson was contemplating in the midst of the crisis with France over unpaid claims. He likewise prevailed on Jackson to soften the claims of executive power made in the protest to the Senate resolution of censure.

Most of all, Jackson made use of Van Buren's skill in assessing political situations and in reading the motives of others. After Van Buren had left on the London mission in 1831, Jackson thus found a "vacuum" in the cabinet which none could fill. One member, Lewis Cass, could never say no, the president complained, while the learned secretary of state, Edward Livingston, knew "nothing of mankind." At the start of the 1828 campaign, before the two had come together, Jackson apparently shared the widespread view of Van Buren as being a sly fox or wily magician of "reputed cunning." Within a short time, however, Jackson became a strong defender of Van Buren. Judging him to be "frank and candid" rather than sly, he defined for a doubting associate the secret of the presumed magician: "His only wand is good common sense which he uses for the benefit of his country." In December 1829, well before Calhoun's mistakes and other events had made manifest to the public the favor that Van Buren enjoyed, Jackson confided to an old friend that Van Buren was eminently worthy of the succession.[16]

Deemed worthy of the succession from an early day, Van Buren retained Jackson's confidence throughout the latter's presidency. With regard to matters of policy, Van Buren's influence was confined largely to that of internal improvements. Here he helped persuade Jackson to veto the Maysville Road bill, passed early in 1830, and then drafted the veto message, which was grounded on the solid republican bases of States' rights, strict construction, and economy in government. As the first important policy initiative of the new administration, it signaled Van Buren's growing influence over Calhoun, who wanted early action on the tariff. The veto also served to strengthen Van Buren's political bases in Virginia and New York. The ideology of the message resounded in the old Republican soul of Virginia, where internal improvements had become the symbolic issue in the war against consolidation. Jackson, it now appeared, was bringing the government back to its true republican tack. At the same time the veto served the interests of New York, for state funds there had already built the Erie Canal and companion projects.

On other policies, Van Buren simply went along. While critics have found in this course further evidence of timeserving opportunism, it was consistent with his earlier political style and with a corporate concept of party government. Less disposed to shape than to react to new issues, Van Buren evinced the spirit of a conservative broker who was assimilating change to the evolving corpus of party commitments. To the policy of Indian removal, which Jackson made so distinctly his own, Van Buren gave support, even though powerful opponents arose in his own state. On the related matter of government lands he accepted both the pro-western principle of liberality toward actual settlers and the presidential veto of Clay's bill for distributing land revenues to the states.

The tariff presented a special problem for Van Buren. Many in the North, including woolgrowers in his own state, favored the higher tariff that he pushed through Congress in 1828; but southern partners in the party opposed it even more strongly. Being out of the country at the time, he played little part in the new tariff of 1832, which precipitated nullification; but he welcomed the compromise tariff of 1833, which gradually reduced duties to the revenue standard. It suited his own conservative inclination that the policy of tariff protection should be "loosened by degrees." More profoundly it answered a deep feeling, so well expressed by a fellow New Yorker in the congressional debates, that the sacred Union of the states should never be balanced "against ten cents upon a pound of wool."[17] Thenceforth Van Buren supposed that the party was irreversibly committed to the principle of a tariff for revenue only.

The nullification crisis uncovered a profound difference between Van Buren and Jackson, but it did not seriously threaten their relationship. The president's proclamation in response to the South Carolina ordinance of nullification struck Van Buren as being totally antirepublican in its consolidating tendency; and the zeal with which Daniel Webster among former Federalists greeted it confirmed Van Buren's fears and caused alarm among his southern friends. Van Buren agreed with Jackson that South Carolina was wrong, but he believed that tariff concession, not force, was the true republican way to meet the crisis. The decentralized nature of the Union and its States' rights origin forever prescribed a spirit of concession. In answer to Jackson's imperious call for the support of New York, Van Buren authored a set of resolutions for the state legislature, which embodied his conciliatory views. Jackson found them unacceptable and, with enormous popular support, proceeded to use the force bill to confront the Nullifiers. At this point, Van Buren failed to see that Jackson's concept of the Union was not old Federalist at all: it was, rather, the expression of a new spirit of democratic nationalism which had developed with the growth of the country and its equalitarian ideals.

Van Buren's role in the war that Jackson made on the national bank reveals most clearly the nature of his relationship with Jackson and the kind of influence that he exerted. It was not true, as the magisterial work of Bray Hammond contends, that Van Buren was the prime mover in the war or that his purpose was to destroy the bank in Philadelphia and to move the banking capital of the country to New York. Whatever his economic views at the time, Van Buren regarded the issue primarily in political terms. Needing the support of Pennsylvania in his bid for the presidency, he simply did not want to lend substance to the charge that he spoke for a self-serving "monied junto" in his own state. The initiative came from Jackson and other advisers, not from Van Buren.[18]

On his arrival in Washington from the London mission in July 1832, he found Jackson already resolved to veto Clay's recharter bill and, as he put it, "kill the bank." Victory over Clay in 1832 on the issue then led to a further step about which Van Buren had grave misgivings. Jackson decided to cease the deposit of Treasury funds with the national bank by October 1833 and to place them with state banks. Sensing that this would create a new storm of controversy, Van Buren wanted Jackson at least to postpone the implementation of the deposit policy until Congress met in December to consider it. But when Jackson remained adamant on the matter, Van Buren ceased further resistance and pledged that "true friends" of party in New York would support the president with "immoveable constancy." Critics at the time bitterly reproached him for giving in, but they wrongly ascribed to him the power to deflect Jackson from his course.

Although Van Buren did not initiate the war on the national bank, he wanted its battles to be fought within the framework of party. One danger, as he saw it, was the possibility of a coalition with Senator Webster. Webster's strong backing for Jackson's proclamation and the force bill was matched by bitterness toward Clay for yielding the principle of protection in the compromise tariff. Webster's eulogies to the Union became liberally mixed with public praise for Jackson, and one cabinet member showed the senator some patronage lists. Finally, at the outset of what became the "panic session" of Congress, the prospect of an arrangement seemed near. On December 15, 1833, Senator Felix Grundy of Tennessee told Jackson he thought it very significant that Webster withheld the votes that Clay needed in order to organize the Senate. Grundy also believed that Webster had little enthusiasm for the issue of executive usurpation, on which Clay prepared to battle the president. Was a coalition possible?

No definite answer has been given, but Van Buren clearly saw a crisis for his idea of party government and his own political fortunes. In Grundy's presence at the White House, Van Buren earnestly importuned Jackson to give up any thought of enlisting Webster's aid. Coming in the wake of nullification, Van Buren reasoned, Webster's pro-Union posture might deepen the fears of southern party members. On other issues, Webster would eventually exact a heavy price, possibly to undermine the party's creed, which was already fixed on bank and tariff issues. Honest rank-and-file members would become confused or demoralized by such a coalition, and therefore all the gains in party discipline since the era of good feelings would be lost. On the spot, Jackson sided with Van Buren's argument and told Grundy to drop the matter. Even in Van Buren's later recollection of the incident there remained the air of triumph: "Between neither of these gentlemen and myself was the subject ever revived."[19]

The sequel of events gave substance to Van Buren's sense of triumph. Webster went over to the opposition and lent support to Clay's battle against Jackson, which culminated in late March 1834 with the censure resolution. Van Buren, meanwhile, led the party's congressional hosts. As presiding officer in the Senate he met the fury of Jackson's foes with dignity and firmness. A dramatic encounter with Clay revealed another aspect of Van Buren's style and influence. Responding to one of Clay's long and impassioned appeals for the vice-president personally to make the president reverse his course, Van Buren vacated the chair, walked with solemnity and purpose to the desk of the Kentucky senator, and then, to the delight and relief of party friends, politely requested of Clay a pinch of his aromatic Maccoboy snuff. While Clay controlled the Senate, Van Buren's friends in the House gave their votes for four key resolutions against the national bank, which sounded its death knell. One close observer of the session thus paid tribute to the vice-president: "To no friend of the Administration, is more due, the meed of public approbation, for fixed and unalterable purpose to sustain it, at its period of greatest difficulty, than yourself."[20] The battle had been fought on party grounds, and Van Buren had proved himself a powerful "instrument" of party. Another measure of his power was the predominant influence he exerted on the make-up of Jackson's new cabinet, which was selected in the midst of the battle.

From Congress, Van Buren carried the battle to New York. There he sought to make the 1834 elections a mandate for Jackson and to define the bank policy as a central element in the evolving party creed. "The fate of this administration," he observed, "if not the character of that which is to come after it depends upon the result of the great question which now agitates the country." Supposing that Jefferson's struggle with Hamiltonians in the 1790s over the bank had given "original form & purpose" to party divisions, he welcomed the opportunity for "resolving political parties into their primitive elements."[21] His draft of an address to the Herkimer Convention in September 1834 accordingly focused on the "history of parties" and pictured the present contest in archetypal fashion as a new battle against the old enemies of freedom.

Within this ideological framework, Van Buren sought especially to impress on Jackson the true meaning of the issue. Invoking Jefferson's theory of an eternal enmity between the selfish few and the patriotic many and linking it to the present party competition, he argued for a politics of conflict as being the highest statesmanship: "Every community that enjoys the least semblance of freedom is kept in contention by the antagonist[ic] principle[s], and no man please[s] both without sacrafizing [sic] principle to expediency." By forcing a fight on party grounds, Jackson had thus done more to cripple the old Tory spirit than any other president since Jefferson. The hatred that present enemies showed was "the best evidence of your orthodoxy," Van Buren concluded, "and the highest compliment that can be paid to your patriotism."[22]

At an earlier time, Van Buren had had serious doubts about Jackson's orthodoxy. As the Democratic Republican coalition began to form in the late 1820s, Van Buren had feared that Jackson was still heavily infected with the "Monroe heresy" and that his stature as a military hero further strengthened the self-image of a political leader above party. Much had also been made of Jackson's letter to President Monroe, which deplored the "monster spirit" of party. At the time of Jackson's inauguration in March 1829 Van Buren still had doubts and, to a close associate, confided having great anxiety that the new president might express sentiments in his Inaugural Address that would be "at war with the principles of the Jefferson school." A recent study contends that Jackson brought to the White House a coherent set of ideas in the Jeffersonian mold. For Van Buren, however, the "principles of the Jefferson school" meant not only Republican sentiments but also a fusing of those sentiments to the idea of party and a politics of conflict.[23]

By the end of Jackson's presidency, Van Buren was more certain of Jackson's orthodoxy. In the judgment of a recent student, Jackson had at last discarded doubts about party that he had imbibed in the era of good feelings. The controversy generated over his policies, which culminated in his fight with the national bank, had drawn more sharply than before the lines of political conflict. But it must also be supposed, given the confidential nature of their relationship, that Van Buren steadily exerted an effort to shape President Jackson's perception of political conflict in terms of party and ideology. It was here, rather than by his impact on specific policies, that Van Buren exercised greatest influence. In any case, Jackson's statement of the matter in 1835 was one that Van Buren could heartily approve: "I have long believed, that it was only by preserving the identity of the Republican party as embodied and characterized by the principles introduced by Mr. Jefferson that the original rights of the states and the people could be maintained, as contemplated by the Constitution."[24] If Jackson was seen by many as a tribune of the people, he inclined here to the view of party itself as the tribune or guardian of the republic.

Most of all, Van Buren could see in the circumstances of his elevation to the presidency a vindication of these views. Upon his arrival in Washington as senator in 1821, he had set about the task of "resuscitating old party feelings." He was particularly critical of President Monroe for not designating his successor through the party caucus in Congress. Fourteen years later, Van Buren found himself to be the successor, designated by President Jackson and fully confirmed by the party's national convention, a device for collecting the will of the party which replaced the discredited caucus. Accepting the nomination as the "honored instrument" of party, he pledged "to tread generally in the footsteps of President Jackson."[25] The nation had come a long way from the era of good feelings toward a new political order. To the extent that Van Buren had helped to fashion the new order and to influence Jackson's thought about it, he was pledging himself to follow in steps he had in part made.

The role that Van Buren played in Jackson's administration, as exemplified most clearly in the bank war, also pointed to the way in which he was to shape his own presidency. With the instincts of a conservative broker he reacted to, far more than he sought to initiate, policies; yet the pattern of reaction was one that incorporated new policies into the party creed and made them thenceforth an irreversible commitment that, as an "instrument" of party, he was bound to preserve. Two matters in the campaign of 1836, noted in the preceding chapter, lent further strength to this conservative inclination—differences within his party over banking and currency and the rising level of consciousness over the issue of slavery. In the wake of his election, finally, Van Buren sensed a widespread yearning for political repose after the stormy Jackson years. Relieved that Jackson was passing from the scene, the wealthy New York merchant Philip Hone voiced a common feeling among Whigs about Van Buren: "He will be a party president, but he is too much of a gentleman to be governed by the rabble who surrounded his predecessor and administered to his bad passions." Similarly, a Democratic senator wanted a respite for the restless nation and hoped a "tranquil" Van Buren might let "the troubled waters subside."[26]

In this spirit the president-elect decided to retain Jackson's cabinet and make no immediate removals at lower levels. Two cabinet turnovers during Jackson's administration, in 1831 and 1834, had added to the disruptive effect of other actions. Besides, Van Buren had played a dominant role in the selection of the members of the cabinet that he inherited. Levi Woodbury of New Hampshire was New England's voice in the cabinet. At the beginning of Jackson's term, Woodbury had seemed to favor Calhoun over Van Buren for the succession; but when Woodbury became secretary of the navy in 1831 and then secretary of the Treasury in 1834, he became identified with the Van Buren interest. Never on close personal or social terms with Van Buren and, indeed, critical of his aristocratic social style, Woodbury easily deferred to the judgment of the president on vital policy matters in the department and dutifully administered its tasks during a very trying time.

The Middle Atlantic States were represented by Benjamin F. Butler of New York and Mahlon Dickerson of New Jersey. Butler, Van Buren's law partner at an earlier day, became attorney general in Jackson's second reshuffling of the cabinet and was prevailed upon to remain. Van Buren needed Butler's personal support and his skill in preparing state papers. Dickerson, a former governor, senator, and long-time political associate of Van Buren's, had moved into the navy post vacated by Woodbury. Amos Kendall of Kentucky remained as postmaster general. Though he owed his appointment exclusively to Jackson, he warmed to Van Buren and became a key political adviser. At the State Department since 1834 was John Forsyth of Georgia. Aristocratic, personable, and utterly loyal to his president and party, he had been rewarded for his powerful support of Van Buren's nomination as minister to England and then for his notable services in Jackson's war on the national bank.

Only one cabinet post was open when Van Buren was elected, that of the War Department. He turned first to Senator William C. Rives of Virginia, hoping not only to earn political capital in the South but also to heal a dangerous division in the party which had been caused by Rives's disappointment in not getting the vice-presidency. Rives's refusal of the

War Department post was a great setback for Van Buren, who then gave it to Joel R. Poinsett of South Carolina, a wealthy rice planter who had had varied government experience and possessed great ability. As a Unionist leader in his state during the nullification controversy, moreover, he was a southerner who was readily acceptable to the North.

The president-elect's decisions were not without critics, particularly within his own party. Senator James Buchanan of Pennsylvania felt that his state, whose support was so critical to Van Buren's election, had been neglected and that his being offered the diplomatic mission to Russia was a poor substitute for a cabinet position. On other grounds, John M. Niles of Connecticut, who was soon to become one of Van Buren's strongest supporters in the Senate, feared that the first politician in the White House was not being political enough. Without having a number of cabinet appointments or spoils at the lower level, he thought, Van Buren "voluntarily tied up his own hands" and surrendered the "stock in trade" needed to build an independent base of power.

But Van Buren had other priorities. Along with a respite for the nation he also wanted political and personal repose. Earlier presidents had found that the demands of hungry spoilsmen far exceeded the supply and that any appointment generally brought more disappointments than satisfaction. In his case the divided state of the party might make conflicting claims even more bitter. He therefore deemed it a matter of "vital importance" to make no big changes. "You can have no conception," he wrote to one of his sons, "of what conflicting interests will immediately present themselves the moment a place is opened."[27]

Van Buren's Inaugural Address likewise expressed the desire for repose. It was essentially a charter for inaction, a call to do nothing more than run the shop. In the "gratifying" retrospect of past achievements, little remained but the task of "perpetuating a condition of things so singularly happy." Accenting this sentiment, another passage is most often cited—namely, his statements of self-depreciation. Compared to his illustrious predecessors, "whose superiors it is our happiness to believe are not found on the executive calendar of any country," the new president pictured himself as a lesser figure of a later age. In part this sounded like the filial pieties of the day and was particularly fitting in Van Buren's case, since he was the first president to have been born after the nation had declared its independence. But it also served to strike a defensive note, as if a politician by trade was unworthy of becoming president. And because he lacked Jackson's popularity, there was also what seemed to be a supplicating tone in his appeal to "the patriotism, the intelligence, and the kindness of a people who never yet deserted a public servant honestly laboring in their cause."[28]

One reading suggests that Van Buren set out to do very little because he did not believe he would be able to do very much: the Inaugural Address was therefore an apology in advance for the failure of his presidency. A deeper and more sympathetic reading of the address, however, suggests a statesmanlike concern for order which he saw fit to place in a broader historical perspective. Giving literary and rhetorical form to the address was an assessment of the "great experiment" in self-government that had begun fifty years earlier with the writing of the Constitution. According to this assessment, Van Buren voiced an ambivalence that was shared by thoughtful Americans of the day.[29] On the one hand, there was pride in the fathers and the boast that their noble experiment had succeeded; on the other, an anxious sense that the experiment would fail if the present age should prove false. The pleasing reflection on past blessings and the deeper delight in contemplating the happiness of a "thousand generations" to come was thus balanced on the solemn sense of present responsibility: "It impresses on my mind a firm belief that the perpetuity of our institutions depends upon ourselves."

On the hopeful side, Van Buren noted several ways in which the sons had overcome the fathers' fears. The people had proved their capacity for self-government by bearing arms and paying taxes to support the government. Greater unity, not dismemberment, had come with "the extension of our territory, the multiplication of States, and the increase of population." Collisions had occurred between the federal government and the states, but these "vibrations of authority" had been followed by a renewed appreciation for the federative system of the Union. By implication, Jackson's undoing of the American System averted the danger of consolidation and restored the balances of the Constitution. Another concern of the fathers, then animated by anti-party feelings, had also been overcome. At first there had been a "common sentiment" that only the "great weight" of Washington's character could "bind the discordant materials of our government" and "save us from the violence of contending factions." But nearly forty years after Washington's death, Van Buren proudly observed, the republic "still preserves its spirit of free and fearless discussion, blended with unimpaired fraternal feeling." Enhancing the sense of pride in this observation was the fact, left unspoken, that Van Buren had contributed a good deal to the party system that preserved the spirit of free discussion.

Two other elements of disorder, which were very much in evidence at the time, received more attention. One was the rising incidence of mob action. Of 115 incidents tabulated by the *Niles' Register* for the

1830s, 89 had occurred during the last three years of Jackson's presidency. Such incidents, Van Buren observed, wounded "the majesty of the law" and tended to undermine the republican experiment. Unlike old Federalists and latter-day Whigs, however, Van Buren was not too concerned. Reaffirming the Jeffersonian trust in the "generous patriotism" and "sound common sense" of the people, he rather believed that they would soon return to "the landmarks of social order." A recent analysis of rioting in Jacksonian America confirms Van Buren's faith, showing that most of the riots were very limited in their goals and essentially therapeutic in effect.[30]

The last and "perhaps the greatest" element of disorder mentioned by Van Buren was abolitionist agitation. That he was the first president to use the word *slavery* in an inaugural address was one measure of his concern. To deal with it, he quoted verbatim his campaign pledge to veto any bill concerning slavery unless he had the consent of the southern states. Politically he "went South," as foes quickly charged; and wider currency was given to the phrase "northern man with southern feelings." Van Buren saw himself, instead, as a northern man with national feelings, committed to the order of the Union as the highest good. In this view, abolitionism constituted the greatest threat to the Union, and he believed the Union to be the indispensable means for securing the "great experiment" of republican freedom.

The fathers, he accordingly argued, had fashioned the Union out of materials "as they found it"—diverse in economic interests, divided into distinct sovereignties, and shaped by habits, opinions, and institutions that were "peculiar" to the various sections. To preserve the Union required fidelity not only to the letter of the constitutional bond but also to "the spirit that actuated the venerated fathers of the Republic." It was the animating spirit, he further supposed, of the old Jeffersonian party which he had worked to restore. So far as they applied to the federal government, two principles of the party were central: to exercise no doubtful power and to exercise even a clearly delegated power in the temper of "concession and compromise."

Van Buren's call for repose, in sum, looked beyond present circumstances to the larger question of order. The image of self-effacement that he cast of himself in the Inaugural Address was one that he wanted all of the people to adopt. In the history of a nation, he assumed, each generation had a different task to perform. The founding fathers had declared independence, had won it on the battlefield, had constructed "inestimable institutions" of government, and had defended them from foreign and domestic foes. Looking back after fifty years to the Constitution, he thought it only remained for his generation "sacredly to uphold those political institutions." The age of heroes, of destroyers and creators, had passed, leaving the prosaic but no less important job of preservation. In the steps of the heroic Jackson, the new president announced the arrival of a new and less heroic age.

As Van Buren left the railway station in Washington after bidding Jackson farewell, he could have been pardoned any thoughts about the road he had followed to the White House. In many ways his own career illustrated the ideal of the self-made man at least as well as Jackson's. Considering the state of the restless nation that he was to govern, moreover, he could have also been indulged any further reflections on the last sentence of his Inaugural Address: "May her ways be ways of pleasantness and all her paths be peace!"

3

THE PANIC OF 1837

Van Buren's hopes for pleasantness and peace quickly faded. On May 10, 1837, only a little more than two months after his inauguration, banks in New York suspended payments of specie; and within a few days, all but six of the nation's approximately eight hundred banks were following this example. This meant that the banks were unable at the time to redeem their own notes in gold or silver. Suspension culminated a process of credit and currency contraction which, by mid 1836, had displaced the boom phase of a growth cycle that had started in 1830. It did not, however, bring the cycle to an end: it was, rather, a temporary interruption—a period of adjustment in prices, specie, and credit between the United States and England—and the banks resumed specie payments the following year. The end of the cycle, which was marked by a severe and prolonged downturn, came in the latter part of 1839.

Politically, however, the panic of 1837 had an enormous impact. It raised urgent questions about economic development and, in close connection, the relationship between the Treasury and the banking and currency of the country. What were the effects of English credit on the cycle of economic growth in the United States? Had the banks, by an overindulgence of the "spirit of enterprise," precipitated the pattern of overaction and contraction? Or were Jackson's policies chiefly to blame? Would the new president sustain these policies or reverse them? Temporarily, at least, the economy recovered from the panic of 1837, but Van Buren's political response involved decisions that gave basic shape to his entire presidency.

All three elements—English credit, banking practices, and Jackson's policies—had contributed to the pattern of expansion to excess and then contraction, which led to the suspension of the banks shortly after Van Buren took office. Credit from England, first of all, provided a basis for the cycle of economic growth. Indeed, the statistics for the rising indebtedness of the United States are striking. From a net balance of trade of $7.9 million in 1830, the annual deficit mounted to $62.2 million by 1836, with imports jumping from $62.7 million to $180.1 million during the same period. In the normal operations of trade as then conducted on the international specie standard, such an imbalance could not have accumulated; instead, the deficit of one year or trading period demanded that there be reduced purchases during the next period and that specie be exported in order to restore the "natural" equilibrium of exports and imports. During the years after 1830, by contrast, the unusually high and prolonged imbalance of trade was sustained "artificially" by the inflow of English capital. The aggregate debt of the nation consequently climbed from $74.9 million in 1830 to $220.3 million six years later. Seen in another way, the economic development of the United States depended upon foreign aid in the form of English credit. Albert Gallatin, a former secretary of the Treasury under President Jefferson and now a leading New York banker, estimated that around $100 million of the English credit ultimately went into state projects of internal improvement.[1]

The rapid increase in the number of banks—from 330 in 1830 to 788 by the end of 1836—reflected in part the solid economic growth of the country, which was made possible by the inflow of credit. A comparison between banking practices at the time with those of an earlier day, however, reveals that banks were very prone to overaction. Before the War of 1812 the number of banks was relatively small, and most of them followed the conservative principles of commercial banking. Their loans were in the form of discounts on commercial paper which matured in 30 to 45 days and were not subject to renewal. The bank notes that were issued to borrowers in lieu of specie were thus relatively sound, for the short-term loans constituted a regularly recoverable, and therefore "liquid," asset. As long as they held a large reserve of specie in their vaults, the banks were able to meet the demands that note holders or depositors placed on them to pay in specie. For the economy as a whole, the bank notes bore a close relation to the amount of goods involved in trade, which made them very "elastic" as currency. Put another way, sound commercial banking simultaneously served a credit and a monetary function.

After the War of 1812 the rising spirit of enterprise demanded an enormous amount of capital to develop the country. Banking, as a consequence, underwent a transformation. All too many instances of wildcatting mismanagement and actual fraud indicated one response to the demand. In other instances the new state banks were nothing more than funnels for funds going into projects of internal improvement. Of much greater importance for its impact on the currency, however, was the deviation of most reputable bankers from earlier commercial practices. Bank credits, which were often extended on bases other than commercial paper, were also made renewable without added security; so that by 1830 the average term of bank loans rose to about six months. Such practices clearly made the bank's assets less "liquid" than before and, along with smaller reserves of specie, rendered less certain the ability of the bank to pay in specie. The general currency of the country, in the process, became far less elastic. No longer related closely to the actual needs of commerce, such a currency essentially sundered the credit and monetary functions of banking. But it was precisely this feature of the "credit system" which champions of enterprise such as Senator Nathaniel P. Tallmadge of New York found worthy of praise. "The credit system is the distinguishing feature between despotism and liberty," he said; "it is the offspring of free institutions; it is found to exist, and its influence is felt, in proportion to the freedom enjoyed by any people."[2]

Contrary to Jackson's intentions, some of his policies gave further stimulus to bank overaction. The surplus in the Treasury began to mount with the retirement of the national debt; on deposit in selected state banks, the surplus enabled them to make new loans. The bank war removed the restraining force that, because of its superior resources, the national bank had exercised over state banks. And Jackson had not succeeded in driving small notes out of circulation and thus creating a "vacuum" for specie to fill.

Meanwhile, an unusually large sum of around $35 million in specie came into the country during 1834 and 1835, much of it from sources that Jackson could neither anticipate nor control. About $3 million in gold came from Europe as a result of the gold revaluation, and another $4.5 million came from France to pay the "spoilation" claims. But Mexico supplied most of the added specie in the form of silver. As a commodity export from Mexico during the preceding decade, silver had flowed through the United States to England and eventually into the China trade. But a change in the pattern of this trade, when linked with the inflow of English capital, served to keep most of this silver in the United States, where, in 1834 alone, around $13 million were retained.

With little vacuum to fill in the circulating currency, the enormous bulk of this specie went into bank vaults as the basis, in multiplier fashion, for further issues of bank notes. The money supply accordingly jumped from $172 million in 1834 to $277 million two years later. During this period, Secretary of the Treasury Levi Woodbury estimated that the amount of currency increased from $6.50 to $10.00 per capita.[3]

Just as capital from England sparked expansion in the United States, the initial impulse for contraction by mid 1836 came from the same source. The power to give involved the power to take away. With specie reserves running low, the Bank of England raised its discount rate in July and again in August. This had the effect, over the next six months, of cutting in half the volume of commercial credits being extended to the import trade in the United States. Without the credits to finance the great imbalance of imports over exports, specie began to flow out of the country; by early 1837 this amounted to around $2.5 million. Since most of this sum came out of bank vaults, its withdrawal produced, again in multiplier fashion, a contraction of bank credit and issues which was painfully proportioned to the earlier expansion. Leading bankers severely curtailed new loans and refused extensions on old ones. Further contraction came from the preventive action of many banks, each of which was seeking to strengthen its reserves by presenting the notes of other banks for redemption in specie. The price of money in New York rose to 2.5 percent a month, and the supply failed to meet the demands of large import merchants who were caught with large inventories, obligations to England, and overdue credits that they had extended to their own jobbers. Many, facing the prospect of bankruptcy, also found it increasingly difficult to pay the duty bonds on earlier importations as they fell due.

Two measures of Jackson's administration in mid 1836 contributed to the contraction, and debate over them came into sharp political focus by the time Van Buren was inaugurated. One was the Deposit Act, passed on June 23, principally through the efforts of Whigs and expansion-minded Democrats. It sought relief from the deflationary forces by "unlocking" Treasury funds which, for a number of reasons, were thought to be lying idle in some of the deposit banks. Laws in many states restricted the amount a bank could loan, usually by defining the limit in terms of a ratio to its capital stock. This meant that some of the largest deposit banks, particularly in New York City, held government funds in excess of the limit that they were able to loan. The Deposit Act accordingly spread out the funds and made them more accessible. One part of the measure required that at least one bank in each state be designated as a depository and that the amount of government revenue on deposit in any one bank could never exceed three-fourths of its capital stock. The number of deposit banks quickly jumped from about thirty to ninety. With regard to the existing Treasury surplus, a second part of the act prescribed that it be distributed among the states in four quarterly installments, beginning in January 1837. As it turned out, around $37 million were available for the purpose, making each installment about $9.25 million.

Because the Deposit Act was inflationary in intent, the president was expected to veto it. But Jackson was apparently prevailed upon to sign it by the argument that a veto, at a time of credit and currency contraction, might defeat Van Buren's bid for election. With the "Specie Circular," Jackson found another way to implement his views. Turned down by the Senate in the form of a resolution sponsored by "Bullion Ben" (Thomas Hart Benton), it came forth on July 11, 1836, as an order from the Treasury. By the order, which Benton helped Jackson to formulate, only specie, not bank notes, could be received in payment for government lands. Jackson thought that the Treasury order would promote his "hard money" goals. By compelling banks to hold more specie in their vaults against expected calls by land purchasers for redemption, the order would have the effect of reducing, by some multiple, the issue of new bank notes.

Contrary to the intention of its chief sponsors, the Deposit Act abetted the forces of contraction. In the execution of the act, some of the Treasury's funds were withdrawn from the old deposit banks in order to bring their holdings down to the ratio, prescribed in the act, of three-fourths of their capital. Even greater sums were transferred to all parts of the country as the Treasury prepared, by January 1, 1837, to distribute to the states the first installment of the surplus. This alone amounted to $9.25 million. While in transit, moreover, none of the funds were available to the banks to help relieve the pressures of contraction. The effect of the withdrawals was particularly severe on the big deposit banks in New York City, for they were already bearing the brunt of reduced credits from England and the outflow of specie. Although the bulk of the transfers was made in bank notes, a recent study estimates that $5.58 million in specie went out of the New York banks and that this constituted the "jewelled pivot" around which contraction finally revolved. Albert Gallatin reached the same conclusion at the time. Ultimate responsibility lay in actions taken in creditor England, but the "proximate cause" of distress was the movement of vast sums by the Treasury under the Deposit Act. Because the operation of the "Specie Circular" involved much smaller sums, estimated at about $1 million, it had far less direct impact.[4]

In a number of ways, however, political opponents argued, with considerable success, that the Treasury order was the main cause of distress and that repeal of it would be the chief means of relief. Politically, it was unrepublican: Jackson's issue of the order after the Senate had turned it down was but another despotic act of a "Treasury Caesar." The refusal of the Treasury to accept bank notes was equally undemocratic, since paper money, not specie, constituted the bulk of the currency actually being used by the people. Economically, the "Specie Circular" defined a very "unnatural" process by deflecting specie from the eastern centers of trade toward which it would naturally flow. In this case a normal flow was of peculiar importance, because added specie in the East could ease the pressures created by the foreign demand. Finally, it was argued that the Treasury order tended to discredit all bank notes and, inescapably, to undermine the confidence on which the "credit system" of banking depended. If the government distrusted bank notes, private holders also might soon insist on specie, which would lead at last to the collapse of the entire system.

After the presidential election of 1836 many Democratic spokesmen joined the Whigs in opposition to the "Specie Circular." Prominent among them were Senator Tallmadge of New York, who was already noted as a special friend of the "credit system," and Senator William C. Rives of Virginia. Among other reasons, it was thought by those close to Jackson, Rives came out against the circular because of his lingering bitterness over not having received the party's nomination for vice-president. In any case, Whigs readily deferred to his efforts during the short 1836/37 session of Congress to do away with the Treasury order. Under the existing arrangements of the Treasury, bank notes were received in one branch of revenue—that of import duties—but specie was mandated in payment for government land. In order to end the specie mandate for government land, Rives thus proposed a bill mandating Treasury receipt of bank notes in all payments to the government, for land as well as import duties. Jackson wanted to diffuse more specie in circulation and to check the issuing of bank notes; whereas Rives hoped that the government's use of bank notes in all its transactions could relieve the banks at a time of increased contraction. The 41 to 5 Senate vote for the bill and the 143 to 59 vote in the House indicated that other Democrats agreed with Rives.[5] For them the present evil of contraction was a more pressing political reality than the past evil of inflation, which was deplored by Jackson.

As one of his last official acts, President Jackson gave the Rives bill a pocket veto. Because Congress adjourned less than ten days after passing the bill, he was able to kill the bill simply by refusing to sign it.

48

But he would have given an outright veto had the timing been different, for he was determined at this point to persevere in his hard-money course, even though many in his own party were opposed.

Two things—the mounting pressure of currency contraction and Jackson's veto of a bill for relief—constituted the immediate political heritage of the new president. Van Buren made no mention of the money problem in his Inaugural Address beyond the vague admission that the nation was "not altogether exempt from embarrassments." He probably sensed no immediate danger. Back in February he had dismissed rather curtly Benton's warning: "Your friends think you a little exalted in the head on the subject."[6] Even the sage Albert Gallatin later observed that he had not considered the problem critical until March.

But deep division in Jacksonian ranks over the "Specie Circular" could not escape Van Buren's attention. From his inauguration in March 1837 until the banks suspended specie payments in early May the central fact about his new presidency was the tug of opposing elements within his own party. Along with the economic merits of the case, Van Buren faced difficult political questions: Did his pledge to tread in Jackson's footsteps mean inflexible adherence to the "Specie Circular"? Or might altered circumstances allow for modifications, if not a total change in policy? How could he best deal with the divisions inside the party? And what effect might this or that decision have upon the image of "non committalism" which had followed him to the White House and threatened his credibility as president?

On one side an apparently large majority of party spokesmen wanted Van Buren to rescind or modify Jackson's Treasury order. He admitted that "bundles of letters" every day urged him to take a new course; and Senator Silas Wright of New York, Van Buren's closest and most trusted adviser, believed that a majority in his state wanted a change. The leading party papers, the *Albany Argus* and the *Richmond Enquirer*, assumed that Van Buren was planning to reverse Jackson's policy. In urging a change, Rives argued that the overwhelming majorities in Congress for his currency bill reflected the true will of the nation and therefore altered the relation in which Van Buren personally stood to Jackson. "This view of the matter," he pointedly said, "at once relieves all the delicacy you might otherwise feel in departing from a measure of your predecessor." Warning the president that "an enterprising people" would never accept a deflated currency, a New York banker friend thought it politically wiser to die of "speculation" than of "convulsion." Even if the actual sums involved in the operation of the "Specie Circular" were small, popular perceptions attached great importance to it and awaited some favorable signal from the new administration. Van Buren was accordingly advised to "bend with the storm."[7]

At the least it was thought that some modification of the circular could be made; this might give relief and yet allow Van Buren to keep faith with Jackson. Three alternative suggestions were made: waive the requirement that actual settlers must pay in specie for the purchase of land; receive the notes of all banks that the deposit bank in the area was willing to credit as cash; or as payment for land, accept certificates issued on specie deposited in eastern banks. These suggestions would provide some relief to the eastern banks that were bearing the greatest pressures from abroad. Such modifications, another New York banker friend thought, could bring relief without violating the "delicacy" that Van Buren felt about "reviewing the acts of your immediate predecessor."[8]

Spokesmen from the other side of the party, who now clearly constituted a minority on the issue, strongly urged Van Buren to retain the "Specie Circular" without modification. Only in this way, it was argued, could Van Buren fulfill the pledge to walk in Jackson's footsteps. Chief Justice Roger B. Taney, who had been very close to Jackson's war on the national bank, confidentially warned that "any measure which could be construed into a departure from the policy of the late administration" would be fraught with "lasting evil." Political considerations alone required close adherence to the "favorite policy" of his predecessor.[9]

With regard to its economic effects, two arguments for retaining the circular were pressed; these began to uncover a profound ambiguity in the Jacksonian heritage. One of the arguments, which was pragmatic in nature, closely linked the circular to the goal of saving the deposit banks, particularly in the West and the Southwest. Specie that was kept in the West by the operation of the Treasury order, it was argued, served to shore up the deposit banks in the area, thus checking the excesses to which they were deemed to be especially prone. Letters from bankers in New Orleans, Nashville, and Cincinnati assured Van Buren that the circular was having this salutary effect. From the Hermitage, Jackson likewise perceived the force of this position and advised Van Buren that "should any of the Deposit banks fail, it will shake your administration to its center."[10] Jackson's victory over the old national bank, which was secured by connecting the Treasury to state deposit banks, would then be put in great peril.

A second argument for retaining the circular was urged on Van Buren; it was ideological rather than pragmatic in nature. Saving the deposit banks, according to this view, was only a secondary part of the Jacksonian heritage; the primary goal remained one of enlarging the amount of specie in circulation. Animating this view were a rising spirit of hostility to all banks and the desire for a thorough reform, if not the actual destruction, of what was considered the "wretched bubbling system" of credit banking. Because the banks, and not government policies, had caused overaction and excess, it was not the duty of the government, during a period of contraction, to meliorate its evils or abort the inevitable process of "cupping & bleeding."[11]

In full agreement was William Gouge, a clerk in the Treasury and, since writing his book on banking in 1833, the high priest of hard money. It lay beyond "the scope of Legislative wisdom," he wrote the president, to avert the evils of contraction which necessarily followed the excesses of expansion. "The fault has been committed, and the evil *must* be endured." Indeed, Gouge was now ready, along with other hard-money ideologues, to carry Jackson's policy even farther. While Rives proposed to repeal the "Specie Circular" and to mandate the Treasury to use bank notes, Gouge wanted to extend the specie mandate to cover import duties as well as revenues from land. As the crisis of contraction mounted, Jackson became more torn and tempted in outlook. One part of him still wanted to save the deposit banks; the other part, informed by a deep hatred of all banks, yearned for freedom from their "corrupting influences."[12]

Van Buren clearly faced a difficult decision. His party was deeply divided; and his personal need to prove that he himself was "committed" to Jackson's heritage was clouded by some doubt (evident also in Jackson's own ambivalence) about what precisely were the priorities of the heritage he was to defend. Two things about his decision indicated its difficulty. First of all, he was more close-mouthed than usual in arriving at the decision. His normal practice as president was to hold regular cabinet meetings at which members were encouraged to discuss the issues at hand. The president himself spoke very little at the meetings and did not have votes taken. As a follow-up he often asked individual members for written statements on an issue before he made his decision. In the case of the circular, however, Van Buren assumed "entire responsibility" for the decision. Knowing the cabinet to be as divided as the party, he did not even submit the issue for consideration. Even Secretary Woodbury was not drawn into the decision-making process; he seemed at times to be in the dark about the president's intentions. In this case he and Van Buren clearly conformed to the presidential style that Jackson had fashioned.[13]

Secondly, Van Buren wrestled with the decision for a long time. At the Hermitage, Jackson grew impatient and feared the worst. Writing on March 30 "with the frankness of friendship," he urged the president to stand firm. Not until April 3 did Woodbury at the Treasury pass on any word of the president's inclination to retain the circular, yet new doubts arose by the end of the month about the firmness of this resolve. On April 24, in fact, Van Buren wrote to Jackson as if preparing to make a change, pointing especially to "the dreadful state of the money market in New York." Woodbury still had the "impression" that Van Buren would not rescind Jackson's Treasury order, but nothing had been made "publicly known."[14]

On May 4, exactly two months after his inauguration, Van Buren finally made public his decision to retain the "Specie Circular." The occasion for his announcement was a meeting with a delegation of New York merchants who came to the White House to plead the critical state of the money market and to urge, as means of relief, that the president rescind the circular and that he call a special session of Congress. Van Buren met the delegation with great dignity, and in like spirit he turned down both requests. With regard to the circular, moreover, he saw fit to provide no explanation for the decision other than the simple declaration that it would be "inconsistent with the public good" to revoke the circular under "existing circumstances."[15] Circumstances might change, of course, but the delegation took his word as final.

After the decision became generally known, most contemporaries found a simple explanation: the new president had deemed it expedient to follow closely in Jackson's footsteps. As a not unfriendly New York paper put it, Van Buren "feared the consequences of taking ground at so early a period of his administration in opposition to his political godfather." A recent study on the politics of Jacksonian finance reaches the same conclusion and reflects the view held by most other historians.[16]

This explanation, however, requires qualification. By following in Jackson's footsteps, Van Buren was following some of his own. One was the old problem of credibility, which his foes had fashioned for him. Van Buren saw, in the circular, an opportunity to face the problem and, with his first big decision, to refute the taunting charge of "non committalism." To yield on Jackson's Treasury order might otherwise tend to confirm the image of a "politician" who lacked courage and principles, who at once excited the contempt of foes and betrayed the trust of rank-and-file party members. Failure to meet the test, the president was reported as saying, would leave him "wholly without moral powers."

Apart from the other merits of the issue, Van Buren wanted to establish his right to rule.[17]

The meeting with New York merchants provided Van Buren with a good opportunity to enhance his "moral powers." By choosing the "public good" over the interests of merchants in his own state, Van Buren could exhibit the disinterested patriotism of a Jackson. Most of all he could gain the moral power that came from reenacting the archetypal experience of Jackson, who had, during his bank fight, received many such delegations of merchants at the White House. Senator Tallmadge of New York, who was so keenly aware of the intense money pressures on the mercantile community, could only regard Van Buren's course as one of "perfect infatuation"; and a far more friendly senator, John M. Niles of Connecticut, expressed genuine puzzlement that the otherwise sagacious Van Buren was squandering so much political capital on the issue.[18] Both failed to see Van Buren's stake in the issue; to him the question of credibility for his presidency was a matter of crucial importance.

Van Buren put his stamp on the decision in another way, for he defended it solely on pragmatic, not ideological, grounds. The evidence simply does not support the claim, made by an earlier study, that Van Buren retained Jackson's circular on the basis of Gouge's hard-money argument. As the crisis of contraction began to uncover a deep ambivalence in the Jacksonian heritage, Van Buren placed first priority at the time on saving the party's commitment to the deposit banks rather than on realizing a total hard-money policy for the Treasury. During the campaign of 1836 he saw no contradiction between the "Specie Circular" and his pledge to give the deposit banks a "fair trial." And now, during a time of contraction, he continued to regard the circular, not as a hard-money device, but as an indispensable means for saving the deposit banks. The argument struck him forcibly that the greatest danger lay in the West and that the demand for specie there kept the deposit banks in sound condition. Back in the East, by contrast, he supposed the money pressures bore most heavily on the mercantile community and did not directly threaten the soundness of the banks themselves. As a New Yorker he apparently could not believe that the banks in his own state were in a precarious condition. To visitors at the White House who argued for change, Van Buren read the letters of western bankers who supported the value of the circular. It was "the only measure," he told one guest, "that could save the country."[19]

With these views he hoped to win Rives's support. Rives had worked with great zeal under Jackson to put down the national bank. Now he took the connection between the Treasury and the state banks to be the true heritage of Jackson and believed that saving this connection required an end to the "Specie Circular." Van Buren shared the goal but differed over the means for attaining it. He therefore sought to convince Rives that his decision to retain the circular was not a new hard-money test for the party creed: in the mounting crisis it was, rather, the way to save the state-bank-deposit system at its weakest point in the West. The collapse of the system was fraught with great political evil, because it would greatly strengthen Whig arguments for bringing back the national bank. "We must take care," he warned Rives, "that we are not obliged to meet Congress & the advocates of a United States bank with broken Deposite Banks, and unavailable funds."[20]

In keeping with the political style of his entire career, Van Buren here tried to mediate intraparty differences. Many hard-money radicals on one side approved his decision to retain the circular because they wanted to wreck the banking system. Rives and Tallmadge, among a few others who were soon to be called Conservatives, wanted to rescind the circular in order to save the system. Van Buren identified with the Conservative goal while adopting the means that the radicals approved. Unhappily for the new president, the mounting pressures in the money market put to a severe test his efforts at bringing harmony to party councils.

The suspension of specie payments by the New York banks on May 10 presented an even more profound challenge. By February 1837 a drop in the price of cotton was precipitating the final phase of monetary contraction that had begun the year before. Many factors in creditor England were involved, but the most important was a dwindling grain reserve, which caused throughout the economy a shift in demand away from cotton, and the need for added specie to pay for grain on the Continent. The price of cotton in New Orleans quickly fell from 16 to 13 cents a pound, and one leading firm—Herman, Briggs, and Company— went under at a loss of from $4 to $8 million, because it was unable, at the lower price, to cover its advances for moving the crop. Soon thereafter, Joseph Brothers, a large creditor in New York, also failed. In the mercantile community a sense of panic caused by other failures soon began to spread to the public at large and led to hoarding and a rising demand on banks to redeem their notes. In New York the final blow came when individual depositors in great number rushed in to withdraw their funds in specie. On May 9 alone, around $652,000 was withdrawn.[21] Within a week, banks all over the country were following the New York example.

In real economic terms, the suspension of specie payments by the banks did not strike with such "devastating fury" as a recent study supposed, nor did it usher in a reign of "chaos."[22] With loans and other assets ample to cover their note and deposit liabilities, most of the banks were not actually bankrupt at all. Because their loans were of longer term and therefore less accessible, the banks were simply unable at the time to meet one of their obligations, namely to pay specie on demand to note holders and depositors. Recognizing the fact that the banks' assets were not as "liquid" as the crisis required, the legislature in New York authorized the suspension for one year by waiving the enforcement of laws that provided for revoking the charters of banks that were unable to pay in specie on demand. Where needed, other states took the same action.

A general suspension did two things to the currency: it immediately drove most specie out of circulation, and it left mainly the notes of banks, unbacked by specie and depreciated in value from 10 to 25 percent in different parts of the country. The action of the several states could not, it was true, alter the guarantee contained in the federal Constitution that all debts be paid in legal tender; but the fact that most creditors were also debtors created a situation in which unbacked paper was widely being accepted in all transactions. State and local governments easily entered into the arrangement, by collecting and disbursing in depreciated notes and by using suspended banks as depositories for their funds. Many mercantile enterprises had been ruined by the crisis, of course, and unemployment became a serious problem in some places for the first time. But agriculture and domestic trade suffered a slighter decline, and a lull in manufacturing had ended within six months. Most spokesmen for merchants actually welcomed suspension as a means of relief after months of contraction in the money market. New bank loans were forthcoming to save some firms and to spark new mercantile activity.

When seen in a larger perspective, moreover, the panic was an interruption, rather than the end, of a cycle of expansion that had begun in 1830. Within a year, specie from England and a new flow of credit enabled banks to resume and business activity to revive. It was not until the end of 1839 that a profound downturn brought the cycle to a close.[23]

In its political effects, by contrast, the panic of 1837 had great impact. Party debate over who was to blame for the crisis reached a new level of intensity. Whigs triumphantly announced the bankruptcy of Jackson's "experiments" on the currency, tracing backward from the "Specie Circular" the alternative evils of suspension, contraction, and excess to his veto in 1832 of the bill to recharter the Bank of the United

States. And underlying the specific errors of policy was "the great fundamental error," or original sin, of executive usurpation. By retaining the circular in opposition to the known wishes of Congress, Van Buren had participated in this original sin and therefore had to bear his share of responsibility for the present evils. Many former Jacksonians, now ready to break from the party, joined the Whig cry: "Let old Jackson go to the devil," one said to Van Buren. "Let us retrace our steps."[24] A new national bank or the revival of the old one, in this view, was the obvious remedy.

Democrats who were loyal to Jackson just as surely blamed the banks, and the hostility against the banks, which had been voiced earlier by the radicals, now gained a wider hearing. Money questions at such a moment tended to become moral questions. The Democratic press thus picked up on the outrage that John Quincy Adams had vented on the suspended banks for perpetuating "a fraud on every holder of their bills." Even the moderate Senator Silas Wright confessed he had an almost "uncontrollable inclination" to damn the banks, preferring the "iron money of Lycurgus" to the paper money of the banks, which were always liable to excesses of expansion and contraction.[25] Many radicals were ready to suit action to their feelings. If Whigs called for a new national bank, they wanted to do away with all banks. At the least they would entirely sever the connection between the Treasury and the banks. Jackson's limited efforts to enlarge the amount of specie had not caused suspension; and a total hard-money policy for the government might prevent a recurrence.

Van Buren did not enter directly into this intense debate, but his early decisions, which had been made in the wake of suspension, assumed that the banks were to blame and pointed toward a policy of divorcing the operations of the Treasury from those of the banks. His immediate task, that of keeping the Treasury afloat under the new conditions, would not be easy. By law, the Treasury could not receive as payment of government dues the notes of any suspended banks; yet suspension had driven most specie into hiding and had left a currency that was made up overwhelmingly of depreciated notes. Another law forbade the Treasury to pay the government's own creditors in the notes of suspended banks, but with the exception of a small sum of specie on hand at the Mint, the only funds available to the Treasury were in the form of depreciated notes held on account in the deposit banks. On the deposit side of its operations, the Deposit Act of 1836 forbade the Treasury to place its funds in suspended banks. The funds that were already on deposit with the banks would presumably remain. With regard to new funds, however, the Treasury would have to keep them itself; yet, there was a need for added safeguards, which only Congress could supply.

Confronted with these questions of Treasury management, which had been posed by suspension, the president issued a proclamation on May 15 for the new Twenty-fifth Congress to meet in special session on the first Monday in September. Because only eleven days earlier he had turned down the request of the New York merchants for a special session, some political friends feared that the proclamation might expose his lack of firmness or "committalism." But the expected taunts of the Whigs did not come, for the suspension on May 10 had totally altered circumstances and therefore had made an appeal to Congress so obviously necessary.

Until Congress met in special session on September 4, President Van Buren assumed full responsibility for operating the Treasury. In the performance of this task he could have gained considerable support for evading the specie mandate contained in existing laws. State and local governments, like individual debtors and creditors, were already receiving and disbursing depreciated notes and were using suspended banks as depositories. Even stronger warrant for doing the same thing was at hand in the example of President James Madison, who had, during the last general suspension from 1814 to 1816, operated the Treasury in conformity with the actual state of the currency, receiving depreciated notes and using the suspended banks as depositories. With little hesitation and full cabinet approval, by contrast, Van Buren decided to conform as much as possible to the specie mandate of the laws. Orders accordingly went out to postmasters, collectors of customs, and receivers of land revenues: they were not to accept any notes of suspended banks, they were to keep the collected funds in their own hands, and they were to disburse the funds to creditors of the government only on the authority of drafts issued by the Treasury.

In day-to-day operations, it was true, the Treasury showed considerable leniency. Because it was difficult for import merchants to pay tariff duties in specie, the Treasury found a way, through certain technicalities, to postpone the collection of most import duty bonds until October, after Congress would have had time in its special session to consider the matter. The Treasury also made a decision not to prosecute the deposit banks, which, under the law, were bound to redeem in specie the government funds on deposit with them. By allowing the banks time to recover, Secretary Woodbury reasoned, they would eventually be able to make good on all of the funds held.

On the disbursal side of its operations, the Treasury also took certain liberties. With a decline in customs collections and a precipitous drop in land revenues—from $24 million in 1836 to $7 million in the following year—the government simply lacked enough specie to meet the demands of its creditors. In this situation the Treasury gave its creditors a choice: either wait for specie to accumulate or accept in payment funds to be drawn from the old deposit banks in the form of their depreciated notes. Most creditors chose to accept the depreciated notes rather than to wait for an indefinite period to get paid in specie. One other means was used. When the deposit banks refused to meet Treasury drafts made on them, or when creditors refused to accept the bank notes, the Treasury allowed the drafts themselves to circulate as money. They were, in effect, a form of non-interest-bearing treasury notes that were made receivable at par in payment of all dues to the government. In these ways a beleaguered Woodbury was able to keep the Treasury going, by paying half in specie and half in paper.

Jackson's initial misgivings over the leniency of these actions added to the burdens of the new administration. Following events very closely, Jackson disapproved the indulgences that were granted to the import merchants. And he did not like Woodbury's gentle treatment of the deposit banks, for he wanted to see them prosecuted at once. Van Buren accordingly instructed Woodbury to write a long letter to Jackson, explaining that the concessions made to the merchants and bankers were tactical in nature and that they in no way weakened the administration's basic commitment to uphold the specie mandate of the Constitution. "We mean never to strike the Specie flag," Woodbury wrote, "however we may be obliged to grant such delays and indulgences as the suddenness of the disaster and its widespread violence may render for a short time expedient and proper." By endorsing this letter in the same terms, Jackson at last realized that Van Buren was holding firm.[26]

Van Buren's efforts to keep the specie flag flying over the Treasury after the banks suspended in May have not received the attention they deserve.[27] Basically they set the course for the remainder of his presidency. Consistent in goal with his decision to retain the "Specie Circular" before the bank suspension, his actions thereafter pointed directly to the proposal that he made at the special session in September for a permanent divorce of the Treasury's operations from those of all banks. In both cases he acted as a moderate with the goal of preserving the basic heritage of the party, yet the force of events increasingly lent to these actions a more radical appearance.

Several considerations strongly supported Van Buren's decision to uphold the specie standard during the period of general suspension. The constitutional prescription for legal tender spoke more directly to the responsibility of the federal than to that of the state and local government. The guarantee of a uniform tariff also ruled out the receiving of depreciated notes, because their value in relation to specie varied so widely from one port city of the country to another. There was also a moral obligation on the part of the federal government to hold up the true standard of value and to serve as a rallying point for banks to resume specie payments. Moreover, the condition at the earlier period of suspension was far different from the one in 1837. While Madison had mingled Treasury affairs with the suspended banks at a time when the nation was at war, was drained of specie, and was deeply in debt, the opposite circumstances obtained under Van Buren. He also faced, in this new crisis, his old problem of credibility. Among many party friends, doubts about his firmness once more clearly put in question his right to rule.

Along with these reasons were two political considerations of great weight. One was the obvious fact that the banks, by suspending specie payment, had separated themselves from the operations of the Treasury. They could not by law serve as depositories, nor could their notes be accepted as tender in payment of government dues. Politically, the fact enhanced the party claim that it had been the banks themselves, and not the policies of Jackson, that had caused the trouble.

Secondly, Van Buren feared that any new connection between the Treasury and the suspended banks might, on the basis of Madison's earlier experience, open the way for a new national bank. By deeply involving the Treasury with the banks during the 1814–1816 suspension, Van Buren thought, President Madison had been driven at last to the conclusion that a national bank was the only way to resolve the Treasury's problems and to force the state banks to resume specie payments. This was, in Van Buren's view, the great error of the otherwise virtuous Madison, a negative archetype to be avoided at all costs. In defense of the "Specie Circular" before suspension in May, he wanted to avoid the need of having to meet Congress with broken deposit banks. Now that the banks were broken, he was determined, in the upcoming special session, not to face gloating Whigs with any kind of embarrassing connection between the Treasury and the banks, such as Madison had made. Van Buren's effort to keep a specie flag flying over the Treasury was not the work of a hard-money ideologue. He sought, rather, as a pragmatic leader, to preserve the heritage of his party, the basic feature of which was Jackson's triumph over the national bank that a beleaguered Madison had created.

Here are to be seen both the strength and the weakness of Van Buren's entire presidency. His own experience and his veneration for Jefferson combined to strengthen the view that the welfare of his party and of the nation were the same. Fidelity to party, in this context, made for principled action and served, among other things, to counter the persisting image of "non committalism." It also made decisions easier. Because he had a corporate concept of party, he thus supposed that the pattern of the party's past commitments would provide the surest guide for present action. Because suspension, for most Jacksonians, seemed to discredit the deposit banks, with which Jackson had replaced the national bank, the clear prescription was to move on to some new arrangement. With the proposal of divorce, Van Buren made his basic response to the panic of 1837.

4

A PROPOSAL OF DIVORCE

In his message to the special session on September 5, 1837, President Van Buren asked Congress for new legislation that would make the Treasury independent of the banks. Under the Deposit Act of 1836 and companion measures, the suspended banks could not serve as depositories for government funds, nor could their notes be received in payment of land or tariff duties. By conforming to these laws after the suspension in May, Van Buren had essentially maintained the operations of the Treasury apart from the banks. Unless Congress replaced these laws with some new arrangement, however, the resumption of specie payment by the banks at some later point would automatically revive their connection with the Treasury. It was with this in mind that Van Buren called for new legislation: in effect he wanted to change the temporary separation of the Treasury from the banks into a state of permanent divorce.

Van Buren's proposal of divorce defined the central domestic issue of his entire presidency. Senator John M. Niles of Connecticut, a strong administration supporter, rightly sensed its seminal importance: "The great issues are now formed for the discussion and guidance of public opinion for years to come." Set forth in 1837 and debated at length, the proposal was finally enacted into law in July 1840. During the course of the debate, opposition to divorce gave greater coherence to the Whig coalition, while the defection of self-styled Conservatives, led by William C. Rives and Nathaniel P. Tallmadge, also drew the lines of the administration party more sharply than ever. The issue of divorce, as

Senator James Buchanan predicted, thus became the "touchstone of parties."[1]

Personal and party considerations entered largely into Van Buren's early decision for divorce. There remained, first of all, the question of credibility, which the Whigs had been raising for years. Taunts of "non committalism" resounded once more, daring the president to come forth with some plan. Political friends were also concerned. Would the president submit a proposal to Congress, one of them inquired, "as the deliberate scheme of the Executive Government"? Should Van Buren fail to recommend "decided measures," Buchanan wrote to Jackson, it might prove "fatal" to his presidency. "For my own part I have entire confidence in his firmness," he continued, "but this quality of his character would be put to the test at the meeting of Congress." By sending Buchanan's letter to the president, Jackson also expressed his concern.[2] When Van Buren decided to retain the "Specie Circular," he had passed the first test of his presidency. Now the question of fiscal agency presented a more severe test. Considerable irony was also involved: the Whig challenge for him to exert presidential leadership assumed that the power of the office had grown, which Whigs had lamented for years.

The party, no less than Van Buren personally, was also on trial. Buchanan clearly stated this widely held perception: "The next step we take as a party in relation to the public revenue, if it should not be successful, will prostrate us & reestablish the B. of the United States." Whigs were finding it easy to lay all the blame on Jackson's rash policies and to call for the return to a national bank. Alarmed by Whig inroads in the West, Senator Felix Grundy of Tennessee urged the administration to come up with some plan of its own "in order that the advocates of a National Bank may be met in argument." Because Van Buren took Jackson's victory over the Bank of the United States to be the point of no return for the party, he faced the imperative task of choosing proper ground on which to battle the Whigs. He saw only two choices: to revamp the Treasury's connection with the state deposit banks or to sever "all connection with Banks."[3]

Two of Van Buren's close associates from New York advised the president to consider a new connection between the Treasury and the state banks. Because the interests of so many people in the state were intertwined with the banks, it was reasoned, they could only see a divorce of the federal government from the banks as an act of hostility that was calculated to destroy the banks. Consequently, a proposal of divorce would drive many people to the Whigs and strengthen the call for a new national bank. Enos Throop, who had long been connected with Van Buren and had succeeded him as governor, thus warned: "I do believe it utterly impossible to resist a National Bank, if the friends of the Administration are compelled at the same time to make war upon the Banking System." Even Senator Silas Wright wavered for a moment. Although he was personally moved by an almost "uncontrollable inclination" to crush the banks, he found that too many of "our honest friends" were identified with them. Divorce "would startle them" and greatly strengthen the Whig cause.[4]

But Wright soon came round to the position, held by most party spokesmen, that divorce was the only ground on which the battle could be fought. The nature of earlier Whig arguments, indeed, left little choice. If the state deposit banks had failed once, they would most likely fail again; to make a new connection with the state banks would merely repeat Jackson's original error in removing the deposits from the national bank. The defense of the party and of Jackson required that the blame be shifted from Jackson's policies onto the banks themselves. Jackson had not erred in removing the deposits from the national bank; instead, suspension showed that the deposit banks had betrayed the trust that Jackson had placed in them. Senator Niles defined the political situation very precisely: "Our opponents charge the difficulties (which both parties admit to be vicious) to the government; we charge them to the banks. This is the issue between us."[5] Politically, in this view, divorce constituted the only alternative to a new national bank.

Van Buren defended his decision for divorce in these political and pragmatic terms. Until the state deposit system "had fallen to pieces of itself," he wrote at length to a doubting ally, he had harbored no idea of changing the fiscal agency of the government. But suspension had created a totally new political situation. The mass of the "Democracy," angry at the banks, would provide no support for reconnecting the Treasury with the banks. Divorce, by contrast, might enlist "a mass of good feeling on our side which will increase in power every day." In defense of the "Specie Circular" before suspension, Van Buren supposed that the party could not confront the Whigs in Congress with broken deposit banks. Consistently with this earlier assessment, he now opted for divorce instead of the state-bank-deposit system: "I am more mistaken in my judgment of public feeling than I have ever been, if we could have stood our ground in an attempt to revamp it."[6] Salvation for the party and the Jacksonian heritage required a new step.

Made in behalf of party, it was a step that precipitated the defection of Conservatives from the party. Already bitter at Van Buren for not having rescinded the "Specie Circular," Rives and Tallmadge now looked to "a bold independent course." Rives rejected the party line, which placed all blame on the banks. In his view, their suspension came from no inherent weakness but from unique causes—the heavy debt to England and the extraordinary influx of specie—which had temporarily thrown the system "out of gear." Tallmadge gave divorce a radical reading and warned that Van Buren had declared war "against all our banking institutions." He also deplored the engine of "party discipline" that the president would bring to bear on the divorce proposal. By the end of June 1837 arrangements were completed with Thomas Allen to edit a new paper in Washington which would be dedicated to "true conservative doctrines." Although Allen protested that he was loyal on all issues other than divorce, Van Buren rightly took the *Madisonian* to be an "opposition paper." Adding to the opposition was Reuben M. Whitney, a special agent for the old deposit banks, who now aspired to the same role in a revamped system.[7]

The defection of the Conservatives resulted in a greater degree of harmony among Democrats who remained loyal to Van Buren. But important differences over certain aspects of divorce remained, generally along radical and moderate lines. On the *deposit* side of divorce, pertaining to the way the Treasury *handled* its funds, the differences were minor ones. All agreed that the Treasury should in some way maintain independent control over its funds. The simplest way would be to keep the funds in its own vaults and then to disburse them directly to creditors of the government. A second way would be to use the banks, but on condition that the funds that the Treasury placed in a bank be in the form of a "special deposit." This meant that the designated bank would keep Treasury funds in a vault, separate from its other deposits; make no use of these funds in its normal operations; and disburse them for a small fee to creditors of the government at the direction of the Treasury. Either way, the Treasury would retain direct access to its funds and would keep them from being used by banks as the basis for extending new loans. This feature of divorce also had great political appeal; the claim could be made that government funds, the "people's money," had been withheld from the selfish use of bank corporations.

On the *funds receivable* side of divorce, by contrast, Democrats differed greatly over the *kind* of funds the Treasury should receive and the likely effect they would have on banking and currency. The more radically minded Democrats insisted that only specie be accepted by the Treasury in payment of all government dues. With the "Specie Circular," Jackson had required that hard money be paid for land; now, radicals wanted to extend that requirement to the payment of import duties and all other types of revenue. The exclusive use of specie by the federal government, it was also believed, would eventually have the effect of destroying what Jackson called the "swindling system" of banking. Daniel Raymond, a contemporary writer on economics, accordingly hailed divorce as the herald of "a most important epoch." He assumed that Treasury use of the bank notes had provided the patronage and the element of confidence on which the banking system absolutely depended. Now, by refusing to recognize "the legitimacy of a single bank note," an independent Treasury would cause credit banking to collapse.[8] In the new epoch there would still be banks, but they would be banks of deposit and discount only, not banks of issue.

William Gouge developed this view most fully. His earlier ideas about fiscal divorce, outlined in his history of banking in 1833, attained final form in a pamphlet published at Philadelphia in June 1837. Brought out privately without the countenance of the administration in Washington, where he served as a clerk in the Treasury, the pamphlet placed central emphasis on the funds-receivable feature of divorce. Because the federal government was the "greatest capitalist" and the "greatest money dealer" in the country, he reasoned, its acceptance of bank notes in great quantity had provided an indispensable basis for their circulation and legitimacy. Divorce would withdraw this support and thus erode public confidence in banking. The exclusive use of specie by the Treasury would therefore bring in its train an eventual hard-money currency for the whole country. In this perspective a decision for divorce would define an irrepressible conflict: "The war between specie and paper is now fairly begun. The result will determine the destinies of the country."[9]

Democrats of moderate outlook rejected radical assumptions. John Brockenbrough, president of the Virginia bank that had served as a depository before suspension, deemed "chimerical" the notion that the exclusive use of specie by the Treasury meant the destruction of credit banking. In his view, the state banks could recover and prosper without the patronage of the federal Treasury. Nor did he share the radical belief that the destruction of credit banking was desirable; to the contrary, he thought that banks of issue were indispensable for "a rising and enterprising country like ours." He favored the exclusive use of specie, not for any destructive effect it might have on banks, but for the purpose of rendering the Treasury's control of its funds truly independent. How much control would the Treasury have, he asked, if the notes that it received were suddenly to depreciate in value because of a new suspension of the banks? Brockenbrough was no hard-money ideologue; and his position clearly belies the claim of an earlier study that divorce "found its only backing among intellectuals and radicals."[10]

Other moderate Democrats agreed with Brockenbrough's analysis of the effect that the use of specie would have on banking and currency. Politically, however, they sensed a danger. Foes of divorce, Senator Niles feared, might seize upon the radical interpretation, picturing the "design & object" of divorce as nothing less than a passion "to discredit & overthrow state banks." In part to avert this political danger, Secretary of the Treasury Woodbury suggested an alternative to the use of specie on the funds-receivable side. He was willing for the Treasury to receive notes, after the banks resumed, on three conditions. The Treasury could accept all bank notes that circulated at par in the area where payment was made. The Treasury could also disburse the notes to creditors of the government who were willing to accept them as cash. Finally, the Treasury would take the notes that were not immediately disbursed and submit them to the banks for payment in specie. In this way, many bank notes might be actually received and disbursed, but only specie would be kept in the Treasury vaults. Independent control of the Treasury over its funds, Woodbury thus thought, could be achieved.[11]

In the political context of the time, however, many moderate Democrats realized that something more was needed than simply the goal of securing to the Treasury an independent control over its own funds. There was also some responsibility for the general currency of the country. If an independent Treasury was the true alternative to the old national bank, then it could only be a viable one if it performed two functions in regard to the general currency of the country, which Whigs were now claiming as the peculiar excellence of the national bank.[12]

One of these functions was to provide a sound and uniform paper for facilitating domestic exchange. The notes of the old national bank had circulated more widely at par than those of the largest state banks, and its virtual monopoly on the buying and selling of bills of exchange had supplied a sound and efficient medium for moving goods across the country. Buchanan accordingly thought the Treasury should provide a paper medium of its own. Drafts, drawn on specie in the Treasury vaults and issued to creditors of the government, might be allowed to circulate indefinitely. Woodbury also thought that the Treasury should be able to make an outright issue of gold and silver certificates, based on specie at hand, and put them into the general circulation. Because government paper of this sort would have uniform value in all parts of the country, it could provide a cheap and less cumbersome medium of exchange than specie.[13]

Treasury notes constituted another important form of government paper. Unlike drafts or certificates, which were based on specie actually in the Treasury, these notes were issued in anticipation of new revenues. Made receivable in payment of all government dues and subject to indefinite renewal, they could be disbursed to creditors of the government and could find their way into the general circulation. By supplementing drafts and certificates, one western proponent argued, the issue of treasury notes might then make the Treasury "a more powerful institution" than the old national bank and forever silence the "eternal Whig clamor."[14] A new national bank was not needed, because an abundance of government paper performed one of its earlier functions.

The second function that was claimed to have been a merit of the old national bank was that of acting as a check on state bank issues. Because of its superior capital, the Bank of the United States normally stood as creditor to the state banks and collected their notes in excess of its own outstanding ones. By frequent submission of these notes to the state banks for payment in specie, the national bank thus exercised a constant restraining force. The deposit of federal revenue in the national bank had also enhanced, by that amount, its restraining power. The operation of an independent Treasury, by contrast, would have less impact. The exclusive use of specie would have some effect, it was true, for it compelled banks to be more vigilant in anticipating demands for specie to pay government dues. Additionally, the amount of specie used by the government reduced by that sum the specie that might otherwise flow into bank vaults as the basis for further issues of notes. Clearly the control that an independent Treasury would exert over the state banks would be limited and indirect.

For this reason, many of Van Buren's advisers wanted to supplement the power of the Treasury over the state banks by other means. Three measures were recommended. One, suggested by Buchanan and Woodbury, called for an amendment to the Constitution, which would give Congress direct power to forbid the state banks to issue notes of less than $20 denomination. Jackson had failed by other means to drive small notes out of circulation and thus to create a vacuum for specie to fill.

Two other ways for restraining the state banks, according to Attorney General Benjamin F. Butler, were already within the constitutional power of Congress. By one of these powers—which was later invoked during the Civil War to assure success for a new system of national banks—Congress could drive small notes out of circulation simply by placing a federal excise tax on them. By a second power, Congress could pass a uniform bankruptcy act, making it specifically applicable to corporations, and could devise procedures for closing banks that failed to resume specie payment within a given period of time. The people were ready for "strong measures," Butler assured Van Buren; and a bankruptcy law could truly be "a national Regulator," indeed, "a much more efficient & valuable remedy than any National Bank." Since the "great argument" for a national bank was its alleged ability "to keep the state banks in check," Butler deemed these two measures, and particularly a bankruptcy act, "almost indispensable to the success of your administration."[15]

In the context of saving the party's heritage, Van Buren made the decision for divorce very soon after the banks suspended specie payments in May. It was not until his message to the special session in September, however, that he made the decision official and outlined the details of the divorce proposal over which radicals and moderates differed. Privately he saw such divorce in moderate terms. For this reason he identified immediately with the views of Brockenbrough, which had been sent to him in late May, and passed them on to a number of other party spokesmen from whom he was seeking advice. Not the least of Brockenbrough's attractions was his Virginia pedigree, his experience as a conservative banker, and his ties to the ruling elite in Richmond, which was generally known as the Junto.[16] At the same time, Van Buren was aware of the interpretation that radicals had placed on divorce and, even more, the zeal with which they were preparing to support it. In keeping with his political style, he sought to mediate conflicting views within the party and to formulate some consensus about the details of divorce. Public silence from May to September allowed time for the task.

The course followed by the administration paper, the *Washington Globe*, reflected the president's strategy. Such a course undoubtedly went against the deepest feelings of its editor, Francis Blair, whose first loyalty remained with the more radically minded Jackson. But Blair had been sympathetic to the Van Buren interest under Jackson and now warmed to the new president. In private, his correspondence with Jackson at the Hermitage pictured Van Buren in a favorable light; in public, his paper generally presented a strong case for Van Buren's policies. At this point he opened the columns of the *Globe* to both radicals and moderates. Letters from radical Democrats were published along with installments of the pamphlet by Gouge, which interpreted the divorce proposal as a hard-money crusade against credit banking. Letters from moderates were also printed, and editorials extolled the importance of state banks and a sound credit system. In like spirit, the paper dealt gently with Rives and Tallmadge, hoping to moderate the effects of their opposition.

Unhappily for Van Buren, the independence being shown by Rives and Tallmadge posed another danger, for it tended to weaken the support that Van Buren had expected from others in the party who were to remain loyal. In Virginia the editor of the powerful *Richmond Enquirer*, Thomas Ritchie, assumed a position of neutrality that was paralyzing. Caught between Van Buren and Rives, whom he hoped might regain Virginia's influence in national affairs, Ritchie at once opposed divorce and any break in party unity. While urging Van Buren not to make divorce a new test of party creed, he also pleaded with Rives to stay within the party: "I charge you, my dear sir, not to woo the Whigs."[17] Within a year, Ritchie had given up on Rives and had accepted the policy of divorce; but at this critical moment in Van Buren's presidency, on the eve of the special session, he withheld the support that the president so sorely needed.

Van Buren faced a similar problem in New York. By branding divorce a radical measure, Tallmadge gave added force to the claim of the radical Locofocos that the president was coming around to their position. Moderates in the party, as a consequence, had difficulty in finding a middle ground. The *Albany Argus* professed its neutrality, but in one important instance the friends of divorce found it anything but neutral. The paper quickly printed a long letter from Tallmadge and the address of an Albany committee, both of which incorporated his views, while a lengthy exposition of divorce prepared by Silas Wright had to seek an outlet in the much smaller *St. Lawrence Republican*. Meanwhile, Governor William L. Marcy expressed "fearful forebodings." He did remain loyal to the party and later accepted the party stand on divorce. At the time, however, he could only see it as a radical measure that might destroy the party. Unable to support divorce, he hoped that Van Buren would indulge differences of opinion and not make it a new test of party creed.[18]

As Van Buren had worked during the preceding decade to revive old party distinctions, he had sought to base his own party on an alliance between New York and Virginia. Now, as he approached a crisis in his presidency, this base of power appeared to have seriously eroded. Would he, with this in mind, back away from the decision for divorce made in May, shortly after the suspension? Editorials in the *Richmond Enquirer* suggested the possibility, thus causing new concern among other party friends about his "committalism." Gideon Welles, who was closely associated in Connecticut with Senator Niles, voiced this concern to Van Buren late in August. "My object is," he bluntly admitted, "to urge the administration to take unequivocal & decided ground. Any hesitation or doubt will overwhelm the administration, and lead to calamitous consequences." Along with the problem of Van Buren's own credibility came the need for the party to have a rallying point. Passing over the special position of New York and Virginia or the notion that a party is only a congeries of state electoral machines, Welles supposed that the Democratic party was a corporate entity of national scope, based on principle, and indispensable to the "welfare of the country."[19]

Welles's letter was not needed in order to bolster Van Buren's resolve on the eve of the special session. It pointed, rather, to Van Buren's own basic views about the position he occupied and the duty he had to perform. He believed deeply in party government and in the corporate experience of the party as the best guide for the welfare of the country. Having helped to shape Jackson's presidency in a party mold, Van Buren also believed it was the ultimate duty of the president to speak for his party and to define new elements in its creed.

Van Buren did, it was true, consult widely with party spokesmen, and he did hold regular cabinet meetings during the period when the divorce proposal was under consideration. But he took no votes in the cabinet and, as usual, reserved final decisions for himself. The cabinet disagreed over the details, and at least two members—Joel R. Poinsett and Mahlon Dickerson—probably favored a national bank. Yet they readily deferred to Van Buren's views of party and presidential power, thus lending substance to Van Buren's claim that there was harmony in the cabinet. In Jackson's footsteps, Van Buren could, with the full expectation of friends and foes, set forth a new course for the nation. Between the relative silence of President James Monroe during the panic of 1819 and the special session in 1837 lay the growth of the party and of the presidency, to which Van Buren had made a great contribution.

In these terms, Van Buren's message to the special session was a striking act of presidential leadership and a masterful political document. With a lawyer's skill he dealt with a wide range of views and ordered them in a way that was calculated to reconcile friends and to meet the challenge of political foes. The message vindicated Jackson, confronted the arguments for a national bank, and assimilated divorce to the old republican ideology. Upon hearing the message read in joint session, Niles expressed great enthusiasm: "It will do your heart & soul good to read it," he told Welles, for it contained "all that the friends of the administration could desire." The immediate response of others confirmed this assessment. By boldly repelling the taunts of "non committalism," Van Buren had raised himself "higher in the estimation of the people." The father of Samuel Tilden hailed the message as "a rallying point" for the party or, to change the figure, an "anchor" thrown out in the storm; while a party spokesman in North Carolina similarly rejoiced that the president had "staggered his opponents" with so strong an alternative to the national bank.[20]

With regard to the causes of the "overwhelming catastrophe," Van Buren shifted the blame from Jackson's policies to the banks. Though there had been "overaction" in all branches of business, it was the banks that had carried the forces of expansion to a speculative pitch by "excessive issues of paper" and other means for "the enlargement of credit." In the natural cycle of things a contraction, "proportioned in its violence," would inescapably follow the excesses of expansion. Other commercial countries had experienced the same pattern, but in the United States there was the added evil of "extensive derangement" in governmental finances due to their connection with the banks. For a time the banks had served well as fiscal agents, but the distribution of the surplus revenue had uncovered speculative practices that showed how the government deposits subserved the private interests of the banks. Nor would the old Bank of the United States have performed any better as a fiscal agent; it had exhibited the same "proneness" to excess and the same "propensity" to make the public interest serve the bank's interest.[21]

Supposing this proneness to be "inherent," and not an "accidental" characteristic of all "banks of issue," Van Buren proposed that the Treasury keep and disburse its own funds. Two modes, more fully described in the accompanying report of the secretary of the Treasury, were suggested for the purpose. The more simple of the two merely assigned "additional duties" to the existing officials—collectors, receivers, postmasters—to handle the funds they received. Cheapness and simplicity recommended this mode, yet Van Buren appreciated the concern that many people had for the safety of funds, particularly at such points as New York, where the sums were large. At these points, according to a second mode, a few new Treasury officials could be designated to keep and disburse the funds collected by others. In all cases, adequate bond would be required for all officials handling the funds.

From the deposit side of divorce, where there was general agreement among party friends, Van Buren turned to the matter of funds receivable. Aware of great divergence here, he worked out a proposal that would speak to both radical and moderate views. His first choice was for the Treasury to receive, keep, and disburse its funds only in specie. This meant that the Treasury would be absolutely divorced from the banks. For those of radical outlook, this also would entail the eventual destruction of the banks. It is no wonder that Locofocos hailed the message, claiming themselves to be "the fathers of the Church" and Van Buren himself as "one of their recent converts."[22]

As an alternative to the use of specie, in which moderates saw political danger, Van Buren suggested a modification that was particularly favored by Woodbury. By using this alternative, notes could be received by the Treasury, after the banks had resumed specie payments, on condition that they be submitted to the banks at frequent intervals for payment in cash. It was assumed that many of the notes might be paid out immediately to creditors of the government and that only the notes that had not been disbursed in a short period of time would be cashed in. While notes would be received and quickly disbursed, only specie would actually be held by the Treasury for any length of time. Although the plan did not create an absolute divorce of the Treasury from the banks, Woodbury's report from the Treasury claimed that it would render the Treasury substantially independent of "the vicissitudes of trade or speculation."[23]

Closely related to funds receivable was the matter of making the Treasury an alternative to the old national bank. While reflecting the divergence of views within his own party, Van Buren's formulation also joined issue with Whigs over the larger question of the government's responsibility to aid and control business enterprise. On the one side he rejected the view that the Treasury ought to provide a paper medium in order to facilitate domestic exchange. There was no more an obligation "to aid individuals in the transfer of their funds," he asserted, than to afford facilities for "the transportation of their merchandise." This meant, for Van Buren, no permanent use of treasury notes, no issue of specie certificates, and no indefinite circulation for treasury drafts. The Treasury was to attend to its own affairs and let business do the same. Radicals rejoiced, for any extensive use of government paper lessened the destructive impact that they supposed specie would have on banking. As a moderate, Van Buren did not suppose that specie would have a destructive effect. Instead, he based his opposition to government paper on the old party ground of checking the "constant desire" of Whiggery "to enlarge the powers of government." In this view the government had no positive duty to aid private exchange.

Control of issues by state banks, in contrast, was a duty that Van Buren thought the federal government ought to perform. Despite the claim of Whig advocates, the restraint of state-bank issues was not a job that a national bank could be relied upon to do. Motivated by the same selfish interests as state banks, a national bank might also yield, during a time of expansion, to speculation and excess. But even if a national bank could control state banks, Jackson had shown a national bank to be politically intolerable: as "a concentrated moneyed power," it ever threatened "the permanency of our republican institutions." In considering other means, Van Buren agreed with moderate-minded advisers that the operations of an independent Treasury would exert some control. Indirectly, the withholding of deposits took away one "stimulus" to new bank credit. The receipt and disbursal of specie constituted another and stronger check, for the "wider circulation of gold and silver" would mean that there would be less specie in bank vaults for expanded issues. Or if the Treasury were to receive bank notes, frequent settlements with banks for specie would supply another check, though in a lesser degree than the exclusive use of specie.

To go along with the indirect controls exerted by such a divorce, Van Buren recommended one of the measures that had been suggested to him for direct federal control over state banks. Congress, he thought, should consider a bankruptcy act covering "corporations and other bankers," which would define procedures for closing all suspended banks that would be unable to resume specie payments within a given period of time. "Through the instrumentality of such a law," he explained, "a salutary check may doubtless be imposed on the issues of paper money and an effective remedy given to the citizens in a way at once equal in all parts of the Union and fully authorized by the Constitution." Unaccountably, a recent study of Van Buren's administration completely misses this explicit call for control.[24] For Van Buren, the federal government had a "duty" to provide some future remedy for the evil of "depreciated paper currency." Because he supposed that the operations of the Treasury would have such a limited effect upon the currency, he considered a bankruptcy law to be a necessary supplement to his proposal of divorce.

Putting the emphasis of divorce on control, not on aid, Van Buren sought to meet the challenge of the national bank and to defend the heritage of Jackson. Indeed, his fuller justification of the proposal invoked a rhetoric strikingly similar to that in Jackson's bank veto message. Divorce conformed to the old republican stricture against "blending private interests with the operations of public business." To calls for a national paper currency or other forms of aid, Van Buren gave a systematic reply: "All communities are apt to look to government for too much." Government control of another sort was needed, at the same time, to create a framework within which "private interest, enterprise, and competition" could fairly operate. The "real duty" of the government was not to aid in positive ways but "to enact and enforce a system of general laws" and to leave every citizen free "to reap under its benign protection the rewards of virtue, industry, and prudence.'' Happiness and real prosperity could only come, as Jackson earlier had supposed, when the blessings of government, like the dews of heaven, fell equally on all.

Along with the proposal of divorce, Van Buren also recommended measures of relief, some of which seemed to violate his strictures against aid to private enterprise. He asked that import merchants be given added time to pay their overdue duty bonds. Similarly he favored some plan that, by the requirement of added interest and security, would give old deposit banks, mainly in the West and the Southwest, more time to make good on the $6 million in Treasury funds that were on account with them. Until these funds should become available, Van Buren proposed a temporary issue of treasury notes to help the government meet its own obligations. Since no "surplus" funds in fact remained, finally, he asked Congress to postpone further distribution to the states under the terms of the Deposit Act. Three installments—each of about $9.25 million—had already been made; so, only the last one was involved.

Easy passage of the relief measures showed a widespread perception of a need for them, while the pattern of support in Congress vindicated Van Buren's moderate outlook and his essential party consistency. Whigs opposed only the measure for postponing the distribution of the funds to the states. Even though there was no surplus to distribute, they wanted the Treasury to borrow money for the purpose and, to that extent, lend added stimulus to recovery. By contrast, the more-radical-minded Democrats, and Jackson among them, opposed the other measures of relief. Anger against the banks and the speculating merchants was still very strong. There was also a fear that the temporary issue of treasury notes might provide the opening for a permanent government paper to displace the specie that the radical Democrats favored. But relief for merchants and bankers, Van Buren rightly argued, involved immediate relief for the Treasury and constituted the best way to assure eventual recovery of the Treasury funds. Additionally, much of the present evil had arisen out of the old connection between the Treasury and the banks. Divorce would usher in a new era and would prevent future occasions for the government to get involved in private affairs.

Unlike the relief measures, Van Buren's proposal for divorce did not pass in the special session. Little trouble was expected in the Senate, where an early vote of 31 to 15 against petitions for a national bank suggested a strong Democratic majority. The narrow party margin of about 15 votes in the House also held firm in the choice of Speaker, as James K. Polk defeated his fellow Tennessean John Bell, who had broken with the Jacksonians in 1834 over the bank issue. Whether large or small, however, these Democratic margins included Rives and Tallmadge among a number of Conservatives who had, before the special session, spoken out against divorce and in favor of a new connection with state banks. Success for the administration thus depended on its ability to make divorce a clear-cut issue with the Whigs, who were expected to propose a new national bank.

But this was precisely what the Whigs refused to do. Instead, they chose to form a coalition with Conservative Democrats in order to defeat the divorce measure and await political developments. An early vote for the House printer signaled this strategy and foreshadowed defeat for the divorce measure. Here, twenty-two Conservative votes for the *Madisonian* prevented the reselection of the Democratic *Washington Globe*; and on the twelfth ballot, the Whigs deserted their own paper, the *National Intelligencer*, and assured victory for the Conservative organ.[25]

In this context the administration pursued a threefold strategy. First of all, the decision was made to initiate the divorce proposal in the Senate, where party strength was greater and where Van Buren's closest and most trusted adviser, Silas Wright, was chairman of the Finance Committee. Secondly, Wright made the scheme for divorce on the deposit side in the most simple form. Instead of creating elaborate new machinery for keeping and disbursing funds, Wright's bill merely assigned "additional duties" to existing officials and placed them under heavier bond. In this way he sought to deflect the expected Whig outcries against a bloated system of patronage and executive power.

The third element in the administration's strategy was the most crucial—namely, the decision to make no proposal at all on funds receivable. Because it was the most controversial feature of the divorce proposal and was likely to spark lengthy debate, Wright deemed it best to put off consideration until the regular session in December and instead to concentrate, during the short special session, on gaining the needed provisions for the Treasury to keep and disburse its own funds. Moreover, no new provisions for funds receivable were actually needed in order to give the Treasury some degree of independence. Until the banks resumed specie payments, only specie could be received by the Treasury. If the banks did resume before Congress took action, the Treasury would be governed by the Currency Resolution of 1816. By this measure, which resumption would revive, the Treasury had discretionary power to receive payments in specie or in the notes of specie-paying banks. If the Treasury were to receive payment in notes, as Woodbury personally desired, it would also possess discretionary power to submit the notes of the banks for payment in specie.[26]

In dramatic fashion, John C. Calhoun and William C. Rives foiled this strategy. On one side, Calhoun introduced an amendment to Wright's bill, which would, over a four-year period, phase in the exclusive use of specie by the Treasury. In form his amendment proposed to phase out the discretionary feature of the Currency Resolution of 1816 and to mandate specie only after four years. Politically, Calhoun signaled his return to the Democratic party, from which he had departed during the nullification controversy, by his effort to bend the new policy initiative to his personal and sectional purposes.

Rives challenged Wright's silence on funds receivable from the opposite side. He proposed to end the discretionary feature of the 1816 resolution and to mandate Treasury use of bank notes. He also wanted the Treasury to make a new connection on the deposit side of its operations by designating from twenty to thirty of the strongest state banks to serve as fiscal agents. Still maintaining that the Treasury's connection with the state banks constituted the true heritage of the party, he warned that the divorce proposal would be defeated and would lead to a new national bank.[27] In effect, he was arguing that he was not leaving the party over the issue; instead, the party was leaving him behind.

With these counterproposals, in any case, the pattern of party realignment over the divorce issue became clear. Calhoun, who had been a bitter personal rival of Van Buren under Jackson, now joined the administration; and Rives, who had been such a stalwart in Jackson's bank war, moved in the other direction. Who could have predicted, a year ago, Niles wondered, such a turn of events?

Compelled to end his silence on funds receivable, Wright did not hesitate a moment in accepting Calhoun's specie amendment and avowing its goal of total divorce to be that of the administration. But the close votes in the Senate clearly confirmed the view that the issue of funds receivable was the most politically sensitive feature of divorce. The 31 to 15 vote against petitions for a national bank quickly gave way to very narrow margins on subsequent matters. Rives's proposal was turned down by a vote of 22 to 26, while Calhoun's specie amendment passed by a bare 24 to 23 vote. On its final reading, the entire divorce bill won by a 25 to 23 vote.[28]

Barely passing the Senate, the bill failed in the House. Another New Yorker who was very close to the president, Churchill C. Cambreleng, was chairman of the Ways and Means Committee and was in charge of the bill. By exercising rigorous party discipline, he pushed the bill through his committee and brought it to the floor of the House. Anticipating some Conservative defection, he courted Calhoun's friends and chose one of them, Francis Pickens, to open the floor debate. By turning his speech for divorce into a sectional tirade, Pickens did the cause little good. Cambreleng managed to get the debate back onto national grounds, but his main problem was simply a lack of votes. On a motion by John Clark, a New York Conservative, the House tabled the divorce bill by a 120 to 107 vote.[29] The defection of sixteen Democrats and the abstention of seven others, along with solid Whig votes, was too much for the administration to overcome.

Meanwhile, the bankruptcy measure met an even keener defeat, for it was never brought to a vote. As a moderate, Van Buren thought it was needed in order to supplement the limited and indirect control that divorce could exert over bank currency. Whigs and many Democrats, by contrast, saw it as a radical measure. Senator Thomas Hart Benton hailed it as such and predicted a "war to the knife" over it. In fact, there was no war and very little debate. Felix Grundy, otherwise a strong administration loyalist, gained permission from the Senate for his Judiciary Committee to drop the matter without even making a report. In like spirit, Philip Thomas, a party stalwart from Maryland, pushed through his House committee a resolution declaring that it was not expedient to consider the matter at the special session.[30] Before the session, Attorney General Butler assured Van Buren that the people were ready for "strong measures." It was quite clear, in any case, that Congress did not share that perception.

Three responses to the defeat of the divorce proposal seemed to reopen the question of fiscal agency, which had confronted Van Buren after the suspension in May. Should he revamp the state deposit banks, accept a new national bank, or persevere in the policy of divorce? Judging that the House vote to table the divorce bill was "a glorious event," Rives believed that Van Buren would give up on the policy and make a new connection with the state banks. Henry Clay held a different view. With other Whigs he had voted with Conservative Democrats against the divorce measure, not because he wanted a new connection with state banks, but rather in the hope of gaining time for opinion to mature in favor of a national bank. It might, indeed, become the central issue in the next presidential election. Upon hearing the news of the House vote, Clay waved his arms excitedly and shouted three "hurras," as if commencing his campaign for president. Senator Niles hoped that Van Buren would persist. With the defeat of the "great reform bill" in the special session, he declared, "the battle has got to be fought before the people."[31]

Van Buren had no thought of changing course. The quality of Dutch stubbornness that critics found in Van Buren was, rather, a friendly observer thought, "his *firmness* and *unyielding* disposition whenever he took his ground." Here, as in his earlier career, he regarded a new position taken by the party to be an irreversible element in its creed. He had opted for divorce soon after the bank suspension in May and had remained committed to the goal of a Treasury that would be substantially independent in its operations from the banks. Some of the details and emphases he had given to the proposal at the special session might be modified, but the larger goal remained. Divorce had been his basic response to the panic of 1837 and, as an act of presidential leadership, one in which he was well pleased. "I think I see my way clear," he wrote to Jackson, "from the difficulties that beset my brief administration."[32] He had met the crisis and kept the faith.

From a proposal set before Congress in September, divorce now became an issue before the people. Although Whigs did not come forth with a counterproposal for a national bank, Van Buren supposed that to be the ultimate issue. Jackson had carried his war against the national bank to the people in 1834 and had won; with equal confidence in the "intelligence, patriotism, & fortitude of the people," Van Buren prepared to do the same thing. "They (the opposition) will press us hard for the first few elections," he told Jackson, "but our foundations are wisely & firmly laid, & our triumph will come in good time."[33] The November elections in his own state, coming less than a month after the special session, would present the first test.

5

★ ★ ★ ★ ★

THE MEANING OF DIVORCE

In a providential scheme of things, man's proposals most often get disposed of in unintended ways. Van Buren encountered a similar process in the special session. He sought, with the divorce proposal and the companion bankruptcy measure, to make the Treasury an alternative to the old Bank of the United States. Politically he wanted to define the issue between parties as divorce versus a national bank and to do battle for his new proposal on old familiar grounds. Jackson had fought the national bank on the broad popular ground of democracy versus aristocracy; and this was the meaning of divorce that Van Buren wanted to carry from Congress to the people.

His political foes did not cooperate. Most Whig spokesmen privately favored a national bank, it was true, and devoted some of their speeches during the special session to a discussion of its merits over those of an independent Treasury. But they did not propose a new national bank, choosing instead to join hands with Conservative Democrats in behalf of reviving the connection of the Treasury with state banks. For the purpose of debate, they also embraced the Conservative view that divorce was not moderate and limited, as Van Buren supposed, but radical in its effect, calculated to destroy state banks and to create a hard-money currency. The issue was not divorce versus a national bank at all: it was, rather, hard money versus the credit system of banking—a currency that would be permanently deflated or one that would expand in response to the needs of recovery and new enterprise. At a time of severe deflation in the wake of the panic, the issue of an expansive currency and the promotion of enterprise possessed great popular appeal. Van Buren wanted to renew Jackson's fight between democracy and aristocracy, but Whigs began to deploy for battle on new and more democratic grounds.

John C. Calhoun played an important part during the special session in shaping the new debate. In breaking with former Whig colleagues and by joining the administration on the divorce issue, he gave it a radical and sectional reading which, because of his stature and powers of expression, made it more inviting for Whigs to exploit. On the funds-receivable side of divorce he was, a Senate colleague observed, the most "Locofoco" member of Congress. "We are on the eve of a great revolution," Calhoun announced, "in regard to the currency."[1] Treasury use of bank notes had given them wide circulation and a legitimacy that greatly strengthened their credit in the public eye. The exclusive use of specie by the Treasury would withdraw this life-giving patronage of the government and would destroy the basis of the credit system. Unlike most other radicals on the issue, however, Calhoun thought that the same end could be achieved by the use of governmental paper, particularly by a permanent resort to treasury notes. Backed by the superior credit of the government, the notes, along with specie, would drive bank notes out of circulation and would constitute the general currency of the country.

In larger perspective, Calhoun thought that the revolution in the United States could, in a precise sense, bring banking and currency back full circle to the pure and original model of Amsterdam. Here, the first banks simply performed deposit and discount functions, with no thought of issuing notes on their own credit. But through time, this model had been subverted—in England and then in the United States by Alexander Hamilton—through the patronage that the government had given to the paper system. Happily, the crisis of 1837 provided a golden opportunity to consummate the revolution. By suspending specie payments, the banks had disconnected themselves from the government and had given to Congress an original perfect freedom, "disentangled from the past," to resolve the issue. "The conflict between metallic and bank currency" had become so deadly, Calhoun said, "that they must separate, and one or the other fall."[2]

On the deposit side of divorce, Calhoun looked to the attainment of sectional goals. The deposit of Treasury funds in the large banks of the commercial North, he supposed, had enhanced the banks' capital and enabled them to control the cotton export trade. Divorce would take away this means and make it possible for the South to establish direct trade with England. Indirectly, the removal of the deposits would also be conducive to another sectional goal, that of reducing the size of governmental revenue. So long as Treasury funds were placed on deposit in the banks, it was clearly to the banks' advantage that the amount of funds be as large as possible. The withdrawal of deposits would destroy this vested interest in large governmental revenues and thus remove an important pressure on the government to raise tariff duties or to undertake prodigal projects of internal improvement. In turn, retrenchment would reduce the amount of patronage and spoils on which Jackson and his party had expanded the power of the executive branch. Divorce, in short, would render obsolete the old Whig issue of executive despotism on which Calhoun had coalesced with Henry Clay.

The only remaining danger to the republic, as Calhoun saw it, was the unfulfilled aspiration of Henry Clay and the "Whig Nationals" to push through his American System of policies for consolidating the nation. At this critical juncture Calhoun announced his break from Whig ranks and his hope of rallying the Democratic party under "the old republican flag of '98." In very brief compass he summarized his reasons for supporting divorce: "I seize the opportunity thoroughly to reform the Government; to bring it back to its original principles; to retrench and economize, and rigidly to enforce accountability." In private Calhoun was even more sanguine about his new position. Standing in the breach of "this great conflict," he claimed to hold "the fate of the country" in his hands.[3] He was not merely joining the administration on the divorce issue; he was bending it and the party to his personal and sectional purposes.

An inner contradiction in Calhoun's thought about divorce made him, in fact, a poor spokesman for the administration and lent further focus to the Whig strategy. He welcomed a severe retrenchment in government revenues as a way to achieve sectional goals. But any great reduction in the amount of specie or government paper that the Treasury used in its operations would weaken, in that measure, its power to drive bank notes out of circulation or even place substantial checks upon them. "The smaller the amount of the revenue, the less will be the influence of this bill," Senator Robert Walker of Mississippi said about divorce. "The cause is too impotent to produce any such effects," James Buchanan agreed. "On the contrary, I fear that it will go but a small way indeed towards checking the extravagant issues of banks, and that its influence will scarcely be felt."[4] By rejecting a bankruptcy act, moreover, Calhoun would take away a supplementary means that Van Buren had proposed for federal control over state banks. Calhoun favored divorce as a way to destroy banks of issue; in fact his views on divorce amounted to a States' rights withdrawal of federal responsibility for controlling the banks.

During the special session the first and most distinctive response of Whig spokesmen to divorce came at this point. Daniel Webster bitterly condemned the proposal for surrendering "the whole duty" of the federal government and leaving "the currency to its fate." The "uniform currency" clause of the Constitution enjoined a positive duty, he argued, while the power to regulate interstate commerce also implied the power to assure a uniform medium for exchange. The old national bank had performed this duty well, Senator Richard H. Bayard of Delaware observed, providing a uniform paper for exchange and restraining state bank issues. In like spirit, Clay could conceive of no "adequate remedy" for the crisis other than a national bank: "The great want of the country is, a general and uniform currency, and a point of union, a sentinel, a regulator of the issues of the local banks; and that would be supplied by such an institution."[5]

Along with a sound and uniform national currency, Whigs argued for a national bank in terms of fashioning stronger bonds for the Union. Between "a sound general currency" and "the preservation of the Union itself," Clay argued, "there is the most intimate connexion." As with many other Democratic policies, Clay thought, divorce contained a disorganizing principle that violated the interdependent and corporate dimensions of the common life: "We are all—People—States—Union—banks bound up and interwoven together, united in fortune and destiny, and all, all entitled to the protecting care of a parental Government." Congressman John Sergeant of Pennsylvania, Clay's running mate in 1832, expressed this Whig emphasis most forcefully: "Sir, What is the Government of the United States for? It is to make us a nation. It is to give us a national character. It is to give us national capacities and advantages—not by consolidation, not by interfering with or destroying the rights, and powers, and privileges of the States, but to facilitate their intercourse, without effacing the lines between them; to give to the citizens the rights, the immunities, and the privileges of free citizens throughout the United States; and, so far as it can, by these acts, to promote whatever is good, and to guard against whatever is evil."[6]

By ascribing such importance to a national bank, Whig spokesmen, during the special session, appeared to be ready to accept the issue as Van Buren had defined it and to battle divorce on the old grounds. Compared to a national bank, in their view, divorce was sorely inadequate to meet the need for a sound national currency. Van Buren acknowledged no responsibility at all in supplying a paper medium, nor did he offer a satisfactory alternative for restraining issues by state banks. Even with a bankruptcy law, which Whigs joined Calhoun in denouncing, the government could only operate on the banks in an indirect, spasmodic, and penal fashion; whereas the national bank, by holding larger capital and by making frequent settlements with state banks, had exercised its restraining influence in a direct, institutional, and sustaining way. Whigs condemned Van Buren, in effect, for abdicating a national responsibility.

But the Whigs then proceeded to make an abdication of their own. Though convinced that a national bank was the only adequate remedy, they did not come forth during the special session to propose one. Instead of pushing their fight against the divorce proposal with the call for a new national bank, they joined forces with Conservative Democrats and cast their votes for the proposal, which was set forth by Senator William C. Rives, to make a new connection between the Treasury and the state banks. Consistency was clearly a victim of this strategy, for these were the very banks the Whigs had so recently condemned as Jacksonian "pets" and had blamed for the derangement of the currency. Short-run considerations simply overrode their concern, as a responsible opposition party, to hold in view a permanent solution to the nation's problems. With little expectation that Congress would renew the Treasury connection with state banks, they coalesced with Conservatives to defeat the divorce proposal and to gain time, as they hoped, for public opinion to swing in their favor. It was "altogether inexpedient, in a political point of view," Bayard bluntly admitted, to press for the chartering of a new national bank.[7]

Whig spokesmen did more than vote with Conservative Democrats; they also adopted Conservative arguments against divorce. For more than a year, Senator Nathaniel P. Tallmadge had spoken out against the hard-money tendency within the Democratic party. Now he saw in divorce the ultimate result of that tendency and, in Calhoun's formulation, confirmation of its radical effect. The divorce measure "strikes at the very foundation of the CREDIT SYSTEM," he warned; it would make "warfare against the banking institutions of the country"[8] and also against the mass of people, for their interests and prosperity were intertwined with that of the banks.

Whigs easily picked up the refrain. "But, sir," Sergeant accordingly said, "it is not a divorce of the Government from banks. It is a divorce of the Government from the people." In theory, Clay supposed, it might be best for the nation to have no banks and to use only specie for currency. But in fact, the experience of the nation had made Americans "a paper money People" and had linked their destiny irreversibly with the banks. Because of the corporate nature of the common life, the people and the banks were, in many ways, identical: as stockholders owning shares, as debtors owing loans, as creditors holding notes, or as citizens dependent upon bank notes as the currency for their daily transactions. By making war on the banks, divorce made war upon the people. "It is not a mere abstraction that you would kick, and cuff, and bankrupt and destroy," Clay said of banks, "but a sensitive, generous, confiding people, who are anxiously turning their eyes towards you, and imploring relief."[9] Relief here meant the deposit of government revenues in the banks and especially the receipt and disbursal of their notes.

The political benefits of Whig abdication were enormous. Support for a national bank involved, as an essential element, some degree of control over the state banks; and Jackson had managed to make his war upon a national bank a contest between democracy and aristocracy. As newborn champions of the state banks, by contrast, Whigs emphasized the importance of governmental aid but not control. The Treasury, by mingling its credit with the banks through the deposit of its funds and the receipt of bank notes, could presumably restore confidence in the credit system, aid the banks to resume specie payments, and stimulate an expansion of currency, which would be beneficial to all. At a time of severe deflation, in short, the Whig call for aid to the state banks made divorce appear to be a radical prescription for the permanent contraction of the currency. The issue was not between divorce and a national bank, as Van Buren insisted, but between permanent deflation and a more expanded currency.

To dramatize the new issue, Whigs warned of the dire economic consequences lurking in a policy of divorce. "I regard a depreciating or diminishing currency as one of the very greatest scourges of man," Congressman Waddy Thompson, Jr., of South Carolina warned. At least by a multiple of three to one, Clay supposed, the hard money promised by the divorce proposal would reduce the amount of currency that a vital credit system could otherwise supply. "All property would be reduced in value to one-third of its present nominal amount; and every debtor would, in effect, have to pay three times as much as he had contracted for."[10] For a nation of property holders and debtors, divorce would mean war on the people.

On the positive side, the economic effects of a vital credit system were just as striking. Tallmadge had always sung the praises of state banks as the agents for enterprise, progress, and freedom. When sustained by the patronage of the government, bank credit was the substitute for real capital in a young and underdeveloped country. The marvels of improvement in New York bore witness, he claimed, to the creative power of bank credit. In reciprocal fashion, credit was at once the product of freedom and the means for extending the fruits of freedom. It gave wings to new enterprise, excited the active virtues of the people, and promised opportunity for all to participate meaningfully in the common life. Credit was the poor man's capital and his means for realizing true equality, not by radical leveling, but by the elevation of all. For a "young, growing, and enterprising People," Clay accordingly called the credit system "the friend of indigent merit." Nor was Webster laggard in discovering the political appeal that enterprise had in democratic America.[11]

Whigs thus made up the issue between parties that was to shape the remainder of Van Buren's presidency. Giving to divorce the radical reading that Calhoun welcomed and Tallmadge deplored, Whigs found in its presumably hard-money implications a perfect foil for their advocacy of democratic enterprise. That Whigs made themselves the special champions of enterprise did not mean, of course, that Van Buren's party was therefore opposed to enterprise. Whig rhetoric shamelessly exaggerated the radicalism of the administration's position and overlooked the wide range of views within the Democratic party. After due allowance is made for exceptions and exaggerations, however, there still remained a substantial debate between parties over the degree of enterprise that was deemed desirable and over the proper role of government in aiding or controlling the undertakings of its citizens.

It was a debate, moreover, that gave to party contests a greater degree of coherence on economic and social issues than had obtained during Jackson's presidency. Put another way, party alignment over divorce tended to remove earlier ambiguities and, in the phrases of a recent essay, to break up the coalition of "note takers" and "credit seekers" that had supported Jackson's war on the national bank.[12] The note takers, Jackson among them, wanted to replace the national bank with a specie policy that would make the currency sound and stable, if not exclusively metallic. Viewing the currency more as consumers than as producers, they favored enterprise at a sober pace.

The Jacksonian credit seekers, by contrast, were moved by entrepreneurial hopes of expansion. They welcomed the end that Jackson had put to the national bank because it lifted the restraints that the old bank had exerted over the state banks. Divorce, with the meaning Whigs gave to it, now tended to draw the credit seekers away from Van Buren's party and to strengthen the position of the note takers who remained. The older study by Bray Hammond was partly right in finding the "spirit of enterprise" at work in Jackson's war on the national bank. With the panic of 1837 and the proposal of divorce, however, the spirit found fuller scope for expression in Whig ranks.[13] The force of events and the strategy of political foes meant that Van Buren would have to fight for divorce on different grounds than those on which Jackson had battled the national bank.

Party constituencies during the course of Van Buren's presidency reflected the lines of the new debate. Whigs generally enjoyed strong support from commercial centers, the larger towns, and other parts of the states that aspired to become more fully integrated into the market economy. The strongest Democratic constituencies, by contrast, were usually found in the less-commercialized parts of the states. Yeomen in the backward areas of New England, planters in different parts of the South, small farmers in the Alabama hills and in Piney Woods, Mississippi, groups in the less-developed sections of the Northwest—all of these generally wanted greater restraints on banking and currency.

Eastern workingmen had other interests. Because wages lagged behind prices, they dreaded the results of currency inflation. There was also a belief that an expanded currency served, by artificially raising domestic prices above the world level, to attract cheaper foreign goods and to destroy the protective effect of the tariff. In general, those who stood to lose by rapid development and change had an interest in a stable currency and in enterprise at a more sober pace. Although somewhat less distinct, the Democrats were disposed to oppose or to proceed with more caution than Whigs on state projects of internal improvement.[14]

But more was involved than just economic matters. Underlying party contests over currency and enterprise were other and deeper concerns which the panic had excited and the divorce proposal had brought into focus. A careful consideration of the rhetoric in the debate is therefore needed in order to uncover these concerns and the fuller meaning of divorce that they conveyed. For all its extravagance and excess, the party rhetoric on either side reposed on an outlook, or "world view," that related economic matters to an ultimate concern for the fate of the republican experiment itself. "It is a great issue," Churchill C. Cambreleng thus said of divorce, "for everything moral, social, and political is at stake." Particularly in times of financial crisis, one historian of a later crisis argues, the question of the money standard becomes at last a question of "what the moral standard ought to be." A close student of ideology, Clifford Geertz, similarly finds intense ideological affirmation to be a function of "social strain"; events that confound normal expectations therefore create an urgent need to render "otherwise incomprehensible social situations" meaningful.[15]

As noted in an earlier chapter, events by the time of the special session suggested the presence of many strains. The violent cycle of currency expansion and contraction, to which the divorce proposal was a response, was only a more dramatic instance of the wrenching forces of change in the economic, social, and political life of the nation as it groped toward a democratic order to the common life. By the 1830s many elements of an earlier and more traditional order had weakened or disappeared, leaving an ambivalence of outlook, blended of hopes for the future and an anxious sense of disorder and unrest. In this context, competing party views about what the republic was or ought to be expressed this ambivalence and placed Van Buren's central domestic policy in a broader framework of meaning.

The concept of republicanism that was lodged in the rhetoric of most Democratic spokesmen provided a distinctive way of relating the present evils to the nation's past experience. Clear expression to this view came in the first issue of a new party monthly, the *Democratic Review*. By the operation of "the great moral law," it claimed, the people were paying the price of a great "national sin." The panic of 1837 had been caused by a "departure from those principles of political morals on which all national happiness and prosperity depend." All of the undesirable changes of the present signaled, in effect, deviation from the unchanging principles on which the moral, political, and economic order of the republic depended.[16]

Pervading the debate over currency and enterprise was, thus, a profound sense among Democrats of degeneration from the values of the early republic. Senator Robert Strange of North Carolina deplored the socially disruptive effect of speculative enterprise, which enticed men away from regular pursuits and engendered a "loose morality" among the people. In like spirit, an old republican from Virginia believed that Americans had enjoyed "real independence," more "genuine happiness," and "better morals" at the time when the Constitution was written. Albert Gallatin similarly found "general demoralization" and not "general happiness" to have been the result of the "apparent prosperity" during the last few years. While disclaiming any desire to crush the spirit of enterprise, Buchanan "would limit it within proper bounds" so that business could be pursued, "as our fathers did," in the expectation of "regular profits" drawn from "years of industry." Calhoun deemed social stability, as guaranteed by re-publican values, to be the only basis for the "moral and intellectual development of the country." Supposing that there was a law of supply and demand in cultural as well as in economic affairs, he warned that an unchecked banking system placed too great a premium on the "inferior qualities'' of money making and thereby withheld social reward for the ''higher mental attainments'' in science, art, and the professions.[17]

Several assumptions about the nature of the republic were inherent in these views. When beginning the experiment, the founding fathers had been fully aware that the existence of a republic rested on the virtue of the people. Essential to this virtue, moreover, was the ascendancy of the ''social principle'' over the ''selfish principle,'' as James K. Paulding had put it, an ascendancy that always prompted the citizen to place the good of the whole above his own self-interests. For assuring the ascendancy of the social principle, Gallatin thought, the best condition of society was one in which the great majority of the people enjoyed ''a modest independence'' acquired by ''industry and frugality.'' With regard to government, republicanism prescribed a limited and essentially negative role, one that withheld special favors to any and extended to all an exact and equal protection of the laws. The job of government was to prevent evil, rather than to try to promote good, and to provide a framework within which uncorrupted virtue could freely express itself. In this connection, finally, Senator John M. Niles voiced the common belief that organized self-interest—in this case the corporate ''money power''—posed the greatest threat to republican freedom. The special favors that money power received soon made it the controlling interest in government and denied equal access to all others. To complete the work of corruption, the influence of the regnant selfish principle finally settled down over the people like a ''subtle poison which is to corrupt the very fountains of our liberties.''[18]

If deviation from republican principles was the way in which Democrats ultimately explained the crisis of 1837, the reaffirmation of these principles seemed to provide a true remedy. Party spokesmen thus elaborated the view, expressed in Van Buren's message, that divorce would be an act of restoration. It was ''as ancient as 1789,'' Niles said, ''as old as the Constitution.'' The Treasury had begun its operations on a sound basis, receiving only in specie and approved government paper. Within two years, however, Alexander Hamilton had subverted this design by his decision to accept state bank notes and to create a national bank on the corrupt model of the Bank of England. The panic of 1837 was ''the natural fruit'' of the Hamiltonian deviation, Senator Thomas Hart Benton thought; yet it also provided a happy occasion for deliverance. By disconnecting the Treasury from the suspended banks, the crisis would enable the government to adopt once more its true and original policy. ''I am for restoring to the Federal Treasury the currency of the Constitution,'' he exulted; ''I am for carrying back this government to the solidity projected by its founders.''

Similar phrasing informed the speeches of other Democrats in Congress and the claim of the *Washington Globe* that divorce was "the second declaration of independence." As a dramatic public event, moreover, the divorce proposal was likely to have a regenerating effect upon the public mind. It would, Van Buren was assured, "excite the patriotism and stimulate the virtue of the people."[19] The purgation of evil elements, in this view of republicanism, allowed the good in the people to rise once more.

Many distinctively Democratic practices could be fitted into this ideological scheme. Belief in a permanent party organization, which reposed on universal suffrage for adult white males, held out the promise of drawing all people into the common life, into the *res publica*. In league with the power of the executive veto, furthermore, the operation of a disciplined party served as a tribune to guard the people, at home and at their work, against the sleepless scheming of the selfish few in the legislative branch. Critics among the Whigs condemned the Democrats for carrying on a politics of conflict which, as they saw it, arrayed one class against another in violation of the corporate and interdependent nature of society. Democrats assumed, instead, that the party itself incorporated the honest people of all classes and guarded the virtue of the republic against the essentially alien principle of self-interest.

Culturally, the party perception was also distinctive. Whigs strongly inclined to "politicize morals," as one historian aptly phrases it, to seek moral reform through political means in order to create a greater moral consensus and cultural uniformity. By contrast, Democrats tended to "moralize politics," to invest with considerable intensity the political effort of guarding from substantial change the virtue of existing arrangements. It was an ideology that was congenial to cultural pluralism, with strong appeal to what a recent student calls a constellation of "outgroups"—Irish, Germans, Catholics, Scotch-Irish in most places, nostalgic southerners, economic losers, nonevangelical Protestants—which arrayed against the Yankee world of Whiggery. Here were "ethnocultural" constituencies which overlapped in many instances the economic constituencies that supported Democrats on the currency issue. The *Democratic Review* thus found parallels to the divorce of banks and the state in the separation of church and state, the political pluralism of the federative Union, and the doctrine of "nonintervention" with the "domestic institutions" of slavery in the southern states.[20]

Democratic rhetoric, in sum, invoked the idea of a republic that was essentially immune from disruptive change in the economic and social sphere. It was an outlook that placed the present evils in a meaningful perspective and held out the promise of restoration. By means of stable currency and sober enterprise the nation could regain its republican health. Adopt Van Buren's proposals, Benton urged, "and the Republic is safe."[21]

Debate during the special session also revealed, however, that Democratic means were not adequate to the ends they were seeking. Calhoun had no problem, of course, because his radical assessment made divorce itself a sufficient means for creating a stable currency of specie and governmental paper. Most other advocates of divorce, on the other hand, ascribed to divorce a much more limited effect upon banks and currency. Indeed, without the bankruptcy law or some other mode of national regulation, there would be far too little restraint on issues by state banks. The only other means for assuring a stable currency was reform of banking at the state level, but the prospects in 1837 were not too good. Wright's hope that there was "yet virtue in the people of the state to bring about the result" was mingled with doubt; far too many people, in his view, failed to see suspension and the currency issue from a moral point of view. Juries routinely acquitted banks in suits brought by holders of their depreciated notes, and the year-long indulgence of suspension given by the state legislatures enjoyed wide support.

Buchanan came close to admitting that the problem lay with the people themselves, not with a presumed "money power." Apparently infected with the "spirit of enterprise," great numbers of people, no less than bank corporations, seemed to be following the "selfish principle," the operation of which was supposed to corrupt the virtue of the republic. The excessive expansion of bank issues could thus be seen as the result of the selfish principle at work among the people, not as a cause of their corruption. Buchanan feared that the crisis would pass without the banks being effectively reformed and that, without some means of controlling them, the nation would be vulnerable once more to a new cycle of expansion and contraction. "We are a strange people," he mused. "The lessons of experience make but a feeble impression on our minds."[22]

While yearning for what they took to be the stable values of an earlier age, advocates of the divorce measure possessed no certain means for mastering the present forces of change. Seen in this perspective, their old republican ideology served far better to express their fear of change than to prescribe a way for dealing with it. To the degree that their means fell short of their professed ends, Democratic spokesmen here evinced the spectacle of a party backing anxiously into the future.

Political foes, by contrast, faced a future of economic expansion in an optimistic way. For a dynamic and democratic age, one historian has perceptively observed, the Whigs spoke to the hopes, as Democrats spoke to the fears, of the people. While Democrats ter:ded to look for the economic model of the republic in the past, Whigs and most Conservatives found that model at work in the forces of the present. In appealing to the values of the early republic, Senator William Preston thus noted, the Democrats vainly yearned for "a golden age, a pastoral state of political simplicity and beatitude, exempt from vicissitudes, amidst perpetual sunshine and perpetual peace." Another South Carolinian, Congressman Hugh S. Legaré, developed this theme most fully in a great speech which Whigs saw fit to circulate widely in the next three years. Writing off the old republican sentiments of the Democrats as representing a stolid and mindless primitivism, he mockingly observed: "I have, sometimes, in the course of the debates, looked around me to see where I really was—whether the shade of some old lawgiver, some Minos or Lycurgus, had not been evoked, to bring a degenerate age back to the stern principles of Dorian polity, to an agrarian equality of property, to iron money and black broth."[23]

Unwilling to serve black broth to his own constituents or to circulate iron money, Legaré rejected as well the old republican judgment that the present age was "a perverse and crooked one" which had, through the seductions of enterprise, sadly degenerated from the virtue of the founding generation. It was, rather, the "great design of Providence" to use the love of money and the spirit of enterprise as means for the progressive development of civilization. Enterprise released the energies and quickened the intelligence of the people, producing an ever greater divison of labor and calling into use the latent faculties of the national mind. Added wealth and leisure, which came with economic progress, provided the basis for higher attainments, for new advances in science, art, and the noble professions. Whereas Calhoun feared that a social premium on enterprise would hamper higher pursuits, Legaré regarded economic pursuits as stepping stones to social and cultural refinement. Taking the divorce proposal in its most radical reading, he concluded that the "true issue" before the country was hard money versus the credit system—ultimately, stagnation versus civilization. Clay agreed that divorce would throw the nation back "for centuries."[24]

In other terms, Whig spokesmen denied that a wider scope to the "selfish principle" in the economic sphere necessarily threatened the existence of the republic. The acquisitive spirit was, rather, an important spring of active virtue, young Abraham Lincoln thought, and it was central to the realization of the "American Dream."[25] The aid of the government to individual pursuits was therefore part of a true republican system, a way to enlarge opportunity, promote virtue, and integrate all citizens into the *res publica*—into the affairs of the common life. The credit that the Treasury extended to the state banks, by depositing its funds in them and by receiving their notes, was not a special favor to the selfish few but a benefit to all.

The contrast of earlier party differences places in a more meaningful perspective the position with which Whigs responded to the republicanism of Van Buren's party. Alexander Hamilton had deemed antithetical the ideal of republican "virtue," held by the Jeffersonians, and the basic fact of self-interest in a commercial society. Making the most of the difference, he had aimed, with his fiscal measures, to fix the government of the new republic on a surer basis than the virtue of the people by appealing to the interests of the wealthy and powerful few. The economic development that would come from his policies would make the nation "grand," but Hamilton had had no thought of promoting virtue. Whigs in the 1830s, by contrast, sought to synthesize the elements Hamilton had held apart. They made democratic the appeal to self-interest and claimed that economic development would also strengthen the virtue of the people. In effect, they invested the idea of republican virtue with a new meaning that was in harmony with the pervasive spirit of enterprise.[26]

This harmony, however, rendered urgent for Whigs the companion task, to use an earlier phrase, of "politicizing morals." Policies of government to stimulate economic activity and promote the "active" virtues of the people were good; but they had to be matched by other policies in order to create a broader moral consensus in society and thereby promote the "passive" virtues as well. With the same thing in mind, Rufus Choate thus looked to the "feminine" as well as the "masculine" element in virtue. One provided a frame of social order within which true progress might come. Professing a fear of economic aid, Democrats stressed the need for guarding the virtue of the people from corruption. Reposing on its basic "ethnocultural" constituency of Yankees and evangelical Protestants, by contrast, the Whig party sought to foster virtue, active and passive, through positive means. Congressman Sergeant stated the difference in a brief and precise way. The role of government was dual: "to promote whatever is good" no less than "to guard against whatever is evil."[27]

While Democrats had misgivings about new changes in the economic sphere, Whigs clearly embraced the forces of democratic enterprise in a hopeful way. In the political sphere, however, Whigs expressed doubts and fears of their own. If dynamic economic development was one force producing social strain, another was the triumph of political party organization. As family and partnership forms of business began to yield to new corporate structures, political organization followed the same pattern. And here it was the Jacksonians who spoke to the hopes of the future, creating key elements of political order—such as permanent party organization, techniques of mass appeal, focus on the executive as the highest expression of a sovereign people—which have subsequently governed democratic America.

Many Whig and Conservative spokesmen, by contrast, yearned for the political culture of the eighteenth-century fathers. It was patrician- and leader-oriented, one in which power belonged by right and deference to the gentlemen elite. Because disinterested, patriotic, and wise, the leader gave true voice to the good of the whole. Through the exercise of independent judgment and conscience, and uncorrupted by the evils of faction and party discipline, he embodied that "public virtue" on which the republic reposed. Underlying the political outlook was a concept of society as a corporate unity in which all interests were related and harmonized. In this regard the Whig impulse to politicize morals at once reflected this consensus idea and anxiously sought to fulfill its conditions by inculcating common values.[28]

With its emphasis on unity and consensus, such a political outlook would seem to rule out a politics of conflict and the legitimacy of permanent party organization. At best, party organization could only be a temporary affair, proceeding in the form of a self-liquidating crusade to vanquish political enemies of the republic and to restore good men to their rightful place of rule. And yet, Whigs entered the conflicts of the new political arena and, by the end of Van Buren's presidency, as the election of 1840 showed, developed great facility at voter appeal and party organization. To the degree that Whigs still yearned for the older antiparty ideals, however, they, too, evinced the spectacle of a party that was backing uneasily into the future.[29]

In effect, Democrats and Whigs divided the elements of their common republican heritage in an age that was far different from that of the fathers. The challenge of profound economic and political change, intensified by the crisis of 1837, gave added force to the sentiment expressed by President Van Buren in his Inaugural Address that the republican experiment was at once a success and yet likely to fail unless the present generation acted wisely. The parties provided alternative means for dealing with this ultimate concern, different ways for the nation to face and back into the future and thereby address the need of the present to effect a meaningful relation with the past. "Republicanism," according to a recent essay, "meant maintaining public and private virtue, internal unity, social solidarity, and it meant constantly struggling against 'threats' to the 'republican character' of the nation."[30] Democrats thought that the greatest threat to republican virtue lay in the connection between organized self-interests and the government. Party government constituted a sentinel for saving virtue; and the divorce of the government from banks was the proximate answer to the crisis. In what follows, it will be clear that Whigs deemed party government, particularly in connection with the executive, to be the central threat to the republic.

Along with the evil economic consequences of the divorce proposal, Whigs deplored its purely partisan inspiration. Anticipating mischief after the banks had suspended, the old Federalist Harrison Gray Otis appealed to Van Buren, his Senate colleague and messmate in the early 1820s, to rise above party to the "majesty of a patriotic chief," to disclaim all connection with Jackson's rash policies, and to reestablish a national bank. To strengthen the plea, Otis also suggested that Van Buren read the eighteenth-century work on antipartyism, Bolingbroke's *Idea of a Patriot King*. It is not known whether the president did the assigned reading, but he clearly did not heed the other advice. Webster accordingly assailed Van Buren, whom he otherwise considered to be so prudent and sagacious, for rejecting a national bank solely on the ground of a "party pledge" to follow in Jackson's footsteps. Decisions about the good of the whole that were made in this way, he warned, would create a government within a government and would place party welfare above the welfare of the people. Professing more of sadness than of anger, Clay condemned the way in which party spokesmen in Congress had surrendered their independent judgment and had made "the ties of party" paramount to "the obligations of patriotism."[31]

Sounding very much like Whigs, many Conservatives resisted, on old republican grounds, the demands of party discipline. Senator Oliver H. Smith of Indiana condemned the "trammels" of party that compelled its members "to act contrary to their convictions." Tallmadge, who had chafed under the "collar of party" for more than a year, bitterly rejected the divorce proposal as a test of party "merely because it bears the stamp of an Executive recommendation." Though opposed to the divorce on economic grounds, Senator John King of Georgia professed much greater concern at the way the administration had proceeded with the issue. As a "party man" and a "real democrat," he felt that a true republican sense of party, based on principle and individual judgment, had been subverted: "The spirit of our fathers has fled. The blood of '76 has run out. Sir, there have been more gray hairs brought upon the head of our youthful and vigorous Republic in the last four years, than ought to have grown upon it in one entire century of quiet and peaceful administration." Personal interest and ambition undoubtedly informed Conservative pleas, and their antiparty cry clearly echoed the refrain of earlier defectors from the ranks of Jackson's party. But the fact remained that their concern for the relation of party to republican values bulked large in private correspondence, where there was less need to mask personal convictions. Indeed, a good case has been made for the view that the antiparty feelings of the conservatives were more important than economic considerations in their break from Van Buren over the divorce issue.[32]

Finally, Whigs assimilated divorce to their earlier strictures against executive usurpation. Divorce, in this view, carried to the ultimate limit that tendency under Jackson—with his bank veto, his removal of deposits, his "Specie Circular"—to wrest the control of the Treasury from Congress and to place the nation's purse exclusively under executive power. An independent Treasury would become a mighty government bank to overshadow the land, Clay warned, and it would entrench a corps of officials who, through patronage and spoils, could perpetuate their own existence. The forms of republican government remained, but its substance would flow to a Treasury Caesar.

To dramatize the evil, Clay invoked the "two currency" argument. Since the Treasury would receive and disburse only in specie, of-ficeholders would be paid in hard money. Meanwhile, the continued suspension of the banks would mean a depreciated paper currency for the people. Clay thus remarked on its unrepublican horrors: "A hard-money Government and a paper-money People! A government, an official corps—the servants of the People—glittering in gold, and the People themselves, their masters, buried in ruin, and surrounded with rags."[33] In fact, officeholders, along with others who had claims on the government, most often got paid by drafts on the funds remaining in the old deposit banks. The image of an aristocracy of officeholders had great appeal, however, and enhanced the Whig claim that Van Buren was not divorcing bank and state but was divorcing the government from the true will and interests of the people.

Political foes, in sum, professed to find in divorce two closely related evils—political subversion of republican principles and economic subversion of the general welfare. They thus defined with skill and ingenuity a basis of opposition to Van Buren's administration which possessed great appeal, for it spoke at once to the ultimate concern of the people for the fate of the republican experiment and to their immediate economic interests. By taking the issue of divorce from Congress to the people, Van Buren hoped to reproduce the archetypal experience of Jackson's war against the national bank. But thanks to altered circumstances, the zeal of political foes, and the defections from his own party, Van Buren actually faced a new situation. Through the years he had assumed that only one party—his own—reposed on a genuine popular base. Blinded in some degree by this assumption, as one sanguine foe observed, he misjudged the political impact that Whigs were having on the divorce issue. The insight, if not the grammar and mixed metaphors, of this observer justifies a fuller quotation: "The whole secrete of Mr. Van B. policy is to keep on the side of democracy & when driven to extremities or compelled to show his hand—or take ground—it is then he strikes so that none shall cut under him—feeling that democracy is like a grass crop always spring up fresh & in good time going to seed & when it reaches this point it is called aristocracy & new crops follow but in boring his hold this time in the great 'Barrel Politics' he has evidently for the present bored too low & will get dregs only."[34]

The election returns, which came in the wake of the special session, confirmed this assessment. Four states that had gone against Van Buren in 1836 by relatively narrow margins—Tennessee, Kentucky, Indiana, Ohio—now went Whig by a very large vote. At the same time, Maine, Rhode Island, and North Carolina reversed position, going from a comfortable Van Buren majority over to the opposition. But much greater attention was given to his home state of New York, where many supposed that the fate of the divorce proposal—indeed his entire presidency—was at stake. Most observers, expecting the outcome to be close, were unprepared for the stunning result: the thirty thousand plurality for Van Buren in 1836 was turned into a fifteen thousand edge for the opposition; 8 of 10 senate seats up for election went Whig; and the lower assembly was lost by 101 to 27.

Several local circumstances contributed to this result. After the panic of 1837, Anti-Masons in central and western New York began to exercise greater influence in the Whig party. Their interests in improvements and their outlook, which was at once evangelical and equalitarian, enabled them to assimilate older corporate and hierarchical views of society with the newer thrust of democratic enterprise. Out of this background came such leaders as Thurlow Weed at the *Albany Evening Journal* and William H. Seward, who had shed the political liability of the old national bank and were looking toward some entrepreneurial version of free banking to replace the existing Safety Fund banks, which they associated with Van Buren and the Regency. Politically, as well, the Regency made a good target to strike. The antiparty rhetoric of the Whigs, which had been especially effective against a group that had controlled the state for a decade, easily attracted Conservative defectors and masked the Whigs' own brilliant efforts at party organization and mass appeal.[35]

Meanwhile, the Democrats, with their ranks deeply divided, faced the new foe. The old leadership of the Regency at Albany, which was headed by Governor William L. Marcy and the editor of the *Albany Argus*, Edwin Croswell, now had to face the Locofocos in New York City, who were returning to the party after an absence of two years. Excited to new assertiveness by the proposal of divorce, the Locofocos gave it their own radical reading and claimed it as the new test of party orthodoxy. With a lifelong commitment to the ethos of party loyalty, Marcy had no intention of defecting, yet he saw that many Democrats in the state who had fought under Jackson's banner were prepared to leave the party. A "reconstruction of political parties" was in the making, he feared, which would bring certain victory to the Whigs in the November elections.[36]

Whig campaign strategy skillfully exploited the situation, pinning the label of radicalism on Van Buren and the party. Two earlier ideas, long since rejected by most New York radicals themselves, came in for special play. One, associated with Thomas Skidmore, favored a redistribution of all property during each generation; a second, identified with Frances Wright, proposed to take young children from their homes and to place them in state boarding schools. Only a fear of "Cholera," one former supporter wrote Van Buren, exceeded "the dread of Loco Focoism." Another "went the whole Wig ticket," he told the president, in order to "kill Loco Focoism." With regard to the currency issue, Whigs easily linked the prospect of permanent deflation to the specter of social revolution. Divorce, with its attendant war on state banks, contemplated an exclusively metallic currency for the country. Many prominent Whig orators were invited into the state to defend democracy and enterprise against the presumed radicalism of the day, but the presence of Webster was most provoking and bewildering to many old-line Democrats. It was "almost too much to bear," one of them wrote Van Buren, "when Webster says the Whigs are the true friends of the people."[37]

Immediate reactions to the stunning Whig victory in New York left Van Buren with much to ponder. Disappointed and bewildered, a friendly Jabez Hammond could only suppose that the Democrats had somehow failed to "bring the true issue before the people." The evils of the time, another party friend observed, "have been successfully charged to the government." James K. Paulding was prepared for the defection of Conservatives, but he simply could not understand why so many yeomen farmers had gone with the opposition. Whigs, by contrast, replied that yeomen and all others had indeed discerned the "true issue" in the contest. The *National Intelligencer* also claimed a victory for "true republicanism" and saw victory as a herald of political regeneration for the whole nation. For all his "personal sagacity and prudence," Van Buren had failed to cast off "the badge of party servitude" and thus become "the President of the Nation." With the proposal of divorce he had chosen, rather, to follow in Jackson's footsteps as "the President of a Party."[38]

In 1834 Jackson had carried his war against the national bank from Congress to the people and had won a decisive victory. The divorce proposal met a different fate in 1837: foes of Van Buren's proposal ascribed to it a meaning that he had not intended and found in it great political appeal. Although he might have considered the meaning distorted and perverse, it was one that he would have to take into account as he prepared for the regular session of Congress in December.

6

A SEPARATION
WITHOUT DIVORCE

In the wake of the "New York tornado," as he called the fall election in his state, Van Buren turned his attention to the first regular session of the Twenty-fifth Congress, which convened in December 1837 and met for more than six months.[1] Two related considerations, urged on him at the outset, gave basic shape to the administration's course during the long and tortuous session. One was the need to counter the image of radicalism that foes had cast for the divorce proposal during the special session and that they had pressed so successfully in the New York election. The other was to encourage the efforts of the banks to resume specie payments. The administration accordingly signaled a willingness to retreat from the position of a total divorce, held at the special session, and to give other assurances to the banks of its benign intentions. Triumph for this policy came by April 1838, when the New York banks announced the decision to resume specie payments; and in the next few months, most other banks followed the example.

Along with this triumph, however, came new setbacks for the administration and a deepening sense of frustration among many of its friends. In spite of a willingness to compromise, Congress passed no divorce bill. The Treasury continued to handle its own funds independently of banks; yet in default of legal sanctions, this mode of operations represented a separation that was not hallowed by a divorce decree. The question remained unsettled, and Whigs raised anew the cry about a Treasury Caesar. Meanwhile, Democratic ideas about bank reform at the state level lost out to an entrepreneurial version of "free banking," which was pushed through the New York legislature by the Whigs. Finally, many party spokesmen began to voice concern over Van Buren's leadership—weak and passive, as they saw it, lacking boldness or initiative, controlled too exclusively by events.

But events, as Van Buren perceived them at the beginning of the new session, left little room for bold initiative. The advice that he had received from either extreme in the party served, rather, to prescribe a middle course of compromise. On the radical side he was urged to persist in the policy of total divorce. Standing on principle was also true political expediency, it was argued; about every ten years the Democratic party "went to seed" or, to change the figure, needed to be "whipped back into its principles." From the other side the president was advised to surrender principles, to give up the divorce proposal, and to disavow the ideal of republican "virtue" with which the proposal had been invested. "The love of country, & of glory, had been swallowed up in the vortex of avarice & private accumulation." Because the people lacked sufficient "virtue" to support such a reform measure as divorce, the president ought to connect the Treasury with the banks once more, encourage an expansion of the currency, and thereby minister to "this all pervading spirit" of private gain. Van Buren still had only one other hope in order to save his administration and to assure reelection: namely, to take counsel with "the spirit of desperation" and therefore make war on a foreign country.[2] Mexico was a likely enemy, as a later chapter will show, while troubles on the northern frontier, growing out of rebellion in Canada, made England another possibility.

Van Buren had no intention of starting a war or making a total surrender of his divorce proposal. He responded, instead, to the advice of Enos Throop, among others of like mind, who voiced a widespread call for some sort of compromise. Because of Whig efforts, Throop reported, a great many people had come to perceive the divorce as a war on the banks and on their daily interests. The companion proposal for a bankruptcy law had also given "great alarm." While reassuring public opinion on these matters, moreover, Throop thought that Van Buren should also exploit the opportunity to aid the efforts of the New York banks to resume specie payments. That the president found such advice congenial can be seen in the fact that he had already made inquiries of his own about resumption, indicating to New York bankers, through Secretary Levi Woodbury, a desire "to promote that object in every mode lawful, just, & honorable." Two cabinet members, Woodbury and

Amos Kendall, reinforced Throop's advice and indicated that the funds-receivable side of divorce was where compromise must come.[3]

While impressed with the need to make some changes in his earlier proposals, Van Buren made no explicit recommendations for compromise in his message to Congress on December 5, 1837. He devoted far less space to financial matters than at the special session, and he observed, in a rather general way, that his own basic views remained unchanged. On this basis, radicals in the party read the message as a new commitment by the president to the policy of total divorce. Its strong statements on the deposit features of divorce reinforced this impression. On the "essential points" of collecting, keeping, and expending funds, he resolved to divorce the Treasury "from all dependence on the will of irresponsible individuals or corporations" and to secure the public money "from the uses of private trade." He was willing for the Treasury to place funds on "special deposit" in some cases, but this special use of the banks was to be solely at the option of the Treasury and was not to be a "fixed part of the machinery of government." Strictures against the "overgrown influence of corporate authorities" also sounded like a continuing crusade against the money power.

Many other people read the message in a different way and praised it as a charter for compromise. In this reading, things not said were as meaningful as the things mentioned, and all were welcomed as means for effacing the radical image of divorce. Praise for the state banks as being "highly useful" to the general welfare accompanied the disclaimer that divorce was "a measure of hostility" to the credit system of banking. No mention was made of the bankruptcy proposal or of any other means to provide direct federal control of the banks. The problem of bank reform and regulation was, rather, one for the states to handle. Most of all, the message maintained total silence on the question of funds receivable. Read in conjunction with the Treasury report, this silence could be taken as a signal for compromise. In the report, Woodbury deemed the kind of funds used by the Treasury to be a question "entirely distinct" from the way in which the Treasury handled its funds. By admitting that there were "shades of difference" among political friends about the proper "mode" of divorce, the *Washington Globe* also opened the way for some compromise.[4] While retaining the support of party radicals, Van Buren's message also responded to the desire of moderates for change. Something of his power as a "magician" still remained!

In the message, Van Buren raised two other domestic matters that had an important political bearing on his central concern for divorce.

One, involving land policy, was skillfully drawn to appeal to the older as well as the newer western states, an area where support for divorce in the special session had lagged behind that of other sections of the country. It called for two things—for a special preemption act to cover the "squatters" who had settled on the public lands since the last measure had been passed in 1834, and for the Land Office to graduate downward from $1.25 per acre the price of unsold and presumably less valuable lands in the older western states. Only a preemption act was finally passed through Congress, but early reports from the West indicated a favorable political response to the entire proposal.

A second matter directly involved Jackson's old enemy, Nicholas Biddle. Here Van Buren called attention to the fact that Biddle's bank, since going under a Pennsylvania state charter in 1836, had illegally reissued around $10 million in the very notes it had originally issued while under its charter as a national bank. Reissue in such great volume clearly gave Biddle a great advantage over the other state banks, because the prestige connected with the old bank notes enabled them to circulate more widely. In opposing these "resurrection notes," as they were called, Van Buren exploited a great political opportunity. It enabled him to stand up against Jackson's old enemy, to appear to be the champion of the other state banks, and to belie the image of a man who was bent on destroying the credit system.

Signals of compromise found in the president's message were also to be found in the divorce bill, which was presented in the Senate by Silas Wright. He chose to discuss as separate and distinct the "two great principles" of divorce—namely, the handling of funds and the kind of funds to be handled—and to make the first principle the chief carrier of true republican doctrine: "A *practical and bona fide* separation between the public treasures, the money of the people, and the business of individuals and corporations." Proposed in the bill was new and elaborate machinery for the Treasury to handle its own funds; this also indicated the administration's resolve to render the Treasury effectively independent on the deposit side. Along with the mints in Philadelphia and New Orleans and the Treasury Building in Washington, four "receivers general" were designated for Boston, New York, Charleston, and St. Louis; they would keep and disburse the funds turned over by collectors and receivers. As a supplement to the system, Wright's bill did enable the Treasury to place funds on "special deposit" with the banks where no government depository was nearby, or where the sums exceeded the bond of the local collector or receiver. In all cases, however, the use of the banks was at the discretion and convenience of the Treasury.

On the funds-receivable side of divorce, it was true, Wright's bill evinced no apparent willingness to compromise. It prescribed specie, "the legal currency of the Constitution," and not bank notes, as the kind of money to be received. On the face of it, the bill thus assumed the position of total divorce that Calhoun's amendment had staked out in the special session, and it seemed to render explicit and unequivocal the matter of funds receivable on which Van Buren's message had remained silent. Several things in Wright's discussion of the bill, however, suggested that the administration was not altogether firm. Speaking in behalf of his Finance Committee, which had developed the bill, Wright observed that he "felt constrained" to prescribe specie precisely because it had been part of the divorce bill passed by the Senate at the special session. Such constrained support contrasted sharply with the hearty endorsement given to the deposit features of the bill. Moreover, Wright proposed to phase in the use of specie over a six-year period, rather than in four years, as Calhoun wanted; and Wright soon showed a willingness to prolong the process two more years. Most of all, Wright recognized that the question of funds receivable, far more than that of deposit, was of "deep interest," one on which there was "great diversity of opinion" and "great delicacy of feelings." Although he was personally committed to the use of specie, he expected intense debate and possible retreat from the specie requirement.[5]

The role that John C. Calhoun played in the session was important, as well as ironic. No one else identified more fully than he with the specie requirement and the goal of total divorce; yet, his course in the Senate, which was marked by strident sectional pleading, contributed to the forces of compromise. For one thing, the debate that he precipitated over slavery caused a delay in the consideration of the divorce bill, which worked in favor of its amendment. On December 27 he responded to antislavery resolutions from Vermont with six resolutions of his own and engaged the Senate in debating them until January 13. The first resolution reaffirmed the compact origin of the Union; the second claimed for the states the exclusive jurisdiction over their domestic institutions; and the fourth defined slavery as a domestic institution. These passed by large margins, as did two others, after changes had toned down Calhoun's language regarding the District of Columbia and the admission of new states. It was the third resolution that brought about the most revealing change. Calhoun wanted to proclaim it a "positive" and "solemn" duty of the federal government to provide "increased stability and security" to slavery. With wide support, by contrast, the amendment of Democratic Senator John Norvell of Michigan struck out Calhoun's call for positive action on the part of the federal government and resolved, instead, that the duty of the government was essentially "negative," namely "not to interfere with the stability and security" of slavery.[6]

Along with the delay, northern Democrats also resented Calhoun's obvious effort to enhance his claim as "the great defender" of southern interests. The "new ally" was "becoming something of a dangerous man," more likely to do harm than good, Senator John M. Niles privately complained. The northern Democrats' speeches and votes on amendments accordingly made it clear that they supported Calhoun's resolutions on a pro-Union rather than on a proslavery basis. On the old republican principle of States' rights, Calhoun defended divorce as a withdrawal of the federal government from either aid or direct control over state banks. By a rigorous application of this same principle, northern Democrats enunciated most forcefully the doctrine of nonintervention with slavery. The duty of the federal government was to leave things alone, neither aiding nor controlling the state institutions of slavery. Nonintervention reflected "a true interpretation of the Constitution," Niles declared; it conformed strictly to the "old republican school of '98" and provided the only basis for Union. While securing the true interests of the South, it combated the Whiggish impulse of the abolitionists to refashion the Union made by the fathers. If Calhoun sought to use the Democratic party for sectional purposes, northern spokesmen insisted on placing the defense of the south on a broad national platform. In doing so, Niles must have taken special pleasure in invoking the slogan with which Jackson had confronted Calhoun and the Nullifiers: "The Federal Union must be preserved."[7]

Another delay in the Senate's consideration of divorce came with the dramatic encounter between Calhoun and Henry Clay. It had been building since the special session, Thomas Hart Benton observed, when Calhoun broke Whig ranks to support Van Buren's proposal of divorce. On February 19, midway through a speech against divorce, Clay launched his assault on Calhoun, bitterly taunting him with desertion, inconsistency, and craven political expediency. It was the sort of thing that Clay did especially well. A body language of gesturing, pacing, and pawing the floor enhanced the effects of a finely modulated voice and his initimable skill in blending passion and reason, statesmanlike concerns and biting sarcasm, good humor and savage personal attack. Not content to confine himself to recent events, Clay went back to the glorious moment for both of them during the War of 1812 and traced Calhoun's tortuous course thereafter as a nationalist and sectionalist, Unionist and Nullifier, statesman and now sycophant of the "sly fox." At a critical moment in the Whig battle for republican liberty against executive despotism, Clay concluded with a flourish, Calhoun "took up his musket, knapsack, and shot pouch, and joined the other party."[8]

On March 10, after three weeks of careful preparation, Calhoun answered Clay's charges. In style, he presented striking contrasts: he stood virtually immobile, spoke in a harsh monotone, and depended for effect on the force of his close-knit arguments. He rightly disclaimed any connection with the sly fox. (Indeed, their personal relations were not restored until Calhoun made a call at the White House in January 1840.) Nor did he rank party loyalty high among the "political virtues." Faithful only to old republican principles, he claimed that he had neither deserted Whig ranks nor joined the Democratic party. Passing over charges of a more personal nature, Calhoun then went on the attack, focusing anew upon ideas that he had expressed in the special session and had outlined more recently in a letter to his constituents. The panic of 1837, in this view, had freed the government from past policies so that it could adopt a totally new course. It was a course, moreover, calculated to promote southern interests, for it linked low tariffs and severe retrenchment to the policy of divorce. To this, Calhoun added an explicit proslavery argument, extolling the superior virtues of slave labor over those of free labor in the North.[9]

Two days later, Webster seized the opportunity to exploit the sectional light in which Calhoun had presented divorce. With a range of Whig arguments both old and new, he condemned divorce as being irresponsible, undemocratic, and un-American. By rejecting the idea of a new national bank, advocates of divorce were abdicating responsibility for creating a uniform paper currency. From a different side he argued that the refusal of the administration to make a new connection with the state banks would mean war on the banks and on the credit system. Striking, at this point, the newer entrepreneurial theme, Webster then praised credit as being a poor man's capital, the only thing that enabled him to rise and to participate more fully in the common life of the republic. More broadly still, divorce would violate the corporate nature of the common life—pitting section against section, the poor against the rich—and would erode the bonds of common interest and affection. "Such tendencies," he said, "we are bound by true patriotism, and by our love of Union, to resist." By mingling the interests of the government with those of the people, he would fashion new bonds of Union and incorporate everyone into the life of the nation. Finally, he linked the issue of divorce to the fate of the republican experiment itself. Standing "as in the full gaze of our ancestors, and our posterity," he solemnly enjoined the responsibility of the present: "Yes, sir, I would act as if our fathers, who formed it for us, and who bequeathed it to us, were looking on us—as if I could see their venerable forms bending down to behold us, from the abodes above. I would act, too, sir, as if that long line of posterity were also viewing us, whose eye is hereafter to scrutinize our conduct."[10] In the familiar role as defender of the Union, Webster made his greatest speech against divorce.

When the Senate finally got back to full consideration of Wright's divorce bill, the prospects for passage had become uncertain. Van Buren, who was following developments closely, thought at first that there would be no problem; but by March 17 he believed that a tie-breaking vote by the vice-president might have to decide the matter. Two administration senators, James Buchanan and Felix Grundy, had been instructed against the bill by their Whig-dominated state legislatures; and two others, Alfred Cuthbert of Georgia and Thomas Morris of Ohio, stood poles apart on the kind of funds to be received. Morris, a hard-money man, disliked even the six-year period for phasing in specie, while Cuthbert leaned away from specie altogether.[11]

The first vote on March 21 brought no surprise, as the bill to revive the state-bank-deposit system, brought forth once more by William C. Rives, failed by a 20 to 29 vote. For many, however, the next move in the Senate was totally unexpected. Cuthbert proposed to strike the specie feature and to revive the Currency Resolution of 1816, which gave the Treasury discretion to receive specie or the notes of specie-paying banks. Apparently caught off guard, administration spokesmen asked for a delay. Little is known about what happened during the next three days, but on March 24 Cuthbert's amendment passed by a vote of 31 to 21. Wright voted with Calhoun in the minority, but 14 Democrats went the other way. The entire divorce bill, with the new amendment, then passed by the narrow margin of 2—27 to 25. Calhoun voted with the Whigs, Conservatives, and instructed Democrats against the amended bill and bitterly assailed its passage as representing a surrender of the substance of divorce. Genuine independence for the Treasury and hopes for currency reform still required, in his view, the exclusive use of specie and government paper in its operations.

There is not enough evidence to explain this crucial turn of events. Cuthbert most likely acted on his own. He had been absent from the special session and therefore had not committed himsef to the specie clause that passed the Senate. In a brief speech he simply explained that he was unwilling for the government to abandon "that medium by which the commerce of the country is carried on."[12] It is not known how much effort Wright made to impose party discipline or what role Van Buren played. The president knew a week earlier that Cuthbert opposed specie and that others believed the passage of Wright's divorce bill might be easier without the specie requirement on the funds-receivable side. There was also a belief that a Senate retreat from specie would encourage the banks to resume payments and thus fulfill an important goal of the administration. Since Van Buren and Cuthbert had been congressional messmates for a time in the 1820s, it is just possible that the "magician" worked quietly with his old messmate to achieve this goal.

One thing was clear in any case. The arrogance of Calhoun and the burden that his sectional pleading added to divorce made it easier for some advocates of specie to retreat. Niles vented all his anger on Calhoun for voting against the bill, rather than on Cuthbert for amending it. "No party can make any dependence or reliance on him," Niles privately wrote; and if the bill should make it through the House, "I shall not regret Mr. C's vote as his influence is not of the most safe kind."[13]

Whether concerted or not, Senate action did have the effect of reinforcing other moves by the administration in April 1838 to abet the efforts of New York banks to resume specie payments. Under the necessity of resuming by May, when the year-long indulgence of suspension was to run out, New York bankers, led by Albert Gallatin, sought support outside, particularly from Nicholas Biddle in Philadelphia. But they looked in vain. Due largely to his opposition, one bank convention had adjourned on December 3, 1837, without taking any action other than to fix April 11 as the date for another convention to meet. Meanwhile, Biddle refused all overtures to set his own deadline for resumption and, under growing pressure on the eve of the new convention, came out flatly against resumption, explaining his reasons in a public letter on April 5 to John Quincy Adams. Seeking to unite all banks in an adversary relation to the administration, he wanted to make resumption a lever for compelling Van Buren to repeal the "Specie Circular," to abandon the proposal of divorce, and to connect the Treasury once more to the state banks. With an arrogance that is reminiscent of the earlier battles against Jackson, he thus urged fellow bankers to remain behind the cotton bales, as at New Orleans, "preparing to resume but not resuming" until Van Buren had surrendered. For the purpose he defined very starkly an irrepressible conflict between the banks and the administration: "The credit system of the United States and the exclusive metallic system are now fairly in the field, face to face, with each other; one or the other must fall."[14]

The anger that this aroused among New York bankers showed that Biddle had failed to unify the banks against the administration. Throop hastened to tell Van Buren that Biddle's "faux pas" presented a golden opportunity to aid the effort of the banks to resume and to efface thereby the damaging image of hostility toward them. Eagerly embracing the political windfall of doing battle against Jackson's old foe, Van Buren orchestrated a number of significant moves. On April 7 administration stalwart Thomas Hamer of Ohio introduced a resolution in the House, affirming that it was both the duty and the intention of the administration to strengthen public confidence in the banks that would decide to resume.[15] No specifics were given on how to fulfill the duty, and the resolution was soon tabled, out of fear that it might prematurely precipitate House debate on the divorce bill.

Other initiatives by the administration soon suggested specific means for aiding the banks. On April 13 Woodbury sent two letters to New York, to be read at the bank convention. One promised that specie would not be kept in the Treasury in excess of current needs, and the other pledged that the Treasury would receive the notes of banks that resumed specie payments and would disburse them, wherever acceptable, to the creditors of the government. Three days later, Senator Grundy introduced a bill to penalize Biddle's bank for any further circulation of the "resurrection notes." Speaking in the bill's behalf, he explicitly repudiated Biddle's letter to Adams and disavowed that the administration had any hostility against the banks. Meanwhile, Governor William L. Marcy asked the New York state legislature to pledge at least $6 million in canal stock to support the banks; and a letter from England announced to the convention that a sum of $4 million in specie was on its way over to New York.[16]

On April 17, 1838, New York bankers announced the decision to meet the May deadline for resuming specie payments. Woodbury rightly claimed a great victory for the administration. Back in 1816, during the last general suspension, President James Madison had deemed that a new national bank was absolutely necessary in order to support resumption by the state banks. Now the banks began to resume without that support, indeed doing so in spite of the determined opposition of Nicholas Biddle and the national bank created by Madison. While avoiding Madison's bad example, Van Buren also enjoyed, for a moment at least, the political opportunity to reenact the archetypal experience of Jackson in battling Biddle and the old bank. Once more, Van Buren wrote Jackson, with great satisfaction, that Biddle had "overshot the mark."[17] A further sense of triumph came as the force of the New York example compelled resumption elsewhere, even in Pennsylvania, where Biddle himself was at last forced to abandon the cotton breastworks.

Clay's response at this point was another significant indication of the administration's victory. Assuming that he would be the candidate of a united Whig party in 1840, Clay sought, with two moves, to cancel the political advantages that the Democrats were deriving from resumption. One was designed to extricate his old friend Biddle from an embarrassing position. For this purpose, Clay introduced and spoke briefly to a petition asking for a new national bank to be established in New York. Buchanan leapt at the chance to define the issue between parties as being that of an independent Treasury versus a national bank, but he clearly leapt too soon. Clay had no intention of following the petition with a formal proposal, for he did not suppose that public opinion had matured in its favor. Privately, Clay assured Biddle that he contemplated no new bank at all and that the petition from New York had been introduced solely to deflect unfavorable publicity from the Philadelphia bank.[18]

Secondly, Clay proposed that the "Specie Circular" be repealed. If suspension in 1837 had rendered it inoperative, resumption now brought it back in force. Clay rightly saw in it an issue of great symbolic importance, because the circular had been the focal point of controversy at the end of Jackson's term and at the beginning of Van Buren's. Actually, the Senate had already dealt with the matter, incorporating Webster's amendment for repeal into the divorce bill. No action had yet been taken in the House on the bill, however, nor was the House's action certain to be favorable. In any case, Clay was in a hurry to take away the political capital that the Democrats had gained from resumption; so, on April 30 he made repeal of the circular a new and entirely separate measure. Unhappily for Clay, strong Democratic support for repeal—indicated by the 34 to 10 vote in the Senate and the 154 to 29 vote in the House—tended to foil his purpose and to spare the Democrats the embarrassment he intended. Democrats plausibly argued that the circular had served well at an earlier time to check bank issues but that it was no longer needed. Moreover, repeal conformed to the spirit of Cuthbert's amendment, which, by reaffirming the Currency Resolution of 1816, gave the Treasury full discretion to receive the notes of banks that paid in specie.

While the Senate passed the divorce bill in March, the House did not call it up for final consideration until late June. There were several reasons for the delay. First of all, as Van Buren complained, the House, as usual, was going about its business in a "dilatory way." Sectional feeling, intensified by a new dispute over abolitionist petitions, was also disruptive. On December 18 Congressman William Slade of Vermont introduced petitions against slavery and, because no "gag" had yet been adopted by the Twenty-fifth Congress, spoke to them in a long and bitter tirade. Cries of order added to the disorder and led to the withdrawal of most southern members, who then arranged for a caucus in the evening. Turning down the more radical suggestions, such as Calhoun's idea of a southern convention, the caucus decided to adopt the Pinckney gag of the preceding Congress. Under the leadership of John Patton of Virginia, the rule was pushed through on December 21 by a large vote, as twenty of New York's Democratic representatives voted with the majority. This meant that the petitions would continue to be received in the House chamber, but then would be tabled without further action being taken.[19]

Party feeling also ran very high during the session. One example was a fight on the House floor between two members from Tennessee, Democrat Hopkins L. Turney and Whig John Bell. Another incident, shocking and "barbarous" as Van Buren put it, was the duel between Jonathan Cilley of Maine and a Whig adversary, William Graves of Kentucky. Invoking House privilege, Cilley refused Graves's request that Cilley retract statements against the national bank and a controversial New York editor. Graves, with the backing of Clay, thereupon challenged Cilley to a duel and designated rifles as the weapons. With neither side feeling that honor had been satisfied after the first shot, the firing continued until Cilley fell mortally wounded on the third round. The natural death of two other Democratic members—one from Maine and the other from Maryland—caused further delay while replacements were being chosen; and a dispute over Mississippi's two seats was not resolved until the end of May. Out of it all, unhappily for the administration, Whigs gained four of the five seats.

On June 19 the House finally took up the divorce measure, though in a form that many had not expected. Instead of considering the Senate bill, which dropped the specie requirement, House leaders brought forth their own bill, which retained the specie feature. The bill clearly expressed the personal conviction of the Ways and Means chairman, Churchill C. Cambreleng; but it also represented, in the view of speaker James K. Polk, the best legislative strategy at the time. Conservative Democrats opposed divorce in any form, while House members who were under Calhoun's influence would only vote for a divorce bill that would mandate specie on the funds-receivable side. As expected, Calhoun "moved heaven & earth" for the passage of the bill, which was so clearly linked to his own political fortunes. But all his efforts were in vain. On June 25, 1838, the House defeated the bill 125 to 111, by about the same margin as at the special session. The six votes that Calhoun had mustered did little more than offset the four new seats that the

Whigs had won in special elections, while about sixteen Conservatives voted in opposition. An overwhelming vote against reconsideration left the issue of divorce apparently dead for the session.[20]

Political foes were jubilant. In a mock funeral procession, Whigs paraded an effigy of the dead divorce bill through the streets of Washington, and Conservative Democrats shared credit for the victory. The *National Intelligencer* praised the ''independent spirit'' of statesmanship which had led Conservatives to defy the trammels of ''party influence.'' Defeat of the divorce bill had been a victory not only for economic wisdom but also for the old spirit of republican virtue.[21] It was generally assumed that, with most banks now beginning to resume specie payments, the Treasury would renew its connection with the banks under the old Deposit Act of 1836, which had governed Treasury operations before the suspension. Conservatives hailed renewal as a vindication of their views, and the Whigs, while privately in favor of a national bank, thought a new connection with the state banks was infinitely preferable to divorce.

But claims for the death of the divorce proposal were grossly exaggerated. Two crucial provisions of the Deposit Act stood in the way of an automatic revival of the Treasury connection. Any bank that had, since July 4, 1836, either issued its own notes or handled the notes of other banks in denominations less than $5 could not be used as a depository of Treasury funds; nor, under the same conditions, could its notes be received in payment of government dues. Of the approximately eight hundred banks at the time, only a very few could qualify, because suspension had driven most coin out of circulation and had compelled the banks to issue and handle small notes. Until the Deposit Act was amended to strike out these small-note provisions, the Treasury could not use the banks as depositories or receive their notes. Congress had failed to pass new laws providing for an independent Treasury, yet the force of the old law meant that the Treasury would continue its operations independently of the banks.

For this reason the last-minute efforts at the end of the long congressional session centered on amending the Deposit Act. Out of this important battle, which historians have unaccountably neglected, the administration won a victory of sorts. Speaking for the Whigs, Webster sought to strike out the small-note provision of the Deposit Act and thus to enable the banks to serve once more as depositories. Democrats in the Senate managed to defeat Webster's amendment, and a like fate awaited it in the House. On the funds-receivable side, by contrast, the administration itself took the initiative in removing the small-note provision and thereby allowing the Treasury to receive the notes of banks that might resume. Wright's amendment for this purpose passed both houses and, in effect, lifted the barrier posed by the Deposit Act to the operation of the Currency Resolution of 1816. The Treasury now enjoyed full discretion to receive the notes of specie-paying banks.

The *Washington Globe* rightly called these efforts "the last Sub Treasury bill."[22] They enabled the administration to salvage the substance of the divorce policy, leaving the Treasury independent of the banks on the deposit side and allowing for that degree of retreat from specie that had been indicated, in the spirit of compromise, at the beginning of the session. Separation from the banks had been maintained, even though it failed to gain the full legal sanction of a divorce decree.

At the end of the long session, Van Buren appeared hopeful, reporting to Jackson that "our friends" in Congress went home in "excellent spirits." Resumption had been achieved without a new national bank; a reconnection with state banks had been avoided; and the substance of an independent Treasury had been saved. Economic recovery had also come with resumption; along with the specie sent over to aid in the resumption, England extended new credits for commercial houses and for state projects of internal improvements. In this perspective one historian has argued that the panic of 1837 represented a period of temporary adjustment in the relations of the United States to creditor England, rather than a serious downturn. Politically as well, Van Buren was pleased by "very favorable" reports that he was receiving from different parts of the country regarding the prospects of the fall elections.[23]

Van Buren also had reason to believe that the Conservative defection had been contained without doing much damage to the party. In New York he wrote Tallmadge off to the Whigs quite early, along with other inveterate "bank Democrats." Meanwhile, Governor Marcy and the *Albany Argus* began to rally more unequivocally to the banner of divorce. At the beginning of 1838, it was true, the governor was still taking Locofoco enthusiasm for divorce as evidence of the party's radicalism. By March, however, he began to realize that the limited scale of government finances made divorce, even with the specie feature, far less important in its effects on banks and currency than was generally believed. The aid that Van Buren extended to New York banks during the resumption crisis also belied the radical image. As a party man, moreover, Marcy bitterly condemned the defection of former friends who had "feasted and fattened by the patronage of the republican party" for so long. Loyalty to party remained, for him, one of the highest virtues. After a rather evasive course of its own, the *Albany*

Argus also came out squarely for divorce: "We believe the time has emphatically come for the separation of bank and state."[24]

In Virginia the equivocal position taken by Thomas Ritchie and the influential *Richmond Enquirer* posed a bigger problem. Still hoping to prevent a split between Van Buren and Rives, Ritchie pushed with increasing shrillness the compromise formula of special deposits, which neither could accept. The central task of the Van Buren men in Virginia was a "campaign of education," as one student calls it, to correct public opinion in the state and to set forth divorce versus a national bank as the true issue. For this purpose a movement in 1838 pressured Ritchie with the threat of a new paper in Richmond that would be unequivocally committed to the administration. Wright added to this pressure by making a quick trip to Richmond somewhat later. Even more persuasive was the outcome of the spring elections, for in these contests the Democrats lost control of the state legislature because Conservatives offered competing slates in several districts. Before Congress adjourned in July, finally, Ritchie failed in a last desperate effort to bring Rives and the president together. By now he was ready to concede that if the issue at last came down to divorce or a national bank, he would "sink or swim" with Van Buren. Clearly, the administration party in Virginia was beginning to close ranks.[25]

Van Buren's visit to Virginia in August confirmed this state of affairs. Traveling in an open carriage with two of his sons, he made his first stop at Castle Garden to share "beans and bacon" with Rives. No political agreement was reached, or probably even attempted, but the visit apparently did great social credit to both host and guest. The president then went to Richmond for conferences with party leaders and on to Norfolk, as a later chapter will show, to launch the South Seas Exploring Expedition. Joined at a later point by the charming Poinsetts, the president made his last stop at White Sulpher Springs.

From there, rumors spread that Van Buren had wearied of fighting banks and that he sought to conciliate Rives with the promise of the vice-presidency in 1840. Fearing the rumors to be well founded, a bitter foe of Rives warned Van Buren that the differences between them were "irreconciliable" and that great harm to the party would come from any effort to "inflate the vanity and self-importance" of the Conservative defector. But all such rumors were without foundation, for the president went to Virginia to assert his position and not to conciliate its opponents. Rives thus wrote in bitterness to a friend: "He seems to be as pertinaciously wedded to his ill-fated policy as ever." In September, shortly after Van Buren had left Virginia, Rives publicly announced, in the columns of the *Charlottsville Jeffersonian Republican*, his position as an "armed neutral" between the two parties. Two years later he formally identified with the Whigs.[26]

If optimistic himself, Van Buren overrated the "excellent spirits" of others. Having wrestled for a year with the yet unresolved issue of divorce, Silas Wright confessed to "mental apathy" and a "sickening almost to disgust."[27] The victory of sorts for the administration at the very end of the session had been a negative one: it had merely prevented a new connection between the Treasury and the banks under the Deposit Act. The battle to give full legal sanction to an independent Treasury still had to be won. In the meantime the operation of the Treasury without these sanctions made the administration vulnerable to the Whig cry of Caesarism. The keeping and disbursing of Treasury funds without congressional safeguards, in this view, gave the president an unchecked control over the nation's purse and an enormous engine of spoils.

Frustration also arose on the funds-receivable side. By a compromise, signaled at the beginning of the long session of the Twenty-fifth Congress and salvaged at the very end, the administration retreated from the specie mandate to the discretionary power in the Currency Resolution of 1816. The administration's friends assumed that the Treasury would use its discretion to receive the notes of specie-paying banks, would immediately disburse most of them to creditors of the government, and then would submit the small remainder to the banks at regular intervals for payment in specie. This, in fact, was the essence of the compromise. But political foes projected a different course, claiming that the Treasury, informed by a radical spirit, would not disburse any of the notes at all but rather would submit them in large quantity and at unexpected moments to the banks for payment in specie. In this arbitrary way a Treasury Caesar could, Tallmadge thus warned, destroy the banking system. Better to receive only in specie, others agreed, than to allow the executive such power. Sensitive to Whig charges of Caesarism, the *Washington Globe* began to question the value of any compromise at all.[28]

There was also discontent within the party over Van Buren's leadership. It was "a general impression," Senator Niles observed, that "the President is too easy & passive & willing to let things take their own course." Lacking "energy & vigor," he acted as if the proposal of divorce at the special session had exhausted his responsibility as a leader of the party. Elam Tilden contrasted the excitement generated by Jackson's bank war with the relative apathy that people were showing toward divorce. More somehow needed to be done to put the true issue before the people, rather than simply to respond to the issue as defined by political foes. The president lacked Jackson's personal appeal, of course, yet a perceptive and sympathetic observer, Jabez Hammond, also thought that Van Buren was not "political" enough and that he seemed content to push his divorce measure by the "weight of principle" only.[29]

A passivity before the public was also matched by what many in Washington regarded as aloofness. "Contrary to all pre-conceived opinions of his character," one journalist observed, "Mr. Van Buren has rendered himself the most inaccessible both to friends and adversaries of all the chief magistrates that ever filled his station." Poor relations with most members of Congress compounded the problem, for Van Buren had chosen to deal with the legislature principally through his most-trusted personal associates, Silas Wright and Churchill C. Cambreleng. Niles here thought "closeness" to be one of Van Buren's "greatest faults." In too many cases Van Buren took actions without consulting senators from the states most directly involved. To improve his relations with Congress, it was suggested that he remove some of his cabinet members and appoint new ones who possessed political constituencies of their own and ties with Congress. This was in some degree the way cabinets had been made up before the Jackson presidency rendered the cabinet more narrowly the voice of the executive alone.[30]

Of the two cabinet changes made in 1838, Van Buren's choice for attorney general did meet the political test. Benjamin F. Butler, who had reluctantly remained at the post for a year, was now allowed to resign. Van Buren looked first to Judge Richard B. Parker, Thomas Ritchie's brother-in-law, with the thought that Parker's expected refusal would yet gain the president political capital in Virginia. He then settled on Felix Grundy, a lame-duck senator who had powerful ties to Jackson, to Congress, and to the Southwest. He also brought to the cabinet the political credits gained by his bill against Biddle's "resurrection notes."

Van Buren's choice for the Navy Department, by contrast, bore out the views of his critics, for it added more social grace to the cabinet than it added political force to the administration. Having welcomed, if not actually encouraged, the aging and inept Mahlon Dickerson to step aside, he then invited Washington Irving to fill the post and urged, in behalf of this request, a desire to renew "personal relations" that went back to the London mission in 1831. When Irving declined the offer, out of fear of the tempestuous sea of politics, Van Buren then gave the post to another literary squire from Tarrytown, James K. Paulding. Related by marriage to Irving and part of the same social circle, Paulding added adornment to the cabinet and soon earned the reputation of being the best dinner host among his colleagues. He also brought considerable interest and knowledge to the department, for he had served on the Navy Board under President James Monroe and for the last decade as the navy agent in New York. But he lacked a political constituency, which Marcy or Niles, who especially wanted the job, could have added to the administration. Although Paulding was an "unswerving republican," Van Buren privately admitted that many in the party might not like the appointment.[31]

An unusual transaction with Biddle's bank also caused embarrassment for the party. To meet the costs of Indian removal, the War Department made an unexpectedly high request for $4.5 million in June 1838 and about $7 million in July, sums well above the ordinary resources of the Treasury. The Treasury might have floated a loan to meet the extraordinary demand, but Van Buren ruled out a new debt at the time as being unrepublican and inexpedient. The only remaining source of emergency funds was to cash one or two of the four bonds that Biddle had issued in 1836 to cover the government's shares in the old Bank of the United States. With regard to the second bond, which was to mature in October 1838 at about $2 million, Biddle agreed to pay it off in three monthly installments, beginning in August. Needing still more money, Woodbury then sought to sell the third bond, which was to mature in 1839, on the European market; but unable to get a favorable bid, he accepted Biddle's offer to pay in full.

In both cases, Biddle arranged for payment in a way he thought to be highly favorable to his own interests. By this arrangement the Treasury would be paid by a credit at the Philadelphia bank, rather than in specie. The Treasury further agreed to use the notes of the bank to meet the demands of its own creditors and to disburse them at a great distance from Philadelphia, mainly in the West and the Southwest. With this arrangement, Biddle boasted that he had wrecked the divorce policy, made his bank a depository of Treasury funds, and gained extended circulation for his notes. In fact, the funds of the Treasury were in the form of a "special deposit," and the connection would automatically cease when all of the funds had been disbursed. Nor was the use of his bank notes exceptional; the Treasury was receiving and disbursing the notes of other specie-paying banks at the time. Nonetheless, the bond deal did take some of the luster away from the administration's earlier victory over Biddle, and public silence by the administration was one measure of its political embarrassment.[32]

The course of legislation regarding state banks in 1838 added a final element of frustration. Though the crisis of 1837 passed without legal provision being made by Congress for the Treasury to handle its own funds, it also passed without the kind of bank reform that leading

Democratic spokesmen deemed proper. Van Buren himself stood, throughout his public life, on the restrictive side of the issue. As a state senator, he had voted against every new bank charter granted by the legislature with the exception of one to aid war-torn Buffalo. During his brief tenure as governor in 1829, he had recommended and then signed into law the Safety Fund System. Among other things, this established a fund, drawn from all the banks in an amount equal to 3 percent of their capital, which was devoted to the security of the note holders of any banks that might collapse. It also created a state regulatory commission of three members. As president, Van Buren professed sympathy with the antimonopoly principle of free banking, but he feared that any law for general incorporation of banks would not be accompanied by adequate restraints. The result would be a great multiplication in the number of banks, leading not to a stable currency but, rather, to "the gratification of the extreme demand for an enterprising and adventurous population."[33] Van Buren wanted enterprise to proceed at a sober pace, and it was in this context that he thought about bank reform.

In this same perspective, Benton and Niles found much to praise in the reform bill that had been passed by the Democratic legislature in Louisiana but had been vetoed by the Whig governor. Three provisions in this bill promised the kind of restraint that Democrats generally desired. One forbade the issuing of notes under $20 denomination; a second prescribed a one-third specie reserve against all note and deposit liabilities; a final provision required that the remaining two-thirds of a bank's liabilities be secured by discounts on commercial paper maturing in sixty to ninety days and not subject to renewal. This meant that a bank's assets would be relatively liquid and therefore accessible to meet its obligations. It also meant that the notes issued on the basis of short-term commercial paper would constitute an "elastic currency," one that would reflect the actual needs of trade and would preclude a ruinous process of inflation. According to the *Democratic Review*, the provisions of the Louisiana bill represented "the true principles of commercial banking." They also marked a return to the conservative practices of bankers during the earlier days of the nation.[34]

More-expansionist views won out in the New York Free Banking Act of 1838. Passed by Whigs two days after the banks had announced their decision to resume specie payments, it replaced the old practice of special legislative charter with a general law of incorporation. Under this law, any number of new bank associations could be organized with only two basic restrictions on their capital formation. One required a new bank to have a minimum of $100,000 in capital stock. The second provided that capital stock, in the form of state bonds and up to one-half in real-estate mortgages, must be placed with the state comptroller in the amount needed to secure in full the notes to be circulated by the bank. Capital beyond the amount for backing its notes in circulation did not have to be placed with the comptroller, nor was there any upper limit to the amount of capital a bank could have.

Other features of free banking in the New York law were in marked contrast with the restrictive provisions of the Louisiana bill. No ban was placed on the issuing of notes under $20 denomination. A specie reserve of one-eighth was required, but this applied only to the notes and not to the deposit liabilities of a bank. It was assumed that the depositor, unlike the note holder, had personal knowledge of the bank and should therefore be free to handle his money as he wished. Most significantly of all, the New York law did not require that any portion of a bank's note and deposit liabilities be secured by short-term discounts of commercial paper. Each bank was left free to decide its own credit policy, whether for short-term discounts or for loans of longer maturity based on securities other than commercial paper. The absence of restraints here expressed most clearly the basic philosophy of the whole measure—namely, that free trade in banking would, in the absence of restraints, automatically draw the proper amount of capital into the business of banking and would thus supply the community with the proper amount of bank currency. It was on this point, a noted historian of banking has observed, that free banking in New York differed most profoundly from the Louisiana bill.[35]

From either side, critics of the law focused at last on its expansionist tendency. Radicals in the mold of William Leggett, a Locofoco editor, condemned the measure for not being "free" enough. The requirement of $100,000 minimum in capital continued the spirit of monopoly, for it denied access to less-wealthy individuals and groups. Although the new banks were styled "associations" by the law, court rulings soon invested them with all the legal attributes of "corporations." Equally "artificial" and unfree was a provision that limited a stockholder's liability to the amount of his shares. In a system that would be truly "natural" and free, Leggett supposed, stockholders would be responsible for all of the obligations held by creditors against the bank.

In two other basic ways the new law violated what radicals took to be essential to free banking—a total divorce of the state government, no less than the national government, from the banks. By receiving and disbursing the notes of the new banks in its own financial operations, the state government lent its credit to the new credit system of banking. The notes to be circulated by the banks were to come engraved from the state comptroller's office, moreover, and this would have the inescapable effect of giving them public character and an undeserved degree of credit. Opposing as unnatural either government aid or control, radicals argued that the new law in fact provided aid to the banks without any concomitant control and that a new round of speculation and excess was bound to be the result. Instead of improving the currency, the *Democratic Review* concluded, the new bank law would mean "a very pernicious aggravation of the evils of the existing artificial paper-money system."[36]

Though radicals thought that free banking in New York was not "free" enough, moderate critics believed that it was too free from needed restraints. Along with state aid they wanted more control. Enos Throop called the law an "enormous political monster" and warned that its provisions for capital in the form of state bonds and real-estate mortgages would spark a new round of speculation and excess. "The act bears internal evidence," Albert Gallatin agreed, "that it was prepared by speculators." While in favor of the general incorporation feature, he thought more restrictions on bank activity were needed in order to protect the community from excess. With no upper limit on capital formation, he feared that too much capital would initially flow into banking enterprise. The experience of the next two years was to bear out this fear, for about half of the 134 new banks formed during that time did not survive.

Gallatin also thought that inadequate security had been required for a bank's immediate liabilities. No provision at all had been made for the depositors, yet their run on the banks in May 1837 was what had precipitated the suspension. He considered the one-eighth specie reserve to be much too small and the security to note holders as pledged in the capital stock held by the comptroller to be somewhat illusory. In time of a business depression, many mortgages and bonds might not even find a market, while the market value of all would most likely fall below the par value of the notes. Finally, Gallatin criticized the act for not prescribing the kind of loans, long term or short term, that the banks could make. Fully committed to the principle of short-term commercial discounts, he saw in this lacuna in the New York law a wide opening for banks to extend long-term loans and thereby to inflate the currency beyond the legitimate needs of trade.[37]

Whatever the shortcomings turned up by its early critics, free banking was to become the wave of the future. After a depression and the prolonged party debates of the 1840s, the idea caught on rapidly, spreading to fifteen states by the time of the Civil War and providing the basic idea for the National Banking Act. Elements of order and stability, which had not been apparent to these critics, emerged in the process and abetted the triumph. For one thing, a recent study shows, the

Democratic critique of banking served to increase appreciation for such things as specie reserves, short-term loans, and liquidity. Other forms of corporate organization began to collect capital for investment in new enterprise, and new savings institutions and insurance companies likewise relieved the pressure on the banks for long-term loans. In the absence of federal control or a new national bank, moreover, an informal but very real system of relations began to develop among the banks of the country, similar to those that had developed earlier among New England banks under the Suffolk System. Here the country banks kept adequate funds on deposit in Boston to clear their own notes and to assure that their notes would circulate at par. After the Civil War, New York assumed a similar relation with many banks all over the country.[38]

In the context of the debate between parties during Van Buren's presidency, the free-banking bill was a Whig coup. In pushing it through the legislature, party leaders skillfully exploited the anti-monopoly spirit, which radicals had for years directed against the system of chartered banks and the Democratic leadership in Albany. Economically, the law was a triumph for the "spirit of enterprise." A Whig address, issued at the end of the legislative session, expressed very explicitly the leading goals of free banking: "to do away with everything like monopoly and special privilege in the hands of any favored class, and to give free scope to the employment of capital and credit wherever and by whomever they could be beneficially employed."[39]

In his magisterial interpretation of the period, Bray Hammond argued that free banking was "the culmination of Jacksonian policy." Jackson, in Hammond's view, had destroyed the old national bank; and Van Buren, by disconnecting the Treasury from state banks, had completed the process of freeing the banks from national regulation. The banking law in New York reflected this impulse for liberation and expressed fully the regnant "spirit of enterprise." Hammond was, in fact, no more than half right: free banking was a consequence of Jacksonian bank policy but not its intention. To "diffuse and expand the opportunities for bank enterprise" was not the aim of Jackson or of Van Buren's administration; it was, rather, the goal of their political foes. Both Van Buren's own proposals at the special session and his emphasis on the restrictive side of bank reform at the state level contemplated the ultimate goals of a stable currency and a sober pace of growth for enterprise. Free banking, as he saw it in 1838, would more nearly subvert than it would fulfill this goal.[40]

By the middle of 1838 Van Buren's presidency was approaching a critical point. The nature of bank legislation in New York matched the failure in Washington to put under law the Treasury's handling of its own funds. Retreat from specie on the funds-receivable side had abetted bank resumption, yet Whigs reaped political benefit with the charge that the president was becoming a Treasury Caesar. Silence on the bankruptcy proposal of the special session, moreover, took away a direct means for promoting the good of a sound and stable bank currency. In response to the "New York tornado"—the stunning Whig victory in the November 1837 election—Van Buren accepted compromise; but it began to strike many as a frustrating one and one that would add to growing doubts about Van Buren's leadership.

Van Buren remained unruffled as usual in the midst of political vicissitudes. Cheerfulness in public was itself a policy of sorts, and visitors at the White House invariably reported that the president was in good spirits. Privately, however, he recognized that the administration and its supporters "still have difficult scenes to pass through."[41] The difficulties of the next two years easily bore out this assessment.

7

THE SECOND DECLARATION
OF INDEPENDENCE

On July 4, 1840, President Van Buren signed into law a bill providing for the total divorce of the Treasury from all state banks. It also provided a structure and safeguards so that the Treasury could handle its own funds, and it mandated specie as the kind of funds that the Treasury could receive, keep, and disburse. The bill passed the Senate in late January and the House on June 30, but Van Buren waited until July 4 to give it his formal approval. Parades, replete with patriotic banners, hickory poles, and volleys of cannon, were timed for the signing; and speeches hailed the measure as the second declaration of independence. "The former delivered the American people from the power of the British throne," Amos Kendall declared; "the latter delivered them from the power of British banks."[1] The proposal made at the special session in 1837 had at last become the law of the land, creating in fact as well as in name the Independent Treasury.

The circumstances attending the triumph of the divorce measure induced Van Buren to give it a new and deeper meaning. The crucial element in its success was another round of suspensions, in late 1839, by nearly half of the nation's banks. If the general suspension in 1837 had prompted the original proposal of divorce, the new suspensions assured its final passage through Congress. But they did more. The bank failures in 1839, which were accompanied by an abrupt end to the flow of English capital, signaled a profound downturn in business activity which lasted for four years. In this context, Van Buren professed to see divorce as involving not only the independence of the Treasury from the state banks but also the independence of the nation from the credit system of England. The goal of a sound and stable currency still required an independent Treasury and the reform of state banks, but it ultimately required a divorce of the nation's enterprise from cyclic fluctuations emanating in England. More than ever, divorce took on an old republican meaning.

A victory for the divorce policy must have seemed fairly remote to its advocates during the last part of 1838. Many were frustrated over the issue by the time Congress adjourned in July, and events during the next year did little to improve prospects for that issue. For one thing, the results of the state elections were ambiguous. Even the relative success of the Democratic party in the North and the West, with the exception of New York State, gave no clear mandate for total divorce. Local issues played a part in Missouri, Illinois, Maryland, New Jersey, and Maine, along with the effects of returning prosperity. Moreover, new governors in the key states of Ohio and Pennsylvania had won election on a platform that professed friendship, rather than hostility, to the state banks. Both favored a policy in Washington that would reaffirm the deposit feature of divorce, drop the specie mandate, and retain the Treasury's discretion to receive the notes of specie-paying banks.

Amos Kendall drew a similar conclusion from the less-favorable election results in the South. Arkansas, Alabama, and South Carolina voted Democratic, as expected; but Virginia, North Carolina, Georgia, Mississippi, and Louisiana went the other way. In a larger perspective, these results reflected the continued movement of the South away from its one-party position under Jackson to a two-party system by the end of Van Buren's presidency. At the time, Kendall saw the outcome as a rebuff to John C. Calhoun's design to fashion a politically united South. Finding this rebuff not altogether unpleasing, Kendall hoped it would make Calhoun "less tenacious of his *particular scheme*" of specie and would dispose him, instead, to accept the view that the Treasury's receipt of bank notes was "more national and more practicable." What made the matter most practicable of all was its likely bearing on the upcoming presidential election. Van Buren's hopes for "an eight years voyage" at the helm of state depended largely upon "the passage of the Treasury Bill in almost any practicable shape."[2] In light of the election returns in 1838, Kendall thought this meant a divorce bill that would continue the retreat away from specie on the funds-receivable side. In effect he urged Van Buren to retain the compromise formula worked out in the last session of Congress.

News of the November 1838 election in New York, which came to Van Buren shortly after Kendall's report, gave added force to this advice. Here the Whigs won a stunning victory. William H. Seward foiled William L. Marcy's bid for reelection as governor and ended the ten-year reign of the Regency. The Whigs also retained control of the state assembly, greatly narrowed the Democratic margin in the senate, and reduced from thirty to nineteen the number of Democrats in the House of Representatives. Van Buren invoked old formulas to explain the defeat—Conservative treachery, ballot fraud, and, especially, the corrupting influence of the banks. "Our story," he wrote Jackson, "is told in one word—money." Marcy, by contrast, believed the Whigs had won because they had burdened purely state matters with the issue of divorce and had succeeded once more in picturing it as being a radical, Locofoco measure. Other party spokesmen in New York reluctantly admitted that, for good or ill, the Whig theme of democratic enterprise had great popular appeal. "The cities and the towns are outgrowing the country," Churchill C. Cambreleng grumbled, "and we have too many of them." John Dix, secretary of state in New York, likewise viewed Whig success as "a commercial victory." Much of the issue was captured in a catchy Whig slogan—"Big Bill Marcy and little bill seward"—for it pointed to the restrictive force of the Democratic ban on bank notes of less than $5 denomination.[3]

The theme of democratic enterprise was precisely the one that Seward was soon to strike in his first message as governor. Speaking in behalf of the credit system and the companion policy of internal improvements, he said: "The augmentation of both prosperity and knowledge may be indefinite; and the security of Republican institutions be constantly increased, if that augmentation be impartially distributed. The spirit therefore that pervades our country and animates our citizens to seek the advantages of competence, is to be cherished rather than repressed."[4]

A second piece of bad news from New York, suppressed until after the election, added to the problems of the administration. It involved the defalcation of around $1.25 million by Samuel Swartwout, the customs collector in New York City. Appointed by Jackson in 1829, Swartwout had regularly taken funds during the next eight years, had used the funds in private speculations, and had then fled to Europe, soon to be followed by the attorney for the southern district of New York. Swartwout was one part of the Jacksonian heritage that Van Buren had never approved of; indeed, his strong opposition to the appointment almost caused his own resignation from the cabinet. The collector's close identification with the Conservative Democrats deepened Van Buren's dislike and rendered even more bitter the prospect that foes of the administration could use the scandal to discredit the idea of an independent Treasury. Here, they could argue, was a collector who, by keeping government funds in his own custody, was able to appropriate large sums for his own selfish purposes. In breaking the news, Cambreleng accordingly advised Van Buren to stress three things in his message to Congress: that the defalcation had begun while the Bank of the United States was the fiscal agent of the Treasury, that it had continued under the system of state-bank depositories, and that most of the funds had in fact been taken before the suspension in 1837 had separated the Treasury from the banks. Since the problem was not due to the form of the fiscal agency, Cambreleng reasoned, the solution lay in newer and more severe penalties for the misdoings of the individual agents involved.[5]

As Van Buren looked to the upcoming session of Congress in December 1838, he complained of "suffering from a cold and a *message.*" It is not known how he dealt with the cold, but things that were said or not said in the message amounted to a renewal of the compromise formula offered at the last session. Total silence on the kind of funds to be received meant that the Treasury would continue the practice of receiving the notes of specie-paying banks. Nor was there any mention of federal control over the state banks. On the deposit side, by contrast, he reaffirmed the policy of divorce and used the Swartwout scandal to strengthen old arguments in its behalf. The defalcation furnished, in this view, "the strongest motive for the establishment of a more severe and secure system for the safe-keeping and disbursement of the public moneys." Additionally, the spectacle of such an individual as Swart-wout diverting "public money to private purposes" made even more clear the "impropriety" of allowing private corporations to bank on the people's money. Public opinion, he claimed, had matured in favor of having the Treasury handle its own funds.[6]

The divorce bill that Cambreleng and Silas Wright presented in Congress reflected the president's views. The deposit features of the bill from the preceding session were revived, with some changes. Instead of having "receivers general" at Boston, New York, and Charleston, "cashiers of customs" would keep and disburse funds, while a "public receiver" at St. Louis was designated to handle revenue from the sale of public lands. Along with other safeguards, the use of public money for private purposes by any Treasury official was made a felony.

On the funds-receivable side the bill dropped once more the specie mandate and allowed the Treasury, under the Currency Resolution of 1816, to receive the notes of specie-paying banks. In an effort to placate Calhoun, one provision was added that would penalize any Treasury official who held bank notes on hand for very long. But Calhoun would have nothing to do with the bill, still insisting that the Treasury receive payments only in specie and government paper. He did not bother to vote when the bill passed the Senate by 28 to 15, and he surely felt vindicated when the House failed even to bring the measure to a vote.[7] For the administration it was the third failure. At the special session of the Twenty-fifth Congress and at the two regular sessions that followed, the House had passed no bill that would have rendered the Treasury independent of the banks.

Further difficulty for the administration came with the expected "windfall," as Van Buren called it, that foes made of the Swartwout defalcation. Conservatives and Whigs overrode the desire of the Speaker and elected from the floor an investigating committee that was hostile to the administration. Six of the nine members paraded a long list of witnesses, went to New York for further evidence, and then submitted a lengthy report on February 27, 1839, which placed most of the blame on Secretary Woodbury and the idea of divorce.

In defense of the administration, a minority report focused more clearly on the central problem at the customs house and pointed to the formula for later reform. Swartwout had succeeded mainly because the clerks and lesser officials who had covered for the defalcation had been appointed directly by the collector and remained personally loyal to him. Reform, along the lines already realized in the Post Office Department and in the Land Office, would replace the older personal style of administration with an impersonal system of checks and balances. Under this new system, all responsible clerks and auditors would be appointed by the president, would be bound to report separately to the Treasury in Washington, and would be made liable to frequent and unexpected inspections by officials from Washington.[8] At the time, however, politics overrode the prospects of reform and made the short session of Congress a forum chiefly for anticipating the presidential election of 1840.

Senator William C. Rives added to the political maneuverings of the session. On December 20, 1838, he called on Woodbury to provide further details about the arrangements that the Treasury had made with Biddle's bank during the summer for cashing the government bonds. In the guise of old Jacksonian orthodoxy, he then launched an attack on Van Buren and Woodbury, taunting them with Biddle's own boast that the administration had abandoned the idea of divorce and had established a new connection with the old national bank. Woodbury's report, ably supplemented by speeches from Wright and John M. Niles, easily dispelled the substance of Rives's charges and showed that the connection had been a temporary one in the form of a one-time special deposit.

127

Debate also made it clear that Rives, in bidding for Whig votes in the Virginia legislature to gain reelection to the Senate, was making a final break with the administration. Undoubtedly, Van Buren would have preferred to avoid a public airing of the bond deal with Nicholas Biddle, but he otherwise seemed to welcome Rives's action. "Mr. Rives has relieved us from all uncertainty as to his position," he wrote Jackson, "and there is an end of that." At the same time, a strong defense of the administration by Virginia's other senator, William Roane, assured Van Buren that the Conservative movement had been excised from the party.[9]

There was also significant political maneuvering on the question of abolitionist petitions. Despite appearances, these moves reflected less a deepening sectional cleavage than the political concern of competing national parties as they looked to the presidential election of 1840. In a secret caucus at the outset of the session, House Democrats agreed to reestablish the gag rule and, under the leadership of Charles Atherton of New Hampshire, pushed it through on December 11, 1838. Three things about the action were significant. First, the leadership of Atherton fully identified the gag with northern Democrats. Secondly, a lengthy preamble to the new gag resolution sounded a somewhat more prosouthern tone than at the previous session. Finally, the anger and dismay of the southern Whigs showed that they had been "ketched," as Niles gleefully observed, or foiled in their desire to be out front on the issue.[10] Because abolitionists identified more strongly with the Whig party in the North, northern Democrats began to exploit this issue in the South. To counter it, southern Whigs sought to be more "southern" on the issue than the Democrats. Paradoxically, their efforts gave further impulse to the developing two-party system in the South and enhanced the prospects of a national party victory for the Whigs in 1840.

Sensitive to the same political forces, Henry Clay assumed a more southern position. On February 7, 1839, he introduced and spoke in favor of a petition from citizens in the District of Columbia who deplored the efforts of outsiders to meddle in the domestic affairs of slaveholders. Clay's move was all the more revealing because he had, in the previous session, condemned Calhoun for needlessly agitating the petition issue. Calhoun, of course, hailed Clay's conversion as an "epoch," but he falsely assumed that it was a victory for his goal of sectional solidarity and a politically united South. Clay rather hoped his speech would prove to be a landmark in his quest for the presidency, enabling him to consolidate the support of southern Whigs in behalf of his nomination by a united Whig party. The narrow focus of a recent study on the politics of slavery within the South overlooks this broader context of national party competition in which the abolitionist issue was handled.[11]

On March 4, 1839, the last session of the Twenty-fifth Congress came to an end. No one was more relieved than Woodbury, who had been roughly handled by the defalcation investigation and Rives's airing of the bond deal with Biddle. For the administration it was a time to take stock, to assess its position very carefully. The Senate bill for total divorce had failed at the special session, and a like fate met compromise efforts during the two regular sessions. The Treasury continued, in fact, to handle its funds independently of banks, but it did so without the sanction of law. It was in this context that the Swartwout scandal had its greatest impact, for it rendered more urgent than ever the need to provide formal structure and safeguards for the Treasury's operations. Meanwhile, Whig foes zestfully contributed to the frustrations of the administration, helping to defeat bills for an independent Treasury and then condemning as despotic the operations that the Treasury was carrying on without legal sanction.

Van Buren seemed for a moment to waver in his resolve, being tempted to drop divorce as a political issue to take back to Congress or to the people. In the elections of 1834 Jackson had gained quick approval for his war on the Bank of the United States, but no such popular mandate had been won for Van Buren's divorce measure. As an alternative, Van Buren considered two different ways for dealing with the problem of governmental finances without having to go back to Congress or to the people. The Treasury might spell out in detail a contract system and, under the Treasury's terms, engage selected state banks to handle its funds in the form of special deposits. Or the administration could, by executive order, reaffirm the independence of the Treasury and elaborate a formal structure and precise guidelines for its operations. Presumably, the law of 1789, which created the Treasury Department, contained the authority for the president to proceed in this fashion.

Three advisers strongly argued against these initiatives on the part of the president. Silas Wright personally opposed any new connection with the banks, however special, and pointed to the great danger of proceeding without congressional approval. He also felt that the use of special deposits might somehow lead to a general deposit system and take the administration back to where it had begun. Worst of all, it would appear to be an "abandonment" of Van Buren's commitment at the special session and would tend to confirm the image of "non committalism" which foes had fixed upon him. Cambreleng agreed, in like spirit, that the administration should not "surrender an iota of principle for the sake of such an experiment." William Gouge just as firmly argued against the idea of elaborating an independent Treasury by executive decree. Although the Treasury Act of 1789 undoubtedly gave this authority to the president, its exercise without the approval of Congress would create a storm of controversy not unlike the one that Jackson had precipitated when he removed the deposits from the national bank. With the approval of the people, Jackson had weathered the storm; but it was clear that Van Buren did not have the same kind of support.[12]

All three advisers urged Van Buren to persevere, indeed to drop further efforts at compromise and to reaffirm the proposal of total divorce. For this purpose, Wright pushed through a resolution to print ten thousand copies of a Treasury document, compiled from consular reports, which showed that most other governments handled their own funds and dealt mainly in specie. Wide circulation of the document, he hoped, might bring public opinion around to the correct views. At the same time, political foes had demonstrated, by votes in Congress and by campaign strategies in the states, that they opposed divorce in any form, even with its retreat from specie on the funds-receivable side. Thurlow Weed, among Van Buren's most severe critics, also began to dare him to step up to the mark and to reaffirm the specie mandate, taunting his compromise efforts as a species of "non committalism." Divorce without the specie mandate, he said, had "an ear tickling sound" that signified nothing.[13]

Other considerations also bolstered Van Buren's resolve. For one thing, he began to savor the prospect of Henry Clay as his opponent in the next presidential election. The Whig caucus in Congress called for a national convention, thus virtually assuring party unity behind one candidate; and movements within the party by early 1839 had convinced Van Buren that Clay would be the nominee. Because Clay had identified so closely with the old national bank, Van Buren believed that a contest with him might at last clarify the true issue between the parties as being one of divorce versus a national bank. Jackson had run against Clay in 1832 on the bank issue, and Van Buren now welcomed the opportunity to do the same thing. "A better candidate we could not desire," he wrote Jackson. "I could not, without apparent affectation, impress you with a just sense of the composure with which I contemplate the result." He felt "so easy in the matter" because he had kept the faith with the party heritage and with the people who had elected him.[14]

To this faith, Van Buren now added new works. As if responding to earlier criticisms that he was too passive and too fatalistic, he began to act in a more vigorous and "political" way. For one thing, he surrendered his initial policy of making no outright removals from office and began to brandish the "pruning knife." It had been an open secret from the beginning that a great number, perhaps a majority, of officeholders were Conservatives, who were opposed, however quietly, to the policy of divorce. Whereas only 3 postmasters were removed in 1837 and 1838, there were 364 removals during the next year and a half. Party workers who were loyal to the policy of divorce particularly hailed changes in the post offices at Albany, Baltimore, Washington, and New Orleans and in a host of lesser offices, even where, as in Dubuque, an outgoing register at the Land Office threatened to commit suicide. The dismissal of some officeholders also produced salutary effects on others who still held jobs, causing many erstwhile Conservatives, or "fence men," to come out for the president's policy and to begin working for his reelection. In an extended correspondence with Maj. William B. Lewis, who had associated closely with the Conservatives, Jackson welcomed and justified the new policy. Arguing that the opinions of all officeholders "ought to correspond with the Executive in all of his important measures," Jackson urged Lewis to resign as second auditor in the Treasury before he was removed. "Rotation in office must from the great pressure of public opinion be adopted by the President," he explained.[15]

In another dramatic action, Van Buren made his summer trip in 1839 far more public and "political" than the trip to Virginia the previous year. At first he planned a swing through the South and the Southwest, where party losses in the elections of 1838 had been greater than elsewhere; but a warning from Tennessee that he might actually weaken the efforts of James K. Polk to dislodge the Whig governor led him to look northward to his home state. By traveling with a small party in an "unostentatious manner," the friendly *Albany Argus* observed, he sought to efface the image that he was a courtier with English servants, horses, and carriage. To the same end he refused to attend dinners or receptions with local elites, preferring, at stops in Maryland and Pennsylvania, simply to greet his "fellow citizens" in public meetings. A relatively nonpartisan tone to the trip was maintained through New Jersey as Whig mayors and the Whig governor joined in extending formal greetings. The carefully planned entry into New York City also had a presidential appearance. Boarding a flag-draped boat at Jersey City, the party moved slowly down the Hudson, hailed by volleys from shore batteries and the frigate *North Carolina*, and was then formally welcomed in a brief ceremony at Castle Garden. From there the president, mounted on a black horse, led a parade through lower

Manhattan to City Hall, reviewing troops and waving to thousands along the streets.[16]

Thanks to Whig foes, the New York part of the trip became overtly partisan. Governor Seward refused to take part in the welcome at Castle Garden, invoking the sacred memory of De Witt Clinton and Seward's own "profoundly different views" on public policy. Snubbed as well by respectable "old Republicans," a sneering Philip Hone later observed, Van Buren was left in the hands of the "Locofoco rabble." Attendance at the Bowery Theater in company with some of its leaders gave final confirmation, Hone also claimed, to the president's radicalism.[17] But Hone's partisan feelings at this point clearly exceeded the facts. The nature of Van Buren's reception more nearly confirmed the force of events during his presidency than his radicalism: in 1836 the Locofoco faction had pointedly refused to endorse his bid for the presidency.

Greeted, in any case, only by "Democratic fellow citizens," Van Buren acknowledged the welcome in this identical phrase and thereby gave a further text for foes to exploit. Seizing upon the phrase, the opposition press, led by Weed's *Albany Evening Journal*, professed patriotic shock and dismay that Van Buren was behaving like a "mere politician" and not like a president of all the people. The towns of Hudson and Schenectady, among others under Whig control, extended no official welcome as the president moved northward; and according to Weed, the "skeleton pageants" gotten up by party sycophants were "artificial and heartless." No credit was even given to the "good feeling" and "enthusiasm" with which the *Albany Argus* thought the people of Kinderhook welcomed home the "boy lawyer" of earlier days. At Saratoga Springs, partisan feeling took a more personal turn as the widow of DeWitt Clinton snubbed the president in full view of a crowded ballroom. With deftness and good sportsmanship, Van Buren turned aside much of the personal rancor. At one point during his stay at Saratoga Springs he left town for a few days in order to let the visiting Clay enjoy a full welcome. And at Schenectady, Van Buren's calm defense of party competition in a republic must have deflated somewhat the antiparty pieties of the furiously partisan Whigs.[18]

Van Buren's opponent in 1840—who was William Henry Harrison, not Henry Clay—has generally been regarded as the first candidate to campaign openly for the presidency. But Whig critics were at least partly correct in seeing Van Buren's trip in 1839 as being one of presidential electioneering. The assessments of friends also focused on the political results of the trip. Kendall found the "spleen" of enemies, no less than the "ardor" of friends, to have been a measure of its success. Another supporter thought that the trip had enhanced Van Buren's "personal popularity" and promised a new beginning for his presidency. Pleased with the "affectionate" and "enthusiastic" reception of the people, Van Buren was ready to renew his commitment to the divorce proposal and to invest it with the force of party creed. Divorce was not merely a fiscal measure, he told a gathering in New York; it also involved "the nature, and to some extent, the existence of republican institutions."[19] He might not have won any votes on the trip, but contact with many voters for the first time since he had entered the presidency apparently strengthened his resolve. If he had wavered for a moment in early 1839, he now seemed to be eager to meet Clay on the issue.

For many reasons, Van Buren was resolved to greet the new Congress in December 1839 with a proposal of total divorce. After a retreat during the last two years from this position, which had been staked out in the Senate bill of the special session, he now intended to renew the call for a Treasury that would be totally independent of the banks in the way that it handled its funds and in the kind of funds that it received. He was also ready to break his official silence of the last two years and to place divorce in the broader context of governmental control. Divorce was not "a mere fiscal measure," he thus wrote to Wright in September, but one that involved such "higher considerations" as governmental "restraint upon overbanking & overtrading." The make-up of the new Twenty-sixth Congress was also thought to be more favorable than that of the old one. The Senate remained firmly in Democratic hands, while the elections of 1838 had brought gains for the administration in the House. But pending the outcome of late elections in North Carolina, Tennessee, Kentucky, and Indiana, Levi Woodbury advised Van Buren that the House vote might turn out to be very close, perhaps ending in a 121 to 121 tie.[20]

While political considerations had brought Van Buren back by mid 1839 to his proposal for total divorce, bad economic news toward the end of the year lent greatest strength to the proposal and assured its final passage. On October 9 Biddle's bank in Philadelphia stopped paying specie, and soon most other banks to the west and south of New York followed its example. This new suspension signaled the end of a cycle of expansion, which the panic of 1837 had only interrupted, and ushered in a severe downturn that did not reach bottom until 1843. Key statistics for the four-year period 1839 to 1843 indicate the dimensions of the downturn. Cotton prices at New York fell from 13.00 cents a pound to 7.85 and at New Orleans from 12.40 to 5.70, with much of the decline coming in the first year. Based on the index of 100 for 1831, commodity prices in the United States dropped rather steadily from a high of 125 in February 1839 to a low of 67 four years later. Annual imports dropped from $159 million at the beginning of the period to $43 million at the end, with about half of the decline realized by 1840. The flow of English capital into state projects of internal improvement virtually ceased. By 1842 nine states had defaulted on the payment of interest for the improvement debt.

Given the debtor relationship of the United States to England, economic conditions in the creditor country precipitated the downturn in the United States. A poor harvest in 1838 caused specie to flow out of the Bank of England in order to pay for grain on the Continent, and this flow reduced the specie reserve of the bank from about £10 million in 1838 to £3 million by early 1839. The rise in the discount rate from 3 to 6 percent reflected this outflow of specie and drastically cut the commercial credits being extended to American houses. At the same time, higher food prices in England brought about a small but significant shift in demand away from cotton and, in conjunction with an incipient decline in textile production, caused a sharp drop in the price of cotton. Biddle got caught in the process. After the panic of 1837 had ruined many brokerage firms, Biddle entered the cotton export trade on a large scale. With resources that were far greater than those of most other dealers, he was able to hold cotton for a longer period and to affect its price in a favorable way. Whether his motives were selfish or patriotic is a matter of dispute, but most students agree that his cotton operations contributed to recovery in 1838. By the following year, however, forces beyond his control overwhelmed the cotton venture; at sharply reduced prices, he was simply unable to cover the advances he had made.[21]

Politically, the different form of the two suspensions was of considerable importance. The impulse for suspension in 1837 had originated abroad, it was true, as the Bank of England sought to strengthen its specie position. But the basic perception of the event in the United States was shaped by domestic forces—the depositors' run on the banks, the preceding pressures in the money market, and the longer debate over the relative effects of the "Specie Circular" and the distribution of the surplus revenue. No such domestic heralds, by contrast, announced the new suspension in 1839. The collapse of Jackson's old enemy had not come from a loss of public confidence or from the impingement of any adverse government policy. Suspension in this form thus made it easy to argue that the banks were unsound and that there was greater need than ever for the Treasury to sever its connection with them. It also fully exposed the vulnerable position of the nation as a whole in its debtor relationship to England.

Van Buren skillfully seized upon this point and made it the key to his annual message in December 1839. At the special session two years earlier he had emphasized the evils of overbanking within the country and the need to separate the Treasury from the banks. Now he placed divorce in a broader context, involving, at last, freedom from "the money power in England," which had forged, through the medium of credit, "a chain of dependence" that linked London, by way of the largest eastern banks, to the remotest area of the country. If properly arranged, he said, the trade between the two countries would be a simple "exchange of commodities," with some flow of specie in or out of the country in order to maintain the natural equilibrium of imports and exports. Unhappily, the massive flow of English capital had deranged this natural pattern, thus creating a great imbalance of trade and rendering the nation liable to fearful expansions and contractions. In the earlier days of the republic a poor harvest in England had provided opportunity for American farmers and the export trade, but now, Van Buren warned, "we wait with feverish anxiety the news of the English harvest" and its likely effects upon "the field of credit" in our country. "Does not this speak volumes to the patriot?" he asked with great emphasis. For Van Buren the new suspension raised, in urgent form, the related questions of an independent Treasury, control of banks, and freedom for the United States from the credit system in England.[22]

With added force, Van Buren revived the proposal for total divorce made during the special session. To place governmental funds in the state banks would not only make the funds hostage to the self-interest of the banks; it would also, in the nature of the credit relation with England, place the Treasury "under the control of a foreign moneyed interest." The use of a new national bank would be even worse, for Biddle's experience had proved that the greater resources of a bank enhanced its power to do evil in the chain of dependence. Van Buren also ended the efforts of the last two years at compromise on the funds-receivable side and called for the Treasury to accept payments only in specie. He explained: "Most of the arguments that dissuade us from employing banks in the custody and disbursement of the public money apply with equal force to the receipt of their notes for public dues. The difference is only in form. In one instance the Government is a creditor for its deposits, and in the other for the notes it holds." True independence required the Treasury to sever the connection totally and to receive, keep, and disburse its own funds in specie.

Van Buren likewise ended his official silence of the last two years and recommended the control of banks and currency. It was the "duty" of the federal government, he now affirmed, "to cooperate with the States" in regulating bank issues. Divorce itself, particularly with the specie feature, was calculated to exercise "a salutary influence" in restraining "excessive issues of notes." Beyond this means of limited and indirect control, Van Buren then suggested to Congress that there be "additional legislation" and "further constitutional grants." Here he apparently had in mind two kinds of actions. One was a federal bankruptcy law, as proposed at the special session, for closing the state banks that had suspended specie payments. The second was an amendment giving the federal government the power to ban notes of small denominations, a goal that Jackson had earlier sought to achieve through the deposit banks. To go with federal controls, Van Buren hoped that the state legislatures would pass reform measures based on the old principle of commercial banking. This would mean that new bank notes, backed by adequate specie and short-term business paper, would provide a stable currency, one that would reflect the actual needs of trade without "inflating or depreciating" the value of money.

Van Buren thus believed, as at the special session, that bank controls and the operation of an independent Treasury could promote the good of a sound and stable currency. Now, in the wake of the second suspension, he thought that something else was needed: namely, the goal of a stable currency required that the United States be liberated from the "false system" of trade with creditor England. The derangement and contraction of economic activity by the end of 1839 inescapably followed the earlier expansion which had been characterized by a mounting imbalance of trade and had been sustained by the inflow of English capital. The duty of the government was not to relieve the present distress or, by using new expedients, to revive the credit relation on which earlier expansion had been artificially sustained. Instead, Van Buren wanted the nation to suffer through the present distress, recover a natural equilibrium in its trade relation with England, and then resist the temptation for any new expansion based on credit.

The president accordingly recommended a policy of "retrenchment and reform" at all levels. By exercising "severe economy," he pledged to reduce by $5 million the annual expenditures of the federal government and to bring the total down to about $20 million by 1840. Import merchants and the states, which were deeply indebted for projects of internal improvement, were advised to pay the old debts of about $200 million and not to incur new ones of such size. In the same austere spirit he urged the nation as a whole to produce more and to buy less. For individual citizens this would mean a return to the "republican simplicity and economical habits" of an earlier age which "reckless extravagance" had corrupted into "a sickly appetite for effeminate indulgence." Through "the patriotism of our citizens," Van Buren concluded, a policy of austerity would bring true recovery to the nation and would also serve "to chasten and invigorate republican principles."

The favorable responses to Van Buren's message underscored its distinctive quality. Marcy praised Van Buren's skill in using "the circumstances of the time" in order to strengthen the proposal of divorce. Niles similarly found the argument based upon the "chain of dependence" to be the most "striking feature" of the message. Another partisan supporter, struck by the message's austerity and ideological purity, rejoiced that "the grand landmarks of our happy Republic" had survived and that "Spartans yet live" to defend them.[23] In its economic bearings the message was clearly very Spartan. At the special session, Van Buren saw divorce—and the goal of stability—in the context of a sound credit system of banking here at home. Now he linked it to independence from the credit system abroad. Substantially, in the future he would eliminate the force of English credit, which was central in the economic development and growth of the young country. Here, indeed, was the counsel of republican simplicity: no promise of governmental relief from the present distress was linked to the prospect of future enterprise at a permanently lower level.

Congress took uneven action on the different recommendations of the message. The call for added means of federal control over state banks went unanswered. On the initiative of Garrett Wall of New Jersey, the Senate did briefly consider a bankruptcy bill; and Thomas Hart Benton, as expected, took the lead in debate. It was a needed supplement, he argued, to the indirect controls that divorce itself would exercise over the currency, "a constitutional, efficient, and innocent regulator." Many northern Democrats shared this view, but most southern Democrats joined the solid Whig opposition in defeating the measure on the basis of States' rights. Opposition on the same grounds led to the defeat of Buchanan's proposal for a new amendment that would have authorized Congress to ban the notes of state banks under $20 denomination. John C. Calhoun and Robert Strange of North Carolina warned that such an amendment would "engraft" state banking institutions on the Constitution.[24] Sensitivity to the domestic institution of slavery clearly made them suspicious of any kind of federal control over state institutions. The old republican emphasis on States' rights thus stood in the way of providing an effective means for achieving the old republican goal of a sound and stable currency.

On another matter directly relating to the credit system in England, States' rights came to the aid of the administration. By early 1840 pressures had begun to build for the federal government to assume the debts that the states had incurred in England in order to finance lavish projects of internal improvement. A key passage from the circular issued by the Barings in London focused on the vital issue: "But if the whole scheme of internal improvements in the United States is to be carried into effect on the vast scale, and with the rapidity lately projected, and by the means of foreign capital, a more comprehensive guarantee than that of individual States will be required to raise so large an amount in so short a time." Anticipating that the Whigs would demand positive action, Benton introduced a set of resolutions on January 6, 1840, opposing such assumption; and by the end of the month, Felix Grundy, back in the Senate once more, issued a report from his committee that was favorable to the resolutions. According to Benton, assumption would violate States' rights and would amount to a new distribution of federal funds to the states; it would spark a new round of speculation, pile up a vast national debt, and bring a new national bank; worst of all, it would place the nation once more at "the footstool of the moneyed power of London." In Van Buren's phrase, Senate Democrats were here refusing to forge new links for "a chain of dependence" on creditor England.[25]

With regard to divorce, victory came quickly in the Senate but much later in the House. On January 6 Silas Wright introduced a bill that took into account the experience of the last three years. The means for the Treasury to keep and disburse its own funds—mints, receivers general, the Treasury Building in Washington—were patterned on the bill that passed the Senate in 1838; Calhoun's original specie clause for phasing out the receipt of bank notes over a four-year period was adopted; and in a provision inspired by the Swartwout defalcation, the private use of public money was made a felony. More sensitive than ever to the charge that the Treasury might circulate its own paper and thus become a monster governmental bank, Wright dropped the provision of the earlier bill, which would have allowed individuals to deposit specie in the Treasury and to use certificates of deposit for purchasing government land. To the same end he retained the requirement that drafts issued to government creditors must be cashed within a limited period of time so that they could not circulate permanently as governmental paper.

With a number of members absent from the Senate, Clay sought to postpone the consideration of Wright's bill. But his motion, along with all other efforts at amendment, failed; and on January 23 the Senate passed the divorce bill by a 24 to 18 vote. Benton's joy was qualified only by the absence of two former Democrats who had, since 1836, opposed his hard-money position in the party. Nathaniel P. Tallmadge, in the process of being reelected senator by the Whig legislature in New York, was late in coming to Washington, while Rives had failed for the time being to gain reelection in the Whig legislature of Virginia.[26]

Favorable action in the House did not come until the end of June. Along with its normal disorders and delays, the House faced the added confusion that arose over five disputed seats from New Jersey. By ruling out, on narrow technical grounds, the votes of two towns—Millville and South Amboy—the Whig governor had claimed for his party all six House seats, which were then chosen by election at large. But five of the six seats were claimed by the Democratic secretary of state for his party, based on the votes of the two towns in question. With rival claimants on hand at the opening session of the Twenty-sixth Congress, the House immediately ran into the problem of organization. After a bitter flurry the House decided to designate John Quincy Adams as temporary chairman and to complete its organization without counting any of the disputed votes. A new delay then arose as the Democrats, who were divided between Benton and Calhoun elements, could not muster votes enough to choose either John W. Jones of Virginia or Dixon Lewis of Alabama for Speaker. Whigs began to desert their nominee, John Bell, on the eighth ballot and, with some Democratic support, elected Robert M. T. Hunter of Virginia on the eleventh ballot.[27]

Administration Democrats were mollified in defeat by the fact that the new Speaker, a States' rights Whig, had favored divorce at the earlier sessions of Congress. Additionally it was thought that the choice of him might attract the support of a few others in his position, particularly Mark Cooper and Edward Black of Georgia. Their votes did help to elect the *Washington Globe* as printer for the House, and the choice of the *Globe*, in Van Buren's judgment, clearly anticipated the final victory of the divorce measure. Unhappily, the victory did not come without further delays. Even though the House finally seated the five Democrats from New Jersey on March 10, the opposition pursued a tactic of further postponement. Debate did not begin until May 20, and another month elapsed before the House leadership won a two-thirds majority for shutting off debate and bringing the measure to a vote. On June 30, more than five months after the Senate had taken action, the House passed the divorce bill by a 124 to 107 vote.[28]

Two of the most ardent champions of divorce rejoiced at its triumph and placed upon it their own special interpretations. Benton regarded it as the consummation of Jackson's original hard-money design to restore "the fiscal action of the Government to its primitive and constitutional course." By acts of Congress in 1789, he argued, the Treasury had been totally separated in its operations from the banks. The "great perversion of the Constitution" had soon begun, however, as Alexander Hamilton

139

had decided to receive bank notes in payment of government dues and to establish a national bank for Treasury deposits. The connection thus made with banks continued, and its corrupting influence almost effaced the memory of the Treasury's original independence. Happily, "the glorious revival of Democracy" under Jackson had commenced the work of reformation by severing the connection of the Treasury with the national bank and by moving toward the exclusive use of specie. Two suspensions thereafter had matured public opinion and enabled Van Buren to move from the "half way house" of state banks to the position of a total divorce. Claiming that he had had "the map of the whole work" at hand in 1829, Benton here spoke as a hard-money ideologue and in a context that deemed Van Buren to be the instrument for fulfilling the purposes of Jackson.[29]

Calhoun assigned a different meaning to the triumph of the divorce policy. It was a victory, not for the Jacksonian party, he claimed, but for the principles of the Nullifiers. In connection with other policies—such as severe retrenchment, the reduction of spoils, a lower tariff—divorce moved ever closer to "the complete restoration of the Constitution." By freeing the South from the credit system at home and abroad, it also restored the natural pattern of foreign trade and would soon enable cotton to control that trade. His report of a personal reconciliation with Van Buren, which was effected at the president's annual New Year's reception, suggested Calhoun's sense of personal triumph: "I said to him," he wrote privately, "that by his course as chief magistrate he had removed the difference in our political relations and that I called to remove that in our personal." Calhoun, in effect, claimed once more that Van Buren had joined the Nullifiers.[30]

Neither interpretation accounts for the course that Van Buren subsequently followed. Contrary to Benton's view that the state deposit banks were only a "half way house" for the party on its road from the old national bank to an independent Treasury, Van Buren entered the presidency with no other purpose than to maintain the connection of the Treasury with the deposit banks. He had had no "map" of the whole work in his hand at the beginning. If his policies thereafter evinced a "perfectly logical development of the left-wing tendencies of Jacksonian Democracy," as a recent study claims, it came principally from the force of events rather than from conscious design.[31] With the divorce proposal he had responded to the panic of 1837, not as a hard-money ideologue, but as an ideologue of party who was intent on saving the heritage of Jackson from its old enemies. A willingness to compromise during the next two years was his response to a clever Whig strategy that refused to accept the issue between parties as one of divorce versus a national bank. Finally, the failure of compromise and its frustrations, capped by a second suspension in 1839, invited Van Buren to revive and strengthen his original proposal.

If not a hard-money ideologue, Van Buren also was not a convert to the Nullifiers and a captive of their sectional purposes. He had originally proposed divorce without having had any consultation with Calhoun and had retreated from its specie feature over Calhoun's strong opposition. Consistently, Van Buren had reacted to events within the framework of party and an evolving creed that contemplated, in his view, national, not sectional, goals.

The pattern of voting in Congress also reflected the force of events more than that of hard-money ideology or southern pressures. A comparison by region of the House vote on the divorce proposal in 1838, when it lost 111 to 125, and in 1840, when it passed 124 to 107, is particularly revealing. In the voting, the old part of the Union east of the mountains was remarkably stable. Thanks to the fact that the disputed New Jersey seats went to the Democrats, the Middle Atlantic States—which also included New York, Pennsylvania, Delaware, and Maryland—cast two votes more for divorce in 1840 than they had at the earlier session; but New England canceled the advantage by casting two votes less. Nor did Calhoun's effort and his overtly sectional appeal change the vote of House members from the Old South, for its thirty votes for divorce at the earlier session were exactly matched in 1840.

The thirteen added votes that assured House passage of the divorce bill came from the newer part of the Union west of the mountains, seven from south of the Ohio River and six from the Northwest.[32] There, local issues undoubtedly played a part, as in Tennessee, where James K. Polk won a great victory in 1839 over the incumbent Whig governor. It was also probable that greater sympathy in the West for divorce resulted from a preemption act of 1838, another in 1840, and Van Buren's repeated recommendations for graduating the prices for land. Most of all, the larger western vote heralded a growing opposition to banking which was to shape state politics in the following decade. Recent studies show how the great entrepreneurial excitement in the West before the panic of 1837 began to decline and, with the second suspension in 1839, to generate an opposite sentiment for "no banks" at all.[33] The conversion of Senator Robert Walker of Mississippi from a mocking critic of "Bullion Ben" Benton in 1836 to an advocate of total divorce in 1840 was one sign of the change.

The change also found expression in the tone and thrust of the debates in Congress. At the special session in 1837, Whig and Conservative foes quickly put the administration on the defensive by condemning divorce as a primitive regression to "iron money and black broth," a hard-money crusade against the "credit system" and democratic enterprise. In the wake of the second suspension, Democratic spokesmen took the initiative and adopted as their theme the Spartan note of austerity that was sounded in the president's message. It was not enough merely to render the Treasury independent of banks; there was a further need to free the nation from the wildly fluctuating effects of the credit system in England. Only in this way, James Buchanan argued in the Senate, could the ultimate goal of stable currency and enterprise be achieved. "We certainly produce too little and import too much," he warned. Such an unnatural imbalance of trade, which was made possible by the "credit system" in England, inescapably defined a cycle of excessive expansion and contraction. On the expansion side, imbalance meant an artificially inflated currency, which raised "nominal" prices above the "real standard" of a world economy that was based on specie. Among other evils it also generated false hopes of permanent expansion, undermined habits of "Republican simplicity and virtue," and plunged the nation into periodic toils of contraction.[34]

Democrats in the House developed the same themes. John Weller of Ohio accepted the present distress, which involved a sharp drop in prices and property values, as a necessary means for restoring trade to a natural equilibrium and for laying the permanent basis for enterprise at a sober pace. "A change in the price of produce," he said in behalf of his constituency of farmers, "cannot effect a change in their principles." With all the zeal of a new convert, Charles Shepard of North Carolina, a nephew of Nicholas Biddle's, expressed the good of permanent stability: "This country does not need an artificial stimulus—the spirit of our people is not broken by the despot's frown; the reward of industry is tempting beyond example; the field for enterprise is rich and varied; the fear is that we may advance too rapidly, that our strength will not be equal to our growth, and that we may be wanting in those great qualities of virtue, stability and moral excellence, which elevate and adorn a nation." A New Hampshire congressman, Edmund Burke, made most explicit the connection of divorce to old republican values: "It is, in truth, a second Declaration of Independence. It involves the great question of the currency; and that question embraces in its scope and effects, the liberties, the morals, and the highest interests of society."[25]

Whig response to the initiatives of the administration looked chiefly beyond the present session of Congress to the upcoming presidential election. There were tactics of delay, to be sure, which held up full consideration of divorce in the House until the end of May. But the Whigs offered no alternative to the divorce bill for arranging the affairs of the Treasury. Suspension had totally discredited Biddle's old bank and had reinforced earlier reasons against proposing the charter of a new national bank. Suspension had also greatly weakened the force of earlier arguments for reviving the Treasury's connection with state banks. Nor was Rives present, in any case, to renew his scheme for state bank deposits. Most Whig spokesmen resigned themselves at some point to the passage of the divorce bill.

The pattern of Whig opposition during the debates of the session was one that refined upon the arguments that were first spelled out at the special session. The issue before the nation was still divorce versus the "credit system," hard-money deflation versus the hopes of democratic enterprise, or, more broadly, a heartless government of self-serving officeholders versus the aid of "parental government" in a time of deepening distress. In a very striking figure of speech, which made the political rhetoric of the day more inflated if not sounder, Clay dramatized the differences between the parties. Standing "without emotion and without sympathy," Clay said, the president "deliberately wraps around himself the folds of his India rubber cloak, and, lifting his umbrella over his head, tells them, drenched and shivering as they are under the beating rain and hail and snow falling upon them, that he means to take care of himself and the official corps, and that they are in the habit of expecting too much from Government, and must look out for their own shelter, and security, and salvation!"[36] Here Clay professed to find in fullest form the evils of spoilsmen politicians, executive despotism, and a policy that was calculated to divorce the government from the true will and interests of the people.

Whig spokesmen called for relief in several forms. One was the assumption of debts that had been incurred in Europe by the states for their projects of internal improvement. With much greater resources the federal government could, by assuming these debts, secure the credit of the nation abroad and, it was hoped, lead to a new flow of capital for sparking recovery and new enterprise. Whigs also supported the proposal, made by Senator John Clayton of Delaware, for a voluntary insolvency law to be applied to individual debtors. As an alternative to the harsh Democratic proposal for a bankruptcy law, it enabled the debtor to yield up all his assets, with the approval of his creditor, and gain total freedom from all past obligations. Clay saw it as a necessary means by which a parental government could, in time of distress, promote the democratic goal of opportunity for all. It made "practical" and "substantial" the right of all to improve their condition and gave real meaning to "the pursuit of happiness." Webster, in like fashion, spoke strongly in behalf of the proposal: "Sir, let us gratify the whole country, for once, with the joyous clang of chains—joyous because heard falling from the limbs of men."[37]

Most of all, Whigs wanted relief from a permanent deflation of the currency, which they supposed to be the inescapable consequence of Van Buren's policies. "All have agreed," John Sergeant of Pennsylvania said in the House, "that the diminution of quantity, and consequent enhancement of the value of money, is injurious." It lowered the value of property, the price of farm produce, and the wages of labor. In a speech that was to be widely circulated during the presidential campaign, Senator John Davis of Massachusetts picked up the distinction that Buchanan had made between "nominal" and "real" prices and charged that Democrats wanted to reduce American labor to the level of foreign countries. In a similar vein, Congressman James Cooper of Pennsylvania moved that the title of the divorce measure be changed to read: "A bill to reduce the value of property, the products of the farmer, and the wages of the laborer, to destroy the indebted portion of the community, and to place the Treasury of the nation in the hands of the President."[38]

On the positive side, Clay argued that the most prosperous condition of society was one "in which there is a gradual and regular increase of the circulating medium." In this view, a mild inflation of the currency would stimulate recovery, sustain new enterprise, and open the way for all to rise. It was "essentially republican," Sergeant added, and essentially American: "The spirit of enterprise belongs to free Governments, and is the offspring of freedom." With renewed force the Whigs sang again the praises of the "credit system" and democratic enterprise, choosing with a sure instinct to make them into central issues in the upcoming presidential contest.[39]

Whigs assumed, in short, that Van Buren's response to the second suspension of the banks had carried him too far and that the triumph of his divorce policy, now fully arrayed in old republican robes, gave them a political target of great value. The choice of Harrison over Clay for the party's nomination was also calculated to enhance its value. While Clay was still identified closely in the minds of many voters with the old national bank, Harrison could far more easily and credibly assume the role as champion of the "credit system" and of democratic enterprise. Jackson saw the matter differently. In mid July, shortly after the divorce measure had been signed into law, he sought to reassure Van Buren that the measure meant not only a triumph for republican principles but also a victory for the president at the polls. "This gives light and strength to our republican cause," he said, "and a death blow to Whiggery, and Harrisonism."[40]

Unfortunately for Van Buren, the paradoxical course of the divorce proposal over the last three years had projected a result different from the one that Jackson had hopefully predicted. The original proposal, made after the suspension of the banks in 1837, met defeat at the polls in the wake of the special session, as the effects of contraction lingered. By contrast, the relative success of the party in the elections of 1838 and 1839 came with economic recovery and the retreat of the administration from its position of total divorce. Now, a second suspension in late 1839 brought final passage of the divorce measure and a new round of contraction. If the earlier failure of the divorce measure accompanied victories at the polls, the reverse of this pattern loomed as a prospect in the big election of 1840. Pointing to the past evils of excessive expansion and contraction, Van Buren invited the nation to look forward to the good of permanent stability that was promised by his policies. This made the present sense of evil and distress a wide field for political foes to harvest, and with the rising excitement of the "log cabin" campaign by mid 1840, the reapers seemed to be very near at hand.

To deal with this unhappy prospect, a rather cynical correspondent suggested two actions for Van Buren to take. He was advised, first of all, to replace Levi Woodbury with a new secretary of the Treasury and to flood the country with new paper money. Though the people were overwhelmingly "republican" in sentiment, it was a sentiment, as the Whigs were discovering, that went with "the gratification of their ruling passion" for wealth and enterprise. The second bit of advice was based on the maxim "No administration had ever sustained itself without some overruling excitement among the people." While both John Adams and John Quincy Adams had violated the maxim and had lost their bids for reelection, others had heeded it and won: Thomas Jefferson had fought a British monarchical conspiracy in 1800; James Madison had begun the War of 1812; James Monroe had reaped further benefit from it; and Jackson, one of its heroes, had sustained the momentum of his presidency by waging war on the national bank. In this light, Van Buren was advised to generate excitement for his administration by making war on England.[41]

Van Buren clearly chose not to follow this advice, but it does serve to place in perspective the basic pattern of his presidency. He followed, instead, a policy of retrenchment at home and peace abroad. The "money power" of England did provide a popular enemy or foil of sorts, for Van Buren's analysis of "a chain of dependence" made the credit system in England appear to be an enemy of the people. Unhappily, the effects of divorce bore down most heavily at home, while all of the "excitement" from the measure was gained by the

Whigs in opposing it. At the same time, as the next chapter will show, Van Buren kept the peace, even though there were provocations aplenty for a president who might be bent on war. By signing the divorce bill into law on July 4, Van Buren wanted to dramatize the claim that it represented a second declaration of independence for the nation. For his presidency, however, it did not assure a second term.

8

PEACE WITH HONOR

As Gen. Winfield Scott was leaving for the Maine frontier, which was threatening by February 1839 to erupt into war over a boundary dispute with New Brunswick, President Van Buren solemnly charged him to seek "peace with honor." Scott succeeded in arranging a truce between the parties, which paved the way for a final settlement during the next administration. At the turn of the previous year, Scott had been sent to the Canadian frontier in western New York to deal with another crisis, one that grew out of the rebellion in Canada and culminated in the dramatic *Caroline* affair. The presence of Scott in the troubled area, Van Buren's profound commitment to neutrality, and official restraint on both sides enabled the crisis to pass. About a year earlier, in February 1837, outgoing President Andrew Jackson had precipitated a crisis in relations with Mexico that was closely linked to his own desire for the annexation of Texas. Van Buren managed peacefully to resolve the strain in Mexican relations and, by turning down the bid of Texas for annexation, to promote sectional peace as well.

On a number of occasions during his presidency, and most recently on the eve of the election of 1840, Van Buren had been advised to get the nation into a war. Instead, he followed with steadfastness and consistency a course that was based on his inaugural hope for the nation that "all her paths be peace." While ready to resist "any invasion of our rights," he was equally prepared to stay out of the affairs of other nations, domestic or foreign, and to preserve "a strict neutrality in all their controversies." Here, more than in other matters inherited from Jackson, he chose to tread in his own steps.

The difference between Van Buren and Jackson came out most clearly in the way in which each of them dealt with Mexico and Texas. Jackson's desire for Texas essentially defined his policy toward Mexico. When his early diplomatic efforts to acquire Texas failed, he assumed a more forceful posture. At the outbreak of the Texas revolt he professed a policy of neutrality, but in fact, little was done to stop the emigration of Americans to Texas, where, on April 21, 1836, they helped Texans to win the battle of San Jacinto. With rumors of a new Mexican invasion mounting by June, moreover, Jackson had ordered troops to take up a position west of the Sabine River. At the same time he urged the minister in Mexico, Powhatan Ellis, to press vigorously for the payment of fifty-seven claims made by United States citizens against the Mexican government.

But rising sectional consciousness in the midst of the presidential contest of 1836 gave Jackson pause. Abolitionist Benjamin Lundy published a series of articles in the *National Gazette*, charging that slaveholders and land speculators were conspiring through Jackson to grab Texas. With copies of these articles in hand, John Quincy Adams voiced the conspiracy theory in the House on May 25, 1836; and the charge gained added force from the fact that the House was, at the very same time, considering the first "gag" resolution against abolitionist petitions. Under these circumstances Jackson decided to put off any recommendations on Texas. Privately, however, the Texas agent in Washington was assured by Secretary of State John Forsyth that Texas remained "a favorite measure" of Jackson's.[1]

After Van Buren's election in November, Jackson pursued, in turn, two strikingly different policies. Until late January 1837 he dealt more easily with Mexico than most observers in Washington expected. His annual message on December 5 thus called for "great forbearance" toward Mexico, even though Ellis was not able to report any progress on settling the claims. In like spirit a special message on December 21 explicitly advised against the recognition of Texas. Among other things, it pointed to the "peculiar delicacy" of the nation's position; United States recognition of Texas before any other country recognized it might raise imputations, however unjust, of the nation's aggressive designs.[2]

Beneath this gentle course toward Mexico lay profound differences between Van Buren and Jackson. The president-elect found the special message a "most interesting measure," not only because he had helped to shape it but also because it promised to allay sectional feelings. Much more sensitive than Jackson to the sectionally divisive nature of the

Texas issue, Van Buren hoped that the "thinking and responsible" people of the South would recognize northern feelings and therefore see the need for indefinitely postponing the issue of Texas. Jackson, by contrast, dealt gently with Mexico precisely because he held hopes by late December of negotiating directly for Mexico's permission to annex Texas. The defeated General Santa Anna was in Washington at the time, on the way from Texas to Mexico, and Jackson sought an agreement with him by which Mexico would remove all objections to the entry of Texas into the Union. At one point during their talks it was thought that Jackson was ready to pay up to $3.5 million as a "quit claim" by which Mexico would free the United States to acquire Texas.[3] Unfortunately for Jackson, Santa Anna's repudiation, after he returned to Mexico, ruled out further hopes for this measure.

Jackson consequently exchanged this easy posture toward Mexico, which Van Buren wanted to continue, with a get-tough policy. On February 6, 1837, Jackson sent a special message to Congress, calling attention to the unpaid claims and recommending a bold policy: deliver one final demand for payment from the decks of a naval vessel and, if this failed, make reprisals on Mexican commerce. Congress had no intention of adopting Jackson's proposals, and the Foreign Relations Committee in the Senate called upon the executive to make one further effort to settle the claims by peaceful means.[4] By his dramatic proposal, however, Jackson succeeded in precipitating the issue of Texas recognition. On March 1, 1837, only three days before he was to leave office, the Senate approved a resolution for the recognition of Texas as an independent nation, and the House appropriated funds for a diplomatic mission to Texas.

Three basic facts about relations with Mexico and Texas faced Van Buren as he entered the presidency. First of all, Texas had been recognized against his own wishes. Secondly, recognition inescapably meant a further escalation of sectional consciousness, for it brought into sharp focus the follow-up issue of annexation. It was therefore no coincidence that, on March 15, Daniel Webster made a strong political speech in New York against bringing Texas into the Union, warning that there would be a growth of southern power, based on the expansion of slavery. Abolitionist agitation also increased, and in a widely publicized letter to Henry Clay, William Ellery Channing gave classic expression to the idea that there was a slaveholding conspiracy to acquire Texas. Finally, Jackson's brusque course against Mexico had rendered urgent the claims issue.

Given these circumstances, Van Buren reversed Jackson's priorities, opposed the annexation of Texas, and sought peaceful relations with Mexico. With Senate support he chose an official of the State Department, Robert Greenhow, rather than a naval vessel, as the means for delivering a new demand for the payment of the claims. The official letter prepared for the mission by Secretary Forsyth was firm and forceful, but a private letter addressed to the Mexican president by Joel R. Poinsett, who had served as minister to Mexico in the late 1820s, was more friendly and conciliatory. Greenhow was received in a very civil manner and was assured that the claims issue would be carefully reviewed. Jackson had forced the claims issue in order to gain recognition of Texas; whereas Van Buren's opposition to the annexation of Texas disposed him to resolve the claims matter in a peaceful way. Supposing that no action on Texas would be taken at least until Congress would convene in December 1837, the new Texas minister to the United States, Memucan Hunt, decided to wait until then to take up residence in Washington.

But the panic of 1837 provided Hunt with an earlier opportunity and brought the Texas issue back into focus. When Van Buren in May called for Congress to meet in special session on September 4, Hunt returned to Washington and prepared to press for annexation. Van Buren received him with "great dignity" and warmly referred him to Forsyth who, as a Georgian, was assumed to share that degree of enthusiasm for Texas that Hunt had encountered in his travels through the Southwest. In Hunt's view, a strong speech against annexation made by Webster in New York on March 15 might be expected to increase southern solidarity. Hunt also believed that the expected defection of Senator William C. Rives over fiscal matters would compel Van Buren to come out for annexation as a means of gaining added support in the South for his divorce proposal. Problems in Texas, no less than Hunt's perceptions, likewise dictated an early decision on annexation. Because the economy, the finances, and the defenses of Texas were in great disarray, annexation would be one solution, perhaps the best. Trade agreements with European countries would be another, but no meaningful negotiations could be undertaken with Europe so long as annexation remained a possibility. Accordingly, on June 26 Hunt was instructed to make a formal request that Texas be made a part of the Union.[5]

On August 4, 1837, Hunt laid the request before Forsyth and appended a lengthy argument in its behalf. Weakness and disorder in Mexico, he argued, placed the sovereignty and independence of Texas beyond doubt. Economic considerations also recommended union, since an independent Texas, tied by commercial agreements to Europe, would threaten the interests of the United States. Finally, Hunt appealed to the nation's ideals by noting that bonds of kinship, affection, and "inbred republicanism" constituted the "principle reason" the people of Texas wanted to link their destiny with the Union.

At the regular cabinet meeting four days after Hunt had made the formal request, the decision was reached with little discussion to turn it down. On August 25 Forsyth then made public the decision and adduced two reasons. First of all, a constitutional question had arisen over the power to annex an "independent foreign state." Louisiana and Florida had been acquired at an earlier time, it was true, but they had been "colonial possessions" at the time of acquisition and had been incorporated into the Union as territories, not as states. Texas, by contrast, presented an entirely different issue, for it claimed the status of a sovereign state. Secondly, Forsyth invoked the force of "treaty obligations" to Mexico under the earlier treaties of amity and friendship. To annex Texas while it was officially at war with Mexico would violate these treaties and possibly saddle the nation with an unwarranted war of its own.[6]

Underlying these official reasons for turning down the request of Texas was sensitivity to the sectionally divisive nature of the issue. Hunt's sanguine hopes had been tempered all along by a perception of Van Buren's "great solicitude" for sectional harmony. Another Texan in Washington also had come to see that the "diplomatic caution" of the administration had arisen "out of deference to the prejudices of the North." No one else in the cabinet favored annexation more strongly than Joel R. Poinsett of South Carolina, yet he easily deferred his private judgment to that of Van Buren and the needs of the party, which was made up, as he thought, of southern planters and the plain republicans of the North. Texas officials misjudged the southern influence at this time and overlooked the force of "party trammels."[7]

Forsyth's course confirmed the fact. He was not only a southerner but also a "political tactician" who ranked loyalty to party among the highest of virtues. While a senator, he had earned his party credentials by defending Van Buren's nomination as minister to England and by fighting with Jackson against the old national bank. As his biographer also shows, Forsyth was loyal to the executive under whom he served; he was a secretary of state who carried out, far more than he fashioned, the diplomatic policy of the administration. His support for Jackson's course in 1836 probably carried him beyond what he privately regarded as a proper neutral course for the nation. Equally, his defense of Van Buren's different policy probably concealed his private desire, as a southerner, to annex Texas. Yet he shared Van Buren's perception of the party as being one of planters and plain republicans; he also shared the real if unspoken arrangement whereby northern support for a "gag" on abolitionist petitions would accompany southern forbearance on Texas.[8] Hunt's hope that a pro-Texas stand by Van Buren would gain southern support for the divorce proposal missed the more fundamental fact of a sectional trade-off that was already at work. The timing of two basic decisions in Van Buren's presidency is profoundly revealing: on August 25, 1837, he announced opposition to the annexation of Texas, and on September 5 he proposed the policy of divorce. And both contributed to sectional peace. The one was an act of forbearance, and the other, by defining a party debate that cut across sectional lines, served as a new bond of Union.

The only remaining hope for Texas lay in the possibility that the relations between Mexico and the United States might take a turn for the worse. By the end of 1837 the claims issue seemed to present such an opportunity. Francisco Martinez, the new minister from Mexico, brought to Washington a response to Van Buren's earlier demands that was totally unacceptable: of fifty-seven claims made by the United States, the Mexican minister mentioned only three. In the annual message on December 5, the president accordingly embraced the "painful duty" to report the failure of the claims negotiations and to place back in the hands of Congress the decision as to the nature, mode, and measure of redress. Would Congress now authorize reprisals and the use of naval vessels, as Jackson had called for a year before? The opposition paper in Washington, the *National Intelligencer*, thought so, reading the message as a call for war to cover up the failure of the administration's domestic policies. Adams found in the "war whoop" another and more sinister motive—namely, a strategy for fulfilling the conspiratorial design of slaveholders to grab Texas. Actions by the two senators from South Carolina tended to strengthen Adams's suspicions about a conspiracy: John C. Calhoun precipitated a debate over abolitionism in late December, and William C. Preston introduced a resolution on January 4, 1838, calling for the outright annexation of Texas.[9]

But peace, both foreign and domestic, was Van Buren's goal. In referring the claims issue, he expressed the hope that Congress would act with "moderation and justice." Senator James Buchanan gave another signal of peaceful intent, putting off for four months any action by his Foreign Relations Committee. Thus free from immediate pressures by the administration, the Mexican government came forth on April 7, 1838, with a proposal to submit the claims question to an arbitration commission under the King of Prussia. Upon the advice of many, and particularly of Poinsett, who assured Van Buren that the Mexican president was acting in good faith, Van Buren accepted the offer on April 21. Peaceful resolution of the issue with Mexico meant, in turn, an end to the hopes of Texas for immediate annexation. The Senate soon tabled Preston's resolution by a 24 to 14 vote; and the Foreign Affairs Committee in the House deemed it unnecessary to make any report at all on the matter. Texas officials only awaited a proper occasion to withdraw the formal request for annexation. On October 12, 1838, the opportunity came when representatives exchanged ratifications for a commission to draw the boundary line between the two countries.

A final indication of Van Buren's commitment to peace was the fact that he indulged without protest the delays that ensued in the arbitration process. On September 11, 1838, the two countries agreed to a convention for establishing the arbitration commission, but a misunderstanding between the minister in Washington and the government in Mexico caused the convention to lapse without being ratified by the Mexican Senate. On April 11 of the following year, Van Buren accepted the excuses for the delay and agreed to renew the original convention. Further delays followed, and it was not until August 25, 1840, that the five-man commission was finally constituted, made up of two members from each country and one designated by the King of Prussia. Only after Van Buren had left office did the commission finally make an award of $2 million. But in accepting the original offer, Van Buren had secured peace with Mexico and, in its relation to the issue of Texas annexation, one basis for sectional peace.[10]

The sectional peace, which Van Buren's course on Texas had strengthened, also won national support for other diplomatic questions pertaining to slavery. One of these involved efforts to gain compensation for slaves who had been liberated in the British West Indies. In 1830 the *Comet*, a slave brig from Alexandria bound for New Orleans, ran ashore in the Bahamas during a storm; four years later the *Encomium*, out of Charleston, suffered the same fate; and in 1835 another vessel out of Alexandria, the *Enterprise*, sought refuge from a storm in Bermuda. In all three cases the British authorities had set the slaves free. With regard to the first, then Secretary of State Van Buren had made a claim upon the British, deeming it "the most immediately pressing" matter before the department. Similar claims had been made for the other two brigs, and on July 29, 1836, Andrew Stevenson, minister to England, strongly pressed Foreign Secretary Lord Palmerston for compensation on all of them.

On January 7, 1837, Palmerston admitted the claims for the *Comet* and the *Encomium*, but he rejected the third one on the ground that the *Enterprise* had come into the Bermuda port *after* August 1, 1834, the day on which British emancipation in the West Indies had become effective. On instructions from Washington, Stevenson rejected the distinction, reasoning that the positive law of the United States over the coastal slave trade, as reinforced by the law of nations, totally overrode the new law of freedom in the British West Indies. While Palmerston persisted in his view, Stevenson worked closely with him over the details of compensation, announcing agreement in May 1839 and funding from Parliament in August. By the end of the year the funds had been transferred to the United States, and on January 25, 1840, President Van Buren relayed the details to Congress: a total sum of $115,000 to cover expenses, back interest, and compensation for 179 slaves at about $479 for each.[11]

Calhoun's response to the settlement served at once to reveal sectional interests and to elicit a clearer statement of national policy. Fearing that the acceptance of compensation for two brigs would imply approval for the principle on which Palmerston had turned down compensation for the third, Calhoun introduced resolutions on March 4, 1840, which explicitly rejected Palmerston's position. By the law of nations, he resolved, a ship that was engaged in lawful commerce—such as the interstate slave trade along the coast—remained under the exclusive jurisdiction of its government while on the high seas and, moreover, carried this jurisdiction into any foreign port where it might be involuntarily driven by distress or storm. Since these conditions applied to the *Enterprise,* compensation from the British was still due. Thomas Hart Benton hailed the unanimous consent that the Senate gave to the resolutions, seeing it as further reinforcement for the administration and also as evidence of Van Buren's success in promoting sectional harmony: "This was one of the occasions on which the mind loves to dwell, when, on a question purely sectional and Southern, and wholly in the interest of slave property, there was no division of sentiment in the American Senate." Nor was there division of sentiment in the administrations that followed Van Buren. The arguments of Stevenson and Calhoun were soon adopted by Daniel Webster in the very similar case of the *Creole* and provided the basis for compensation in 1853, not only for the *Creole* but also for the *Enterprise.*[12]

The case of the *Amistad* brought out greater sectional divergence, yet the proslavery handling of the matter was consistent with other policies and earlier practices. On June 28, 1839, two slave dealers, José Ruiz and Pedro Montez, bribed officials in Havana to issue clearance papers certifying that fifty-two Negroes who had recently been brought over from Africa were in fact ladinos, or Spanish-speaking slaves in Cuba, who were merely being transported to plantations eastward along the coast. Four days after the *Amistad* had left Havana, the African Negroes, led by Cinque, staged a successful mutiny, killed the captain, and commanded the slave dealers to steer the ship to Africa. By night, instead, Ruiz and Montez steered in the opposite direction, and on August 26, the *Amistad* became adrift in Long Island Sound near Montauk Point, where it was seized by an American survey ship. With salvage prize in mind, the commander of the American ship, the *Washington*, escorted the *Amistad* to New London, Connecticut, where the Negroes were placed in jail to await official action. At the same time, Ruiz and Montez headed for the aid of the Spanish consul in New York.

When news reached Washington, the Spanish minister, Angel Calderón de la Barca, formally requested the State Department to surrender the ship and the Negroes to Spanish authority for return to Cuba. He based the request principally on provisions of the Treaty of 1795, by which the United States had bound itself to extend good faith and credit to the official actions of the Spanish government, which would include the official acts of Cuba. In this case it meant that the United States government could not "get behind" the Cuban documents that had cleared the *Amistad* at Havana. Jurisdiction over its ships that were stranded abroad, the Spanish minister insisted, belonged exclusively to his own government. On the surface, at least, it was an identical argument to the one that Van Buren was using in protesting the way the British had dealt with American slaves in the West Indies.

With President Van Buren out of town at the time, members of the cabinet who were then present in Washington—John Forsyth, Amos Kendall, and Levi Woodbury—quickly agreed to accept the Spanish position. Upon his return, the president endorsed this action and instructed Attorney General Felix Grundy to prepare an opinion supporting it. Meanwhile, Forsyth wrote to the district attorney in Connecticut, William S. Holabird, conveying the wish of the administration that the *Amistad* matter be kept out of court and under executive control. By early September, instead, a complex series of suits, involving salvage, the status of the Negroes, and the claims of the Spanish government, were brought in the district court at Hartford. At about the same time, lawyers for Cinque brought a civil action in New York against Ruiz and Montez. Under these new circumstances, Holabird was instructed to plead in court for the return to Cuba of the *Amistad* and the Negroes on the basis of the United States' obligations under the Treaty of 1795. Confident that the decision of the court would be made on this basis, Van Buren ordered a naval vessel to stand by to take the Negroes back to Cuba. Along with them he also proposed to send the two ranking officers of the *Washington* to serve as witnesses. With a like purpose of being rid of the whole affair, he also asked the district attorney for the southern district in New York to give legal advice to Ruiz and Montez.[13]

The decision of the district court in Hartford was different from what the administration had expected, and further appeals kept the *Amistad* matter in litigation for another year. On January 23, 1840, Judge Andrew P. Judson, a Van Buren appointee, awarded salvage prize for the ship and its material cargo. With regard to the Negroes, the cabin boy for the murdered captain, one Antonio, was ordered back to Cuba on the ground that he was in fact a ladino, a slave under Cuban law, and therefore was covered by treaty obligations. By "getting behind" the clearance papers issued in Havana, however, the court declared that the remainder of the Negroes were, in fact, kidnapped Africans, and it assigned to the federal government the responsibility of transporting them back to their native country.

Upon instructions from Forsyth, Holabird appealed the decision, invoking once more the force of treaty obligations. But to no avail. In April the circuit court upheld the decision of the lower court except in one detail, which was to strike out the order for the federal government to transport the Africans to their homeland. When the case reached the Supreme Court, Henry D. Gilpin of Pennsylvania, who had replaced Grundy as attorney general, presented the administration's case on February 22, 1841. Answering his arguments, which he based once more on the Treaty of 1795, were Roger Baldwin and John Quincy Adams, who had at last been persuaded to participate in the case. Both ruled that the treaty had no relevance to the Negroes in question, for the fraudulent clearance papers at Havana masked a bald attempt to place kidnapped Africans in slavery. The decision of the majority, given by Justice Joseph Story, likewise "got behind" the clearance papers. "Fraud," he strongly concluded, "will vitiate any, even the most solemn transactions." By upholding the decision of the circuit court, the Supreme Court had made no provision for the return of the Negroes, thirty-nine of whom had survived the long ordeal. Somewhat later, Arthur Tappan and a few other abolitionists arranged for them to be transported back to Africa.[14]

The participation of Adams doubtless enhanced the sectional impact of the *Amistad* case. The unsuccessful efforts by southerners in Congress during the 1840s to provide compensation for Ruiz and Montez was another indication. But the way in which the case was handled kept it from posing any serious threat to the sectional comity that Benton praised Van Buren for securing. Samuel Flagg Bemis, who was otherwise sympathetic to the animus that Adams felt toward "northern men with southern feelings," admitted that Van Buren's responses were no more proslavery than those of earlier administrations had been. The political effects of the *Amistad* case were also lessened because its final disposition was made in the courts rather than by direct executive action. Woodbury, the only northern member to participate in the original cabinet decision, clearly appreciated this fact. "Perhaps," he wrote Van Buren, "nothing is lost in point of public policy by letting the judiciary take all the responsibility . . . which they may choose to exercise." Finally, his administration accorded full respect to the judiciary after the case had landed in court. Responding to the importunities of the Spanish minister for Van Buren to assert total control, Forsyth very properly reminded the minister that the Constitution "secured the judicial power against all interference on the part of the executive authority."[15]

Two crises with Britain posed the greatest threat to peace during Van Buren's presidency. One grew out of a rebellion in Canada. The stage for the rebellion was set on March 6, 1837, when Parliament approved the stern resolutions of Lord John Russell against self-government in Lower Canada. Feelings against the British also intensified in Upper Canada, where the governor, Sir Francis Bond Head, had needlessly interfered in the electoral process and was standing ready to overrule the elective assembly. His actions gave particular offense to the Scotch-Irish in the area and to many former Americans who had settled there, bringing republican ideals, Anglophobia, and a spirit of dissent that was informed by their evangelical religion.

For a number of reasons, United States citizens along the border were tempted to get involved in the rebellion. Mingled with their ideals of republicanism was the long-held belief that a free Canada would want to join the Union; and the closer economic ties formed by the Erie Canal gave further substance to this belief. Many also regarded Canada as a prospective counterbalance to the probable annexation of Texas. Meanwhile, unemployment in the wake of the panic of 1837 was providing fertile ground for the growth of the filibustering spirit. And should trouble arise, the president possessed little power to prevent individuals or groups from violating the neutrality that the United States government felt obliged to maintain toward British Canada. The Neutrality Act of 1818 pertained chiefly to maritime affairs and was penal, rather than preventive, in its basic provisions.

The test of neutrality soon came. In late November 1837 rebellion broke out in Lower Canada, under the leadership of Louis Joseph Papineau, and on December 5 Upper Canada followed the example. Two days later, Forsyth dispatched letters to the governors and federal officials in the adjacent areas, urging them to use whatever means were in their power to prevent citizens from abetting the rebellion. But most efforts failed. Small groups of Canadian rebels and American recruits quickly projected an attack on Hamilton, which is at the western end of Lake Ontario, and on another site across the river from Detroit. A much larger group assembled in the Niagara area. Having failed to capture Toronto, William Lyon Mackenzie and a small force crossed over to Buffalo and began to recruit, promising a cash bounty of $100 and 300 acres of land to any American citizen who would help him establish a free republic in Canada. On December 15 the small army of rebels and recruits, placed under the command of a prominent New Yorker, Rensselaer Van Rensselaer, occupied Navy Island on the Canadian side of the river about a mile above the falls; and by Christmas the force had grown to about one thousand men. Van Buren learned of these events through private letters and newspaper reports, but formal definition of the crisis came in a letter on December 23, 1837, from Governor Head in Upper Canada to the British minister in Washington, Henry Fox. In this letter, Head advised Fox of the growing force on Navy Island and solemnly urged Van Buren to compel its withdrawal.[16]

Before Van Buren could reach any decision on how to deal with the situation at Navy Island, a much more dramatic incident took place, that of the *Caroline*. The *Caroline*, a steamship of forty-five tons, was owned by William Wells of Buffalo and was licensed to operate on the Niagara River between Buffalo and Schlosser, a small town on the New York side opposite Navy Island. On December 29 the vessel made at least three landings at the island, unloading men and supplies before engine trouble compelled it to take mooring in Schlosser. Fully aware of the vessel's activity during the day, the British took swift action during the night. A force of seven boats and around fifty men crossed over to Schlosser, boarded the ship by force, drove off the guests and crew, set fire to it, and towed it out to the middle of the river, where it soon sank. During the melee a stage-driver from Buffalo, Amos Durfee, was killed as he watched from the dock. Different information, however, shaped local opinion at the time and added to the electrifying effect of the incident: between twenty and thirty innocent men had been murdered in cold blood, it was rumored, and sent tumbling with the vessel over the falls. At a distance, even the *National Intelligencer* felt that peace was in danger. Closer at hand, a reporter for the *New York Herald* in Buffalo more clearly sensed the local feeling: "Surely war with England was unavoidable."[17]

The president hoped not, and his actions helped to avert it. He learned of the incident late on January 4, 1838, as a small dinner party for Whigs was assembling at the White House; and his delay in appearing before his guests, which was caused by an emergency cabinet meeting, led some of the guests facetiously to speculate that he was preparing a message of resignation. But when he did appear, pale and somewhat shaken, these speculations ceased. He requested a private conference with Clay and General Scott, who were among the guests; he then asked Scott to go to the Niagara frontier under the instructions that Secretary of War Poinsett was preparing. According to these instructions, the governors were asked to call out the militia where Scott deemed proper. Because the executive had no legal authority under the Neutrality Act of 1818 to use the military in preventing the activity of citizens, Poinsett mainly urged Scott to "use your influence."[18]

Scott managed quite well. Suspicious in any case of the militia, which was "infected" generally by a sympathy for the rebels, he relied instead on other means and principally, as he put it, on "rhetoric and diplomacy." At Niagara he leased boats that might otherwise have been used to provision Navy Island or to provoke new incidents. On January 13 he persuaded Van Rensselaer to withdraw, pointing out that superior British forces rendered the position hopeless. To groups that were apparently still bent on action, he pleaded earnestly for them to follow a neutral course; and his knack for self-dramatization, which was enhanced by an imposing stature, military bearing, and full-dress uniform, doubtless made the plea more eloquent: "I stand before you without troops and without arms, save the blade at my side. . . . I tell you, then, except it be over my body, you shall *not* pass this line." From Niagara he traveled to other points on the frontier as far west as Detroit; and though minor incidents occurred in his wake, the border had settled down by March. The president's choice of Scott for the mission had been vindicated.[19]

Actions taken in Washington after Scott's departure also reflected Van Buren's peaceful intent. In response to the official protest of the British minister about the "strange and unlawful proceedings" at Navy Island, Forsyth repudiated the course of "our misguided citizens" and assured Fox that the president intended to use all constitutional powers to restrain them. On January 5 Van Buren accordingly issued a proclamation exhorting a neutral course and warning that "no aid or countenance" would be given by the government to any citizen who might be arrested in Canada. In a special message on the same day, Van Buren asked Congress to revise existing legislation and give to the executive the power to prevent individuals from violating the nation's neutrality as well as to punish those who might do so.[20]

With regard to the *Caroline* affair, the president was firm but not warlike. Although the incident produced in Van Buren "the most painful emotions of surprise and regret," Forsyth indicated to Fox that time would be allowed for Canadian officials to explain their part and for the government in England to make a proper response. The special message to Congress on January 8 regarding the *Caroline* was also tentative: Van Buren had called out the militia to prevent any new "outrage"; he had formally protested the matter to the British; and he was asking Congress for whatever additional funds it thought the occasion might require.

Congress answered the president's requests in reverse order. After a brief and somewhat partisan debate, which generally seconded the president's peaceful purposes, Congress authorized $625,000 in new defense funds. On March 10 the House then reconsidered and passed a new neutrality law, which the Senate had approved in January. It extended to inland frontiers the maritime provisions of earlier legislation and empowered civilian officials—but not the military—to arrest the actual flow of arms, vehicles, and supplies beyond the national borders. Because of sensitivity to freedom of speech and of assembly, however, the law withheld power from the executive to prevent groups from organizing and making plans. Though limited in scope, the new law did have a reassuring effect upon the British minister.[21]

Unfortunately, the new law did not prevent further incidents of an unneutral sort or another major crisis by November 1838. Secret societies sprang up along the border and looked to new incursions. In March the Canadian Refugee Relief Association was formed in Lockport, New York, and two months later it avenged the *Caroline* by seizing and burning a British vessel, the *Sir Robert Peel*, on its way to Oswego, New York. In June, refugees from Canada, together with American sympathizers, formed the Sons of Liberty and undertook minor ventures in the Detroit area. But the Hunter's Lodge was by far the largest of the new societies, claiming a membership of fifty thousand at its peak. Formed earlier in Vermont and reorganized at Cleveland in mid September, it proclaimed a republic for Upper Canada, projected a new bank, and with the promise of land and bounties, recruited forces for two invasions. Execution in each case fell tragically short of the plan. One of the invading forces, crossing the St. Lawrence River at Ogdensburg, New York, on November 11, quickly ran into trouble and surrendered to superior British forces at Prescott, Ontario, six days later; 157 prisoners were taken. A second attack at Windsor, Ontario, from December 1 to 4 ended more disastrously, with 25 deaths and 44 prisoners.

Van Buren responded to these new incidents on November 21, 1838, with a second and more strongly worded proclamation of neutrality. Other forces abetted the impact of his proclamation and began to signal a reaction in public opinion, particularly in New York. The fate of the invaders at Prescott and Windsor bespoke a growing military presence in Canada, while news that prisoners had been executed or transported to Australia provided another deterrent. The resumption of the banks and a measure of economic recovery by the end of 1838 also weakened the filibustering spirit. Ideologically, Lord Durham's report in early 1839 spoke to much that was at issue in the rebellion, since it called for a united Canada and a larger measure of self-government. Juries in the area began returning guilty verdicts against those who had violated neutrality, and Mackenzie himself was given a sentence of eighteen months by a judge in Canandaigua, New York. The removal of the postmaster in Oswego because of his sympathies for the rebel cause also suggested that support for divorce was not the only test of party loyalty.[22]

The more peaceable spirit among the people on the border by 1839 had informed the attitude of Van Buren from the beginning. On January 23, 1838, even before the issue of the *Caroline* crisis was taken up, Van Buren privately assured a friend that all rumors of a warlike mood in Washington were "wholly unfounded." Lord Palmerston rightly judged Van Buren to be a "Friendly Spirit" who was acting in "perfect good faith," and Van Buren reciprocated the feeling. He also shared the sentiment of another member of the British government, Thomas Spring-Rice, who supposed that a war between "the two great Anglo Saxon nations" would be at once "unnatural" and disastrous. One of Spring-Rice's early biographers believed that Van Buren's love for the law created a special affection for England and that his tour as minister in 1831/32 had deepened his respect for the ruling class. A long passage in his *Autobiography* expanded on these views and passed severe judgment on politicians who appealed to the latent anti-British feelings of the people. By sending his son John as representative to the coronation of Queen Victoria, the president was expressing feelings of a different kind. In a letter to Palmerston that was personally delivered by Van Buren's son, the president assured the foreign secretary that peace would be easy "if the wishes of the men in power in both countries were alone to be consulted." Domestically, Van Buren sought, by the divorce measure, to foil the "money power" of London and its chain of dependence; on the diplomatic front, he was for friendship and peace.[23]

In this spirit, Van Buren cooperated with British authorities at crucial moments. With the outbreak of rebellion in Lower Canada in November 1837 he quietly approved the British request to march troops from Halifax to Quebec through territory that was being claimed by

Maine in the boundary dispute with New Brunswick. At different times while on the frontier, General Scott shared information with officials in Upper and Lower Canada. On the eve of the raids at Prescott and at Windsor, Forsyth turned over to Fox information that was in the former's possession about the activities of the secret societies and the disposition that Poinsett had made of American forces. At the same time, Van Buren allowed the British to increase their naval forces on the Great Lakes in excess of the limits imposed by the Rush-Bagot disarmament agreement of 1816. Canadian officials reciprocated, often enforcing laws with leniency, welcoming a representative from the State Department to inspect the prisons, and after the excitement had died down, releasing the remaining Americans who had been captured at Prescott and Windsor.

Van Buren was better at passing the crisis, however, than at resolving the diplomatic issue of the *Caroline*. On January 5, 1838, one day after news of the incident had reached Washington, Forsyth made a strong protest to Fox, demanding explanations and redress. Deeming Fox's response unsatisfactory, Van Buren instructed Forsyth to take the issue directly to the home government. On May 22 Stevenson accordingly laid the matter before Palmerston, asking for a disavowal of the act and payment for damages. Here Van Buren then allowed the matter to rest, without putting further pressure on Palmerston, and thus evincing once more, as critics claimed, his tendency to "let sleeping dogs lie." In any case, no official explanation or apology came from the British government during the remainder of his presidency.

With the matter thus unresolved, a new crisis had arisen by the end of 1840 over the case of one Alexander McLeod. Because Palmerston had given no official reply to Van Buren's protest regarding the *Caroline*, made in early 1838, the status of the men involved in the raid was still undetermined. The state of New York, thus assuming that the men were individually responsible, arrested McLeod on November 12, 1840, for the murder of Amos Durfee and put him in the Lockport jail. There an angry mob prevented his release on bail and pushed for a speedy trial. At Washington, Fox was at once bewildered and outraged and was unable to accept the fact that a federative system of government could allow one of the states to interfere in a matter that he regarded to be one solely between two foreign nations. In an angry note to Forsyth he demanded that McLeod be released, claiming that he could not be held individually responsible for the performance of a "publick act" in "Her Majesty's service."[24]

Forsyth rejected Fox's argument on the ground that the jurisdiction of New York was "perfectly independent" in its "appropriate sphere" and that no principle of international law or natural justice could exempt a murderer from that jurisdiction. The political situation in New York at the time reinforced Forsyth's States' rights inclinations, for the Whig governor, William H. Seward, was boldly defending the sovereignty of his state. Tensions mounted as the date of the trial drew near, and in early February 1841 Palmerston ordered Fox to ask for his passports and to return home should McLeod be found guilty.[25]

As it turned out, Fox did not have to leave Washington, and the McLeod matter soon passed. The new Whig administration that succeeded Van Buren tended to agree with Fox that the McLeod case, because it involved an international dispute, was a national, not a States' rights, matter. Most important of all, a state court in Utica, New York, acquitted McLeod of the murder charges in October 1841. Van Buren kept the peace at the time of the *Caroline* incident, but the McLeod case showed that he had not resolved the diplomatic issue. No official British explanation or apology for the incident came until the negotiations got under way that ended in the Webster-Ashburton Treaty of 1842.

This treaty was also what finally resolved the Maine–New Brunswick boundary dispute, a dispute out of which arose, by February 1839, the greatest threat to peace during the Van Buren presidency. The dispute was as old as the nation itself, for the boundary defined by the Treaty of Paris in 1783 was not indisputably clear. According to the treaty, the line went up the St. Croix River to its source; from there due northward to the "highlands" that separate the waters that flow into the St. Lawrence from the rivers that flow into the Atlantic; and then southwesterly down these highlands to the upper Connecticut River. But locating the "highlands" soon became a problem; of more immediate importance, none of the maps in 1783 showed a St. Croix River. A recent study argues that the treaty makers in 1783 probably intended the boundary to be determined by a special commission at a later date.[26]

A special boundary commission in 1798 dealt with one problem but left the other unresolved. It settled on the Schoodic as being the St. Croix River named in the 1783 treaty and fixed a monument at its source. Profound disagreement arose over the location of the "highlands," however: this is what eventually came to be known as the "rivers question." From the St. Croix monument the American commissioners ran the line northward to the headwaters of the Restigouche River and then in a southwesterly direction down the highlands between the St. Lawrence and the Atlantic to the upper Connecticut. According to this boundary the lower St. John River was in New Brunswick, but the entire upper part of the river was in Maine, including the two main tributaries—the Madawaska on the north and the Aroostook to the south.

The British drew a much more circumscribed boundary for Maine, basing it on a totally different view of the "rivers question." They rejected the American claim that the Restigouche, which flowed into the Bay of Chaleurs, and the St. John, which flowed into the bay of Fundy, were "Atlantic rivers" at all in the meaning of the 1783 treaty. By this narrow interpretation the Penobscot River to the west was the first Atlantic river. The British commissioners in 1798 consequently located the "highlands" well to the south of the St. John River at Mars Hill, and from there they drew the northern boundary of Maine westerly along the Penobscot and Kennebec highlands. By this line, Maine would possess none of the upper St. John River, not even its main southern tributary, the Aroostook. Between the boundary drawn by Britain and the more-extended claim made by Maine lay a disputed area of about twelve thousand square miles.[27]

The area remained in dispute from 1798 to 1842. Two efforts to settle it under Jefferson's administration failed when they got mixed up with the question of neutral rights. An arbitration award by the King of the Netherlands, made in 1831, came much nearer to being successful. Unable to locate the "highlands" of the 1783 treaty, the arbiter proposed a compromise. By it, Maine would have received the area from the St. Croix monument up to the St. John River and then the entire right bank of the river from that point, including the important Aroostook valley. This would have left New Brunswick in control of the entire left bank of the upper St. John, including the Madawaska tributary. The British readily approved the award, for it met their vital interest in having an overland military route from Halifax to Quebec up the St. John and Madawaska valleys. The War of 1812 and, more recently, the rebellion in Lower Canada had underscored the need for the route during the winter months when the St. Lawrence was frozen.

The response of the government in Washington to the award essentially defined the situation that Van Buren had inherited. President Jackson favored the award and was ready to compensate for Maine's surrender of the area north of the St. John with federal lands out west. But the state of Maine bitterly objected to the award, and the Senate went along with her views. Added to normal state pride was the force of party competition, for neither party was willing, given the excited state of opinion, to yield an inch to the British. Opposed to any kind of compromise at the time, Maine spokesmen favored, instead, the creation of a new boundary commission, confident that its findings would confirm their reading of the 1783 treaty. And if the British refused to accept these findings, Maine wanted the government in Washington to commit armed forces to defend its extensive boundary claim.

When Van Buren reached the White House, he found himself caught in-between. Privately he favored compromise along the lines of the Netherlands' award, for he appreciated the vital interest of the British in a military road. He also came to share the view of most thoughtful observers that Maine's true interests lay in developing the area south of the St. John, particularly the timber- and soil-rich Aroostook valley. As president, however, he was unprepared to press his own views against a state that was so obviously united in sentiment. He was also a party man, indebted for the past support of the Democracy in Maine and closely tied to John Fairfield among its leading spokesmen.

In this situation, Van Buren's first diplomatic exchange with Britain evinced once more the pattern of letting sleeping dogs lie. On January 10, 1838, Minister Fox submitted a proposal from his government to set up a new survey commission, with the express condition that its failure to determine the line of the 1783 treaty would automatically bind both governments—and the state of Maine—to proceed with direct negotiations for a compromise line. The Whig governor, Edward Kent, quickly reminded Van Buren of what the latter already knew—namely, that Maine would not consent to have the issue submitted to compromise negotiations. The president accordingly responded to the British on April 27, 1838, with a counterproposal, which accepted the idea of a new survey commission but rejected the proviso for a binding follow-up negotiation.[28] He felt that Britain would not accept his counterproposal, but it could at least gain some time and hold off Maine's expected demand for bolder actions.

But time was running out as tensions mounted in the disputed area. While British authorities began a survey for a rail route up the St. John toward Quebec, Maine was completing a road of its own across the Penobscot highlands into the Aroostook valley. And because timber was one of the prizes, Maine authorities expressed growing concern over the "trespass" of New Brunswick lumberjacks into the area. Equally, New Brunswick was concerned over Maine's effort to enumerate the population in the Madawaska settlements. Reacting swiftly to that effort, Governor William Harvey arrested the census taker and issued a proclamation claiming, on the basis of "original possession," that the British had exclusive jurisdiction until there was a final settlement. Washington could not allow this claim to go unchallenged, yet it was but another example of a problem that was still not resolved.

In this context a crisis arose, which was thenceforth known as the "Aroostook War." On December 14, 1838, the outgoing Whig legislature authorized a scouting party to report on instances of timber trespass in the Aroostook region. Based on the report of hundreds in the area and $100,000 in timber already cut, the new Democratic governor, John Fairfield, took swift action without notifying Governor Harvey in New Brunswick or President Van Buren. On January 23, 1839, Fairfield dispatched an armed posse of around two hundred men to drive out the intruders. After his posse had arrested several trespassers, the leader of the posse was then arrested on February 11 and placed in a Fredericton jail. In announcing the arrest, Governor Harvey issued a proclamation, based on the earlier claim of original jurisdiction, stating that New Brunswick had the right to expel the armed posse of Maine by force.

Upon hearing this news, an outraged state legislature approved $800,000 in emergency funds and the call for ten thousand militia; and by the end of February, Governor Fairfield had sent the force northward from Augusta with a stirring speech, invoking the "spirit of '76" to defend the sacred soil of Maine. After he had set these forces in motion, Fairfield then notified Van Buren of the *fait accompli*, demanded unqualified support, and warned of the alternative: "But should you go *against* us upon this occasion—or not espouse our cause with *warmth* and *earnestness* and with a true *American feeling*, God only knows what the result will be *politically*." The Augusta correspondent of a Boston paper stated very concisely the dilemma of the peace-loving president: "Van will mortally hate to go to war; and he will also be very reluctant to lose the vote of Maine." Several state legislatures pledged support for Maine; and Jackson soon assured the president that his "feeble arm" was ready "to chastise the temerity of British insolence." But the conservative press of the country, including some newspapers in New England, deplored the spectacle of a nation being drawn into war by the uncontrolled action of only one state.[29]

The president's response was firm, even-handed, and peacelike. Decisions that were reached in an emergency cabinet meeting and then expressed in a note to Fox were carefully summarized in a special message to Congress on February 26. While condemning the "lawless and desperate" trespassers and approving Fairfield's right to drive them out, Van Buren criticized Fairfield for not having notified the governor of New Brunswick about the action of the posse. Rejecting out of hand the British claim of original jurisdiction, the president pledged the full support of the federal government if force were to be used against Maine. Finally, he warned Fairfield that the federal government could not sanction Maine's armed occupation of the Aroostook with its militia and would not come to the aid of the state if incidents arose out of a prolonged occupation.

On the basis of these views, Van Buren then worked out a memorandum of understanding with the British minister in Washington, which each of them was to urge upon the local authorities in Maine and New Brunswick. While the final question of jurisdiction was to be dealt with by the home governments, three local actions were recommended: New Brunswick should not seek to expel Maine's timber posse by force; Maine should withdraw its militia from the Aroostook; and further trespass should become a joint responsibility. An angry crowd in Bangor greeted these proposals by hanging the president in effigy, but outside of Maine, the proposals were welcomed by men from both parties, and Palmerston praised Van Buren's "wise and enlightened course."[30]

Strong bipartisan support in Congress also worked for peace. Four resolutions from Buchanan's Foreign Relations Committee followed very closely the views in the president's special message. Of particular note was the fourth resolution, sustained by a 26 to 18 vote, that Maine could expect no aid from the federal government if its militia in the disputed area were to provoke an incident. "Sir," Buchanan observed, "if there must be war, let it be a national war." Whig spokesmen overwhelmingly agreed with this sentiment, being repelled by the notion that one state could commit the entire nation in a matter so grave as war. John M. Niles believed that the Senate resolutions would remove a "false impression" in Maine and "undecide her." The recommendation of Congress that a special mission be sent to London also expressed a peaceful intent. To be sure, the appropriation of $10 million and the authority to raise fifty thousand volunteers gave a warlike appearance, Fox observed, as if Britain were poised to reconquer her former colonies. But Fox was reassured by Van Buren's "friendly feelings toward England" that the president would strip the act of its "offensive and mischievous character."[31]

Peace on the frontier, however, depended on more than the will for it in Washington. Van Buren accordingly turned to General Scott once more, urging him to go to the scene and seek "peace with honor." In Augusta, Scott conferred daily with party leaders, corresponded with Governor Harvey, whom he had known since the War of 1812, and secretly shared these communications with Governor Fairfield. Scott especially saw the need for Maine leaders to transcend party feelings and to accept the memorandum of understanding that had been worked out in Washington. For this purpose he arranged a dinner for spokesmen of both parties and, sitting across the table from the Democratic governor, let it be known that he was a Whig but that he shared a common aspiration for peace. Scott's vanity probably allowed him to place too much significance on this one incident, yet it did help to create a more conciliatory atmosphere. On March 21, 1839, Scott then presented to Governor Harvey the terms for a local truce. If Harvey would agree to use no military force against Maine's trespass posse in the Aroostook, Governor Fairfield would withdraw his own militia from the area. Pending a final settlement by the home governments, it was also understood that the Madawaska settlement would be in New Brunswick's "sphere" and that Maine would have a predominant interest in the Aroostook. Finally, the problem of trespass in the disputed area would be a joint responsibility until the boundary had been drawn. After Harvey had agreed to the terms on March 23 and Fairfield two days later, Scott published the exchange of letters on March 26 in the *Augusta Journal*.[32]

The "Aroostook War" thus came to an end before it could precipitate a real war. It was very fortunate that the Maine militia stopped at the Aroostook and that the British forces remained at the Madawaska. The distance between them kept little incidents from leading to larger conflict while diplomatic efforts were being made. Once more, General Scott had played an important role; and behind that was Van Buren's firm resolve for peace. Although seen as the head of a party identified with States' rights, he held the national good above the wishes of a state that was then controlled by members of his own party. It was with this in mind that one friendly observer gave him "the meed of high applause."[33]

In the wake of the crisis, Van Buren explored new ways to bring about a permanent settlement. Upon the recommendation of Congress he considered a special mission to England, with Daniel Webster at its head. Webster's appointment might help to transcend the "pernicious effect" of party competition on foreign relations and to persuade Maine to make concessions. He dropped the idea only after Palmerston had indicated a desire that all negotiations remain in Washington. In order to facilitate new negotiations, Van Buren sought to impress on Maine spokesmen the need to back away from their claims to an extended boundary and to accept some compromise as the "leading and most promising mode of settlement."[34] On a special trip to Maine for this purpose, however, Forsyth discovered that a revival of intense party feelings ruled out the prospect for any consensus at the time.

With Maine still unwilling to consider a compromise settlement, Van Buren turned to another means for resolving the issue, which would by-pass her consent. On July 29, 1839, Forsyth laid before the

British a proposal for another survey commission, which contained a significantly new feature: unlike earlier proposals, this one included a stipulation for follow-up binding arbitration. This meant that should the new survey commission fail to agree upon the 1783 treaty line—a result that everyone who was familiar with earlier negotiations fully expected—each party would then be obliged to accept the award of a third party arbiter. Because the agreement for setting up the new commission was to be made by treaty, it would be binding upon Maine.[35] In 1831 the Netherlands' award had been turned down out of deference to the wishes of the state; now Van Buren was resolved to proceed with binding arbitration as a last resort. He did not want a repeat of the Aroostook crisis.

For several reasons, nothing came of his proposal. Palmerston, though he saw in its provision for binding arbitration a new resolve on Van Buren's part to override Maine's obstruction, thought that any preliminary survey would be a waste of time. Given Britain's vital interest in a military road and its view of the "rivers question," there was simply no way that the British and American commissioners could ever agree on the 1783 treaty line. Palmerston thus held out for a direct negotiation. Meanwhile, the spirit of negotiation in Washington was becoming very frayed; Fox and Forsyth spent most of their time and patience engaging in bitter exchanges over presumed violations of the Maine–New Brunswick truce. Politics also worked against the agreement. The upcoming election of 1840 was not a good time for negotiating, and after being defeated, Van Buren found it easy to leave the matter to his successor. Finally, consideration of the boundary dispute gave way by December 1840 to the more volatile McLeod case.[36]

Only with the Webster-Ashburton Treaty in 1842 was the boundary dispute finally resolved. By passing the crisis in 1839, however, Van Buren made an important contribution to the process. Here, as in other instances, he had a right to feel that he had helped to secure "peace with honor."

9

RUNNING THE SHOP

In regard to key questions in foreign affairs, President Van Buren took a direct and active part. He also remained involved in the affairs of the Treasury Department, particularly in the aspects of its operations that bore upon his proposal of divorce. On other and more routine matters of administration, by contrast, Van Buren allowed virtual autonomy to department heads. The Post Office, Navy, and War departments had secretaries—Amos Kendall, James K. Paulding by mid 1838, and Joel R. Poinsett—who possessed considerable ability, expertise, and administrative vision. Much of their work had been defined by commitments made during Jackson's administration, and financial stringency had imposed further limits. Within these limits, however, each met his responsibility well and even managed to initiate some reforms. Further insight into Van Buren's presidency and the life of the nation can be derived by fuller consideration of these departments.

At the head of one department, Van Buren had inherited a man who has been long regarded as "a truly superior Postmaster General."[1] Kendall was born on a farm near Dunstable, Massachusetts, on August 16, 1789, the son of a local pillar of the Congregational Church. By hard work and sacrifices made by all of his family, he had been able to receive a good education, which was completed in 1811 when he graduated from Dartmouth at the head of his class. Moving westward after the War of 1812, he had served briefly as the tutor to Henry Clay's children, had practiced law for a time, and in 1816 had settled down in Frankfort, Kentucky, as editor of the *Argus of Western America*. Here his trenchant style and crusading spirit made it an important paper, particularly on political issues growing out of the panic of 1819. In 1826 he had broken with Clay, thrown his support to Andrew Jackson in the presidential contest of 1828, and had received, for a reward, appointment as fourth auditor of the Treasury.

From this relatively obscure position he had exercised great influence during Jackson's administration, becoming a central figure in what foes called the Kitchen Cabinet. Along with political skills, Kendall also possessed great administrative ability, characterized by a "love of order," a "firmness of character," and "an inexhaustible capacity for business and mental labor." Appointed by Jackson to the Post Office in 1835, he had soon set in order a department that was foundering in debt and disarray. The rapid extension of mail service into the West had been one reason for the debt; but loose accounting and bidding procedures, under the influence of powerful contractors, had also played a part. Kendall had quickly introduced remedies, some authorized by acts of Congress that he had helped to shape. He soon adopted new accounting and bidding procedures and created a special auditor for the Post Office. To the inspection system he added a new check-and-balance mechanism which required each contractor and postmaster to file separate reports of their mutual transactions with the department in Washington. Both were thus made to feel that the "eye" of Washington "was constantly upon them." Within two years Kendall had proudly been able to report that he had turned a deficit of $600,000 into a surplus of $800,000.[2]

Three things distinguished Kendall's tenure under Van Buren. Thanks to the surplus, first of all, Kendall had managed to extend postal service. There was one notable casualty, it was true, for his experiment with a pony-express delivery system from the Atlantic to the Mississippi had had to be dropped. Otherwise the number of post offices had grown from 12,097 in 1837 to 13,468 in 1840; and by this later date the total annual mileage of postal service had reached 36 million, about 10 million more than when Kendall had taken over. Of this total, about 90 percent was being handled by traditional means—carriage, horse, sulky—and the remainder by rail and coastal steam lines. Not that Kendall was old-fashioned in this regard; indeed, his later success in business with the Morse telegraph showed him to be very progressive. He had continued to use the older conveyances in many cases because the new companies were being too greedy, in his view, for government subsidies. While railroads were carrying the mail in England at an annual rate of $90 per mile, Congress found it necessary in 1839 to fix $300 as the minimum rate in the United States; and even at this figure, many lines were refusing to adjust their schedules to accommodate the Post Office.

Meanwhile Kendall did not use the New York–New Haven steam line at all, because Cornelius Vanderbilt was holding out for an annual rate of $30,000 for the same service that a predecessor had provided for $4,000. Van Buren shared Kendall's outrage at such "attempts at extortion" and therefore approved the continued use of the old conveyances.[3]

Van Buren also approved Kendall's ideas about changing the postal rates. The basic structure and rationale of postal rates had been fixed during the 1790s. A fee of 6 cents was charged on a single-sheet letter, and the fee increased at this rate for each additional sheet and for transport through five distance zones. In contrast to this very high rate for letter postage, which was designed to make the Post Office self-sufficient, newspapers and other printed materials were rated for only two distance zones and at no higher than 1.5 cents each. Additionally, editors were allowed to make free exchanges of their papers with others through the mail; and the franking privilege added greatly to the volume of mail. Poor transportation and communication in the early years easily justified this rate system: by disseminating news and information, it helped to enlighten the republic and to fashion new bonds of Union. For the fledgling press in the West, the Post Office actually served as a free news service.

By the 1830s, however, improvements in transportation had taken away much of the earlier justification, while intense party activity had led congressmen greatly to abuse the franking privilege. Complaints also arose that the Post Office Department was, in effect, subsidizing the circulation of the big newspapers. Most of all, the more commercialized and populated East, which bore the greatest burden of the letter postage, felt that it was not fair for the Post Office to tax eastern business in order to extend mail service westward. During one short period in 1838, Kendall estimated, printed matter and franked materials constituted 95 percent of the total weight but was paying only 8 percent of the cost.

In June 1839 Kendall sent an associate to study the postal reforms in England; and on the basis of these findings, a report in 1840 proposed that several basic changes be made. First of all, it would lower letter postage by 25 percent, reduce the number of distance zones, and rate the postage by weight in multiples of one-half ounce. At the same time it proposed to double the postage on newspapers and to restrict the franking privilege to the executive branch. Finally, Congress was urged to study further the rate problems on the rail and steamship lines. Nothing came of these proposals at the time, yet they clearly reflected the administration's sensitivity to the need for change and contributed to the agenda for later reform.[4]

Finally, Kendall's personal battle with one of the most powerful contractors, Stockton and Stokes, raised an important issue of independence for the executive branch. Soon after assuming his duties, Kendall ruled against a claim of $120,000 made by the contractors; poorly kept records and questionable bidding practices convinced him that the sum was an overcredit on the books and not a legitimate obligation of the Post Office Department. The contractors then turned to Congress, which, on July 2, 1836, passed a bill authorizing the solicitor of the Treasury to make a final settlement. Disposed to be generous because of close personal ties with Stockton and Stokes, the solicitor ordered the Post Office Department to credit the contractors not only with the $120,000 in question but with an additional $40,000. Kendall promptly complied with the first part of the award but not with the second, for he could find no basis at all in the records for the additional sum. Stockton and Stokes went back to Congress for relief, and the Senate adopted a report from the Post Office Committee recommending that the additional sum be credited. Kendall once more refused to comply. Reasoning that the Senate's action was only a recommendation, which lacked the force of law, he thus stood "with the moral weight of the Senate against me."[5]

At this point Van Buren got involved. Shortly after taking office he had come under heavy pressure from party leaders in the Senate to make Kendall pay the additional $40,000 awarded by the solicitor. Van Buren turned back this pressure, however, and stood by the postmaster general. He also supported Kendall's decision to reject a writ of mandamus, which was issued on June 7, 1837, by the circuit court in the District of Columbia, ordering the payment of the award. In a letter to Judge William Cranch, Kendall based his refusal on a sweeping Jacksonian concept of executive power, at once unitary in nature and independent of the other branches. The act of any executive officer was ultimately the act of the president, he argued, and therefore was not liable to direction from the judiciary. He wrote: "The Executive is ONE—one in principle—one in object. Its object is *the execution of the laws*. It is not susceptible of subdivisions and nice distinctions as to its duties and responsibilities."[6]

The Supreme Court heard the mandamus case at the January 1838 term. Attorney General Benjamin F. Butler defended Kendall's course on two grounds. First of all, he argued that the circuit court in the District had no right to issue a mandamus, because Congress had never by positive enactment clothed any of the circuit courts with that power. Secondly, Butler contended that Kendall's handling of the solicitor's award was "executive" in nature, that it involved the exercise of "discretionary power" and was not merely a "ministerial" act. The opinion of the majority, written by Justice Smith Thompson, ruled against Kendall on both parts of the argument presented by Butler. Even without a positive enactment by Congress, Thompson held, the circuit court in the District possessed the power of mandamus by virtue of the unqualified cession of that power by the sovereign state of Maryland at the time the District was created. In this particular case, moreover, the court ruled that the solicitor's award had imposed upon the postmaster general a "merely ministerial" act and that he had no discretion at all. Kendall accordingly bowed to this ruling of the Supreme Court and promptly credited the additional $40,000 to the account of Stockton and Stokes.[7]

As a result of this decision, Van Buren made one further move in behalf of executive independence. Upon the advice of Kendall, in his December 1838 message Van Buren asked Congress to pass a bill that would explicitly take away the mandamus power from the circuit court in the District. Such a measure would thereby place the court in the District on a parity with all other circuit courts across the country. Parity could have been achieved in another way, of course, by a measure of Congress that would clothe all of the circuit courts with the mandamus power. Clearly, however, the parity that Van Buren wanted was the kind that took from the judiciary at the seat of government the power to interfere with the executive in the performance of its duties, even those of a "ministerial" sort. Running the shop, in this view, meant defending at certain points the power of the presidency that he had received from Jackson. But the matter came to rest at this point; the House took no action on a bill passed by the Senate in conformity with the president's recommendations.[8]

With regard to the Navy Department, Van Buren made a partial but significant exception to the practice of not interfering in the work of the departments. Within a year he added to the pressures for the resignation of Mahlon Dickerson, who was a holdover from Jackson's administration, and brought in Paulding to put back in order a department that was having severe problems of discipline and morale. Assuming his duties in July 1838, the new secretary made this his central task and thenceforth enjoyed the unwavering support of the president. Paulding also displayed ability in maintaining regular naval operations at an acceptable level during the period of depression. Two other achievements during his tenure were notable. One was the introduction of steam power to naval vessels; the other was the South Seas Exploring Expedition, which laid claim to the discovery of Antarctica.

The bungling of preparations for this expedition was what had led to Dickerson's departure. The original idea of the expedition, formally proposed by President John Quincy Adams, was to chart the northwest coast of North America; but by the end of his term it had grown into a large-scale exploration of the South and Polar seas, which was designed to advance the interests of science as well as those of navigation. On May 14, 1836, Congress formally approved funds for getting the expedition under way. Unhappily, controversy and confusion delayed its departure for more than two years. Dickerson was apparently never fully committed to the expedition. As something of a "Sunday botanizer," he did not fully appreciate the importance of sending a large contingent of prominent scientists on the expedition. He also disagreed violently with Capt. Thomas ap Catesby Jones, who was first designated to command the enterprise, over the number and size of the ships, the officers to be included, and the role of Lt. Charles Wilkes (later of *Trent* fame during the Civil War), whose experience in coastal surveys had qualified him to head the scientific corps. The procurement of scientific equipment in Europe caused further delay, as did the need for overhauling the ships' galleys in Brooklyn to prepare them for the polar climate.

The final and most humiliating delay came in November 1837 when twenty-three officers refused to serve and about a hundred and fifty seamen deserted the ships. Jones resigned the command, and Secretary Dickerson, ill and weary of the whole affair, began to think of resigning, particularly after growing unhappiness in Congress pointed to an investigation of the matter. Chief responsibility for getting the expedition to sea then devolved upon Joel R. Poinsett at the War Department. He quickly ordered the fleet of six ships to Norfolk for final preparations, passed over the seniority list of wrangling naval officers to choose Lieutenant Wilkes as the new commander, and prepared final instructions. At last, on August 18, 1838, the expedition set sail, with the president and Poinsett among those on hand to bid it Godspeed.[9]

Meanwhile, the new secretary of the navy was tackling other problems in his department. Several things had recommended his appointment to President Van Buren. He came from a prominent Tarrytown family, and his social gifts complemented the cabinet circle headed by Forsyth and Poinsett. Furthermore, the antiabolitionist thesis of his recent book on slavery had found favor in the South. Since Dickerson came from neighboring New Jersey, Paulding's place in the cabinet also maintained the sectional identification of his predecessor. Despite his modest disclaimers, finally, Paulding brought to the department a considerable knowledge of naval affairs. His interests, which went back to his father's days as a seagoing merchant and more recently had found expression in literary sketches of naval heroes, were matched by twenty-three years of administrative experience, first as secretary to the Board of Naval Commissioners under President James Monroe and then, since 1823, as the navy agent for the port of New York.

Paulding's first step in dealing with the disciplinary problem was unusual. He gave anonymous direction to the publication of articles in the *Washington Globe* that were critical of naval officers. The "discipline and morale" of the navy were at a low ebb, the articles contended; envy among officers had replaced the esprit de corps that had come out of the War of 1812; "cruises" in Washington among congressmen had often counted for more than duty at sea; midshipmen "skulked" from serving at half pay while recuperating from pretended illness at White Sulphur Springs; and a low and sordid "love of money" had replaced the "love of glory" in serving the country. Dickerson was also damned with faint praise: his leniency with naval officers had its origin in those amiable personal qualities that otherwise constituted "the charm of social life." Paulding felt that it would help "to have the Navy hauled over the coals a little," while the president also stood to gain. A dramatic initiative by the new secretary might help efface the political embarrassment that had grown out of the two-year bungle of the expedition.[10]

The problems that Paulding had to face were longstanding ones that had been caused by many things in addition to Dickerson's incompetence. By 1820 Congress had begun to lose its interest in the navy which the glories of the War of 1812 had aroused. Politics entered largely into other matters. There was no law that fixed the size of the officer corps in relation to the number of vessels in service; and the political appointment of midshipmen added to the surplus, amounting to around two hundred on half pay by 1840. Promotion therefore came slowly, and it became easy for officers to turn down undesired cruises. Believing that regular duty at sea was indispensable for "the character and discipline of the service," Paulding kept asking, though without success, for Congress to increase appropriations in order that more of the officers could be used. Nor was he any more successful in renewing the call of earlier secretaries for a naval academy. While there were too many officers, Paulding had inherited the opposite problem in regard to recruiting and retaining a high quality of seamen. The democratic and enterprising spirit of the age apparently was making naval service less attractive than ever.[11]

Within these limits, Paulding worked with commendable interest and zeal. In response to particular instances of insubordination or weak command, he personally addressed letters of reprimand and ordered them to be read on all ships and stations. One such letter, involving a Lt.

William Leigh, clearly expressed his sense of proper order: "The Secretary of the Navy deems this a proper occasion to remind every officer of the American Navy that the basis of all military organization is the nice gradation of rank and command and the respect and subordination which every inferior is bound to observe towards his superior officer. The nature of the system forbids any equality of rank or command whatever." Paulding dismissed a number of midshipmen for "skulking" from duty and ordered many others to sea as cruises became available. No respecter of persons, he also took on one of the heroes of the War of 1812, Capt. Isaac Hull. He rebuked the captain for allowing two of his wife's sisters to accompany him to the Mediterranean and ordered him to leave them at the base station. He also returned to Hull's command four young officers whom he judged the captain had dealt with unfairly. After a year at his Navy Department post, Paulding seemed more determined than ever to carry through with his mission. "The President stands by me manfully," he wrote, "and please God, if I live, and Congress does not counteract me, I will make both high and low young and old know who is their master, before I have done with them." Though Paulding did not solve the big problem facing him, an earlier student of naval affairs has rated him highly for his efforts.[12]

On an issue of executive independence that involved his department, Paulding won a clear victory. It arose out of a conflict with the widow of Stephen Decatur over a pension claim. The same session of the Twenty-fourth Congress that had passed a general pension bill had also provided her with a special pension. At first she chose to file under the general act, but shortly after Paulding had assumed his duties, she also filed for the special pension. When Paulding turned down her claim for a second pension, she applied for a writ of mandamus from the circuit court in the District; and, upon the refusal of this court to issue the writ, she appealed to the Supreme Court, which heard the case at the January 1840 term. Chief Justice Roger B. Taney, speaking for the majority, ruled against the widow's request, arguing that Paulding's decision was an "executive" act, involving discretionary power, rather than merely a "ministerial" act. Thus, the very distinction on which Kendall had lost two years earlier provided the basis for Paulding to win.[13]

Despite financial stringency, Paulding managed to maintain the basic operations of the Navy Department and to support new initiatives. The budget of $5.7 million for 1837 fell by about a million over the next two years before rising again to the earlier level in 1840. Within this budget the five regular squadrons—West Indies, Brazil, Pacific, East Indies, Mediterranean—continued in service. The first steam frigates for the navy—the *Mississippi* and the *Missouri*—also entered the service. Paulding's own feeling about this achievement was a mixture of nostalgia for the old all-sail Navy and of the pressures generated by the new "steam fever."[14] In large part his reservations were justified, for the cumbersome sidewheels that propelled the new frigates made them suitable only for coastal and harbor defense. The triumph of steam awaited further improvement in the screw propeller.

The most distinctive feature of Paulding's tenure was the exploring expedition. Its itinerary reflected, among other things, the growing commercial interests of the nation. Leaving Norfolk in August 1838, it sailed across the South Atlantic to the Madeira and the Cape Verde islands and then back to the coast of Brazil by November, charting parts of the coast as the scientists took specimens of the fauna and the flora. Rounding Cape Horn during its summer season, the expedition made its way up to Callao, Peru, by June 1839; and from there it proceeded across the South Pacific, working through several island chains on its way to Australia. With Sydney as the point of departure, Lieutenant Wilkes and three of his vessels then probed southward and, during January and February 1840, cruised for about fifteen hundred miles along the ice barrier guarding the coast of Antarctica, laying a claim to its discovery that the world soon recognized. "The discovery of a new continent," the president later boasted, "is one of the honorable results of the enterprise." Traversing the Pacific once more by way of Hawaii, the expedition explored and charted along the coast northward from San Francisco, and then headed for the Philippines, the China Sea, and Singapore, where it arrived in June 1841 with the bulk of its work done. A year later it completed its circuit of the globe, sailing into New York Harbor after a journey of 87,780 miles.[15]

Most of the scientific materials that were collected on the expedition had already been forwarded to the United States. The maps and charts, particularly of the Pacific islands and reefs, proved to be of high quality and consequently freed American shipmasters from their previous dependence on English cartography. With regard to the massive volume of specimens, Peale's Museum in Philadelphia was the initial repository for the collection, but in 1841 it was transferred to Washington. There the new building for the Patent Office served as one custodian; another was the National Institution for the Promotion of Science, a private organization that had been founded by Secretary Poinsett and chartered by Congress in 1840. As soon as the specimens could be unpacked and put on exhibit, they attracted wide interest, and the visiting Ralph Waldo Emerson declared them to be one of the best sights in the country.

Final custody of the materials was not provided until well after Van Buren had left office. Poinsett and Paulding, who soon became involved with the National Institution, both hoped that it would be designated as the permanent repository. They also hoped that their organization would be endowed with the Smithsonian Fund, a sum of around $500,000 that had been given to the United States by an English donor in 1838 for the promotion of science. Congress was of a different mind, however, and in 1846 it created an entirely new institution with those funds, which was to bear their donor's name. But Poinsett and Paulding did have the satisfaction of seeing the new Smithsonian Institution model itself somewhat after their own organization and, upon the expiration of their charter, become the permanent custodian of the materials that had been collected on the exploring expedition. The discovery of a new continent had been one "honorable result" of the expedition, as Van Buren claimed; but surely the supportive role of his two able department heads had also been honorable to the cause of science.[16]

The interest and time that Poinsett gave to the exploring expedition were remarkable in light of the heavy burdens of his own War Department, which was responsible for about half of all expenditures under the Van Buren presidency. The task of Indian removal, which had been undertaken by Jackson, was far from complete, and the Seminole War in Florida was making the heaviest demands on the army. Removal also compounded the problem of defense on the western frontier: to the duty of protecting white settlers from the Indians was added the job of protecting the Indians from each other. A number of crises on the Canadian frontier represented another grave concern. And all important questions required his personal attention, for he had no assistant secretary or even a top-level administrative assistant. Until the following decade, indeed, the secretary was the only civilian officer of authority in the department. Finally, Poinsett's desire to effect some degree of reform in the discipline of the army added to the job. "The Army is in a sad state and requires regeneration," he privately observed. The enterprising spirit of the times and the republican bias against armed forces worked against recruiting good soldiers, while the demand for engineers in railroad construction and other improvement projects lured many of the best West Point graduates away from service.[17]

Out of a varied background, Poinsett brought to the War Department considerable interest and knowledge of military affairs. Born in 1779 of an old South Carolina Huguenot family, he had studied medicine in Edinburgh and, what was more to his liking, military science at Woolwich, England. His interest in military affairs deepened during a five-year tour of Russia, western Asia, and much of Europe during the course of the Napoleonic Wars. Diplomatic missions to Argentina and Chile provided further opportunity for him to observe fighting at close hand. Back home, an interest in internal-improvement projects connecting South Carolina to the West marked his seven years in the state legislature, but his two terms in Congress after 1821 were undistinguished. In 1825 Poinsett left the country once more, serving as the first minister to Mexico. His close identification with the liberals greatly limited his effectiveness, however, and led to his being recalled four years later. Botany, more than diplomacy, benefited from this tour, as he brought home a Christmas flower, the poinsettia, which still bears his name. During the nullification crisis he worked in close connection with President Jackson and Gen. Winfield Scott to organize the Unionist militia in South Carolina. After the crisis he married a wealthy widow, Mary Pringle, and settled down at her "White House" on the Pedee to the life of a gentleman rice planter.[18]

Despite concern over his health, which at times became very frail, Poinsett welcomed Van Buren's call for him to take over the War Department. Poinsett's obvious abilities, as well as his close identification with Jackson, the South, and the Union, recommended him for the post. Other things enabled him to blend harmoniously into the new administration. His charming wife enhanced his own social assets and made him very companionable to others in the cabinet. With relative ease he adapted his own separate views to the necessities under which Van Buren was laboring, for Poinsett recognized that Jackson's heritage would not allow the new administration to "walk straight" for awhile. Poinsett accordingly gave up his own strong desire for the annexation of Texas and for a new national bank. He also accepted Van Buren's concept of party government, even though it had driven Congressman Hugh S. Legaré, among other former Unionist colleagues, into the opposition and had drawn the prince of the Nullifiers, John C. Calhoun, in as an ally. While respecting Legaré as a person, Poinsett deemed him "an unstable man in politics," adding that "politics here mean party."[19]

The most basic fact about Poinsett's tenure, one that never allowed the administration to "walk straight," was the war in Florida, which had been inherited from Jackson. Two southeastern tribes, the Choctaws and the Chickasaws, had already moved to Oklahoma in a relatively peaceful way before Van Buren had become president; and a third, the Creeks, were by 1837 in the process of emigrating after a brief military campaign had been waged against them. For three basic reasons, by contrast, the Seminoles were resisting emigration. Many chiefs had not been a party to the removal treaty of Payne's Landing in 1832; they deemed it a fraud. As an offshoot from the more powerful Creek tribe, with whom a deep enmity had developed, the Seminoles also feared becoming new neighbors in Oklahoma with the Creeks. Finally, the Negro problem constituted the most powerful reason for not emigrating. Mingled with the approximately four thousand Seminoles were from one thousand to fifteen hundred Negroes, who were made up of three groups—free allies, slaves to the Indians, and recent fugitives from the plantations of Florida and Georgia. Among other things, the superior agricultural skills of the Negroes and their facility with language gave them great influence over the Indians, and the Negroes used this power to oppose removal, fearing that the departure of the Seminoles would leave them behind for reenslavement by the planters in the area.[20]

As the January 1836 deadline for removal approached, mounting tensions cast doubt upon the possibility of a peaceful resolution. On December 28 all doubts were dramatically dispelled: Osceola and another chief murdered the Indian agent outside Fort Drane (near present-day Ocala), while a company of 110 troops under Maj. Francis Dade, which was moving up from Tampa Bay with reinforcements, was ambushed and massacred; there were only 3 survivors. In his report to the House on May 25, 1836, the secretary of war formally blamed the outburst of hostilities on the failure of the Seminoles to comply with the treaty obligations.[21]

Although there were occasional truces, the war lasted until 1842. At the outset, a lack of supplies and of coordination among forces in the area let slip the opportunity to surround great numbers of Indians and Negroes between the Withlacoochee River and Tampa Bay. By the time that Gen. Thomas S. Jesup took command in December 1836, the conflict had become a guerilla war fought by detached forces over an almost impenetrable terrain that was as unknown to the army, Jesup later observed, as the interior of China. But he undertook the task with vigor, stretched depots across the peninsula from Tampa Bay to the St. John River, and because of unrelenting pressure, reached a truce agreement with many chiefs on March 6, 1837. By this so-called Dade Capitulation, the Indian chiefs agreed to cease hostilities and to assemble close to Tampa Bay in preparation for the emigration. In return, Jesup promised to keep white planters out of the area, to pay a fair price for the Indians' ponies and cattle, and to agree that the bona fide Negroes of the Indians—their own slaves and allies—would be allowed to go with them to Oklahoma.

Unhappily, actions on both sides soon caused the truce to collapse. Osceola, among the chiefs who were not party to the truce, merely welcomed the respite that it gave for planting spring crops and awaiting the summer season, when renewed fighting would be most difficult. At the same time, Jesup gave in somewhat to the pressure of white planters, allowing them to come in to look for their cattle and runaway slaves. Restive Negroes and Indians began to abandon the camp, as a consequence, and on June 2 Osceola prevailed on all the others to leave. Around seven hundred, Jesup ruefully reported to Washington, had "precipitately fled." All was lost, he further observed, principally because of the influence of the Negroes and the local planters. Poinsett, who had hailed the Dade truce at the very moment when he had taken over the War Department, now had to take on the burden of the war.[22]

During the next year, Jesup essentially broke the power of the foe. With nine of the army's thirteen regiments in Florida, he was in command of about five thousand regulars; additionally, he claimed the service of around four thousand volunteers and militiamen, along with a small band of Creek warriors. Three things highlighted his achievement. One was the capture of Osceola and a few other of the most-hostile chiefs in October 1837. That Osceola was captured under a flag of truce evoked a flood of criticism from humanitarian circles and Whig foes. George Catlin's striking portrait of the chief, which was painted before his death in January, added to the outcry and helped to create a legend. The judicious assessment of a recent study, however, lends support to Jesup's contention that the murder and massacre that opened the fighting, along with the violation of the Dade truce, had already put the contest beyond the normal rules of war. A second feature was the biggest single battle of the war, at Lake Okeechobee, which was fought with a regiment under Col. Zachary Taylor on December 25, 1837. Though his casualties—26 dead and 112 wounded—were almost double those of the enemy, his forceful presence had chastened many other Indians and Negroes in the area and had driven them into Jesup's camp at Jupiter Inlet. Finally, during the year, Jesup had succeeded in detaching most of the Negroes from the remaining Seminoles and thereby had removed a great obstacle to the emigration. In addition to the 240 Negroes captured directly by the army, many recent fugitives surrendered for want of food, and upward of 100 were captured by the Creek warriors.[23]

With these achievements in view, Jesup considered it a good time to end the war. On February 11, 1838, he accordingly wrote to Poinsett, proposing that the administration cease making further efforts at removal and that it confine the remaining Seminoles within an area of southwest Florida bounded on the north by Pease Creek and on the east by the Kissimmee River and Lake Okeechobee. He reasoned that the Negro problem had basically been solved, that the whites would never want the lands of the proposed reservation, and that the remaining Seminoles still possessed the will and the means to continue the conflict. Unless the policy of "immediate emigration" was abandoned, Jesup concluded, "the war will continue for years to come, and at constantly accumulating expense."

On March 1 Poinsett responded in the negative to Jesup's proposal. It was "useless" to consider the question an open one, he wrote, for it was "the settled policy" of the nation, which the new administration felt bound to follow. A recent letter from Jackson might also have impressed on Poinsett the need for the administration to prove itself, for Jackson bluntly wrote that "it has been a disgraceful war to the American character, and its Army." In his annual message, Van Buren provided other arguments. The past treachery of the Indians and their continued forays into the white settlements had ruled out any real security for citizens until the Indians had been "totally expelled." The honor of the nation also prescribed "good faith" in fulfilling all treaty obligations. Most of all, an exception in the case of the Seminoles would be "of evil example in our intercourse with other tribes." At the time when Jesup made his proposal, a much larger number of Cherokees were resisting removal, and from lands that were far more coveted by the whites than those in southwest Florida. Because the fate of the Seminoles was related to the whole policy of Indian removal, Van Buren decided not to deviate from the steps of his predecessor.[24]

Jesup voluntarily relinquished his command in May 1838. By this time he had killed or captured for removal between twenty-five hundred and three thousand Indians, about three-fourths of the total. During his tenure, around four hundred Negroes were turned over to planters in the area, most of whom were authentic runaways though some undoubtedly were Indian slaves or allies. At one point, Poinsett himself urged a Georgia planter, one James C. Watson, to purchase the Negroes who had been captured by the Creeks. On the basis of such facts, abolitionists later charged that the war in Florida was nothing but a "Negro catching" expedition for the army. Other facts, however, greatly weaken the charge. More than four hundred Negroes actually emigrated to Oklahoma, including a group of about sixty whom Watson had purchased but could never get possession of. By the time Jesup left, moreover, it became the fixed policy of the army to send all Negroes, even runaways, to Oklahoma and to compensate the owners. Meanwhile, debate of the issue in Congress during Van Buren's presidency took place along party rather than sectional lines. It was not until late 1841 that Congressman Joshua R. Giddings raised the abolitionist charge. Jesup may have been a good "Negro catcher," to use Giddings's phrase, but only because he saw it as a necessary preliminary to the removal of the Seminoles.[25]

After Jesup's departure the war dragged on for four more years, ending on August 18, 1842, by a proclamation of President John Tyler. Under its terms, approximately three hundred Seminoles who had survived were allowed to remain within a reservation in southwest Florida, as originally defined by Jesup. Overall the war cost fifteen hundred American lives, between $30 and $40 million, and incalculable suffering for everyone involved. Van Buren's lengthy consideration of the war in his last annual message was one measure of its burden. With careful understatement a recent study assesses the matter well: "It was a sad and distressing affair."[26]

In contrast to the ordeal with the Seminoles, the removal of other tribes was relatively peaceful and inexpensive. Because most regular troops had been transferred from the Northwest to Florida, Poinsett was especially anxious to achieve a peaceful emigration of the Sacs, Foxes, Potawatomies, and Winnebagos beyond the Missouri. To effect this goal he decided to deal personally with them; therefore he invited Black Hawk and Keokuk, among other chiefs, to Washington in October 1837. He rightly supposed that the trip would impress them with the size and power of the nation; and he brought the negotiation to a successful conclusion with an impressive public ceremony. Though one hostile observer, John Quincy Adams, thought that the secretary was "cold, stiff, and formal," Poinsett privately felt it was one of his best public acts. "My peace council was a thing to be seen," he wrote a friend. At the least he thought he had "staved off a frontier war for which I am not prepared."[27]

The Cherokees were by far the largest group east of the Mississippi, numbering around seventeen thousand by the beginning of 1838. Disagreement between the Ridge party, which was reconciled to emigration, and the much larger Ross party, which was not, had held up negotiations with the government; as expected, many chiefs took no part in the talks that led, on December 29, 1835, to the Treaty of New Echota. While the government considered the treaty to be binding on all, only a relatively small number offered themselves for emigration before the May 23, 1838, deadline. On April 6, as a consequence, Scott was assigned the task of rounding them up for removal; for that purpose he received two regiments of regulars from Florida and authority to call for three thousand militia from the four states—North Carolina, Georgia, Tennessee, and Alabama—in which the Cherokees were located. Because Poinsett was seriously ill at the time, Scott drew up his own instructions and received, he later claimed, the "carte blanche" of the president.[28]

Scott executed the task in a flexible way. On the scene by early May, he circulated a handbill among the Indians, in which he asked for peaceful compliance with the treaty, reaffirmed the determination of the government, and reminded them that "thousands and thousands are approaching from every quarter, to render resistance and escape alike hopeless." A week later, on May 17, he issued an order to his own troops, asking them to blend charity with understanding on their mission of force. As the operation got under way, a steady flow of Cherokees began to come from their villages to intermediate points and then onward to three large encampments, which were located on the Hiwassee River near Athens, Tennessee; Ross Landing, near Chattanooga; and Gunter's Landing in northern Alabama. If Scott was right in claiming that the roundup had been relatively peaceful and humane, it was also true that there had been many isolated acts of cruelty, particularly among the militia, as a result of their inexperience, prejudice, or greed for the Indian lands.

By June 1838, upward of three thousand Cherokees had left the camps for the westward trip before a severe drought caused Scott to postpone further movements. During the delay he made an effort to keep the camps in good condition. Though it placed new and unexpected demands upon the Treasury, adequate provisions were supplied to the Indians, and thanks to the cooperation of the chiefs, good discipline and order were maintained. Indeed, by August, Scott felt free to send all of the militia home. With the full support of Poinsett and the president, finally, Scott made the most important decision of all, that of giving to the chiefs the full responsibility for conducting the exodus. This meant that the provisions fund was given directly to them, rather than to private contractors, and that the army itself was freed from the need to provide an escort for the entire trip. The chiefs were true to their word, and after a break in the drought by October, they began the long and painful journey across the "Trail of Tears." Even under the best of conditions, the removal of the Indians from their ancestral homes was full of sadness and suffering. But a historian who was most sympathetic to the Indians' plight has praised the sensitive way in which Scott and the regular army played their part.[29]

President Van Buren likewise praised Scott's "commendable energy and humanity." Having accepted removal as a commitment of his party and the presidency, Van Buren also sought to defend its "wisdom and necessity." Voicing the conventional wisdom that "mixed occupancy" was bad for everyone, he hoped that separation would provide the basis for Indian progress toward higher civilization. For the purpose, he fully supported the educational initiatives of the new Indian commissioner, T. Hartley Crawford, to establish manual schools in every village and to place, at some central location, a training school for teachers.[30]

Meanwhile, Poinsett gave attention to the military problem on the frontier of protecting whites from Indians and the Indians from each other. On December 20, 1837, he proposed a new plan which called for establishing two lines of forts. Forts along the "exterior" line were to be placed within Indian Territory on the Red, Arkansas, Kansas, Des Moines, and upper Missisippi rivers. The presence of troops within Indian Territory would, it was reasoned, promote peace among the tribes and provide a deterrent to raids on the white settlements. At some distance to the rear an "interior" line of forts would be established to provide refuge for settlers in times of trouble, a mustering point for the militia, and quarters for the "disposable forces" who were held in immediate reserve. Accordingly, Fort Gibson was to serve as the exterior post on the Arkansas and Fort Smith as the interior one. Much father to the rear, finally, Poinsett proposed that there be a heavy concentration of reserves at Jefferson Barracks, near St. Louis, which would serve the entire western frontier.[31]

On the basis of his ideas for the West, furthermore, Poinsett drew up a master plan for the defense of all frontiers. Along with the concentration of regulars at Jefferson Barracks to serve the West, he proposed another at Lake Champlain for the Canadian frontier; at Carlisle, Pennsylvania, for the Atlantic north of Chesapeake Bay; and at the headwaters of the Savannah, in Georgia, for the South Atlantic and the Gulf Coast. The demands of the war in Florida never allowed deployment of the army at these points, but Van Buren's strong approval of the plan led to requests for added funds to commence construction of permanent barracks. He saw in the plan a way to defend extensive frontiers with forces that were inescapably limited by the financial stringency of the time and the subsisting republican feeling against a large standing army. The concentration of regulars at four points might also improve the discipline and professionalism of the army, which, Poinsett feared, was seriously weakened by being diffused.[32]

Despite popular feeling against a large standing army, Congress was finally persuaded by July 1838 to authorize an enlargement of regular forces from about eight thousand to over twelve thousand troops. Many of Poinsett's recommendations were incorporated: a new regiment was created; the thirteen existing regiments were increased in strength; more emphasis was placed on artillery and mounts for infantry; the Engineer Corps was doubled; and plans were completed for the separate Topographical Corps. Added funds were provided to improve instruction at West Point and to extend from one to four years the service required from cadets after graduation. The base pay for soldiers was also raised from $6 to $7 per month.[33]

But even with these increases, the crisis on the Maine frontier by early 1839 had impressed Poinsett and Van Buren with the need for further changes. Since seven of the army's fourteen regiments were in Florida and some others were in the West, there were only three regiments left to deploy on the entire Canadian frontier. Maine officials, who were condemning the "inactivity" of the army, could not have known, Poinsett privately reported to Van Buren, that any effort to mobilize the army in New England would have resulted in "a very silly exposure of our weakness." Van Buren's commitment to peace with Britain in 1839 was thus reinforced by the realization that the nation was simply unprepared for war.[34]

In this context, Poinsett devised a plan for reorganizing the militia, which his biographer has rightly considered a statesmanlike measure. Deeming the existing militia system to be totally deficient in "discipline, subordination, or knowledge of arms," Poinsett proposed to create an "active or movable force" of a hundred thousand men and a "reserve or sedentary force" of the same size. Each year the "active" militia would be mustered in army camps, placed under the discipline of regulars, and given, at federal expense, from ten to thirty days of rigorous training. After four years in the "active" militia the men would then go into the "reserve" and would be on call for an additional four years. In time of crisis, Poinsett argued, the regular army of about twelve thousand men could be quickly reinforced by two hundred thousand militiamen who would possess discipline and a knowledge of arms.[35]

Unhappily for Poinsett, the plan fell a victim to severe political attack. In the background lay a pervasive democratic bias against the kind of professionalization that Poinsett stood for, a bias that was, during the following decade, to threaten the existence of West Point itself. To this was added the force of local interests and of politics identified with the old militia organization. Most of all, the ingenuity of Whig foes, particularly in the South, managed with considerable success to link the plan to their longstanding indictment of executive despotism. The plan would break down the barriers of States' rights, it was charged, would place a standing army of two hundred thousand at the disposal of the president, and in combination with his direct control of the Treasury, would fatally consummate the process, begun under Jackson, of uniting purse and sword. Frequent repetition of these charges began to take a political toll. Thomas Ritchie warned Van Buren that the Whigs had won the spring 1840 elections in Virginia solely on the basis of this issue and that it loomed ominously over the upcoming presidential contest.[36]

Faced with this prospect, Van Buren saw fit to withdraw his earlier endorsement of the militia plan and, by a fine splitting of constitutional hairs, to reclaim his orthodoxy in regard to States' rights. In a long public letter he claimed that he had not actually examined the final details of Poinsett's proposal, which had been sent directly to the House in March 1840 at the request of that body. Nor was this oversight all that unusual, for he simply lacked the time to review all of the responses made by department heads to requests from Congress. Had he examined this particular one, however, he would have interposed his objections on constitutional grounds. Congress did possess the power to "organize, arm, and discipline" the militia along the lines that Poinsett proposed, but the "training" of the militia was a power that was reserved exclusively to the states. Clearly, the "politician" in Van Buren here overrode statesmanlike considerations.[37]

Poinsett's silence on his militia proposal after the election of 1840 signaled its demise. In regard to other matters, by contrast, his final reports to the president pointed with pride to solid achievements. During his tenure more than forty thousand Indians had been moved west of the Mississippi, a greater total than under any other secretary of war. Meanwhile, peace had been maintained on the extensive frontiers, and the ordeal in Florida was nearing an end. He also claimed that he was leaving the army in much better condition than he had found it. Recruitment in 1840 raised the total force above ten thousand men, which was much nearer to its authorized strength than it had been before. The practice of stationing regulars in large numbers when possible had also contributed to "a high state of discipline." On the side of economy, Poinsett reported that expenditures were down from $20 million in 1837 and 1838 to less than $10 million for 1840. During the same period the average cost of maintaining a soldier in service had dropped from $400.15 to $375.96.[38]

Poinsett's reports can be taken as a fair summary of Van Buren's entire presidency. The commitments that had been made by Jackson defined the basic tasks to be performed, while the financial stringency growing out of the panic of 1837 set severe limits on the way in which the tasks could be performed. But within these limits, Poinsett, as well as Kendall and Paulding, proved to be able administrators, who ran the shop quite well and vindicated Van Buren's trust in them.

10

★ ★ ★ ★ ★

THE LAST STEP

What has caused the great commotion, motion, motion,
    All our country through?
    It is the ball a rolling on, on,
For Tippecanoe and Tyler too—Tippecanoe and Tyler too,
And with them we'll beat little Van, Van, Van,
Van is a used up man.

The campaign of 1840 did not turn out the way Van Buren had envisioned it the year before. In a letter to Andrew Jackson he then had welcomed the prospect of a contest with Henry Clay on old party grounds. Clay, who had been defeated by Jackson on the national-bank issue in 1832, might easily be cast once more on the unpopular side; while Van Buren, whose Independent Treasury was claimed as the true alternative to the national bank, could be seen as the champion of democracy against the old Federalist aristocracy. Most of all, he felt so easy about the contest because his central measure had "fulfilled the expectations" of those who had elected him. Having shaped his administration in the steps of Jackson, he was looking to reelection on the same basis.[1]

Unhappily for Van Buren, his foes confounded his hopes with a great commotion, turning to a military hero, adopting log cabins and hard cider as popular symbols, and generating a degree of public excitement that seemed to blur old issues. To a bewildered old republican, Peter V. Daniel of Virginia, it was a "great effervescence" in the "political cauldron" which contained strange new elements. Large balls, patched over with Whig slogans, were often rolled at the head of giant parades, mocking the earlier boast of Thomas Hart Benton that "single and alone" he had set the ball in motion to expunge the resolution which had censured Jackson. Massive rallies, composing "acres of men," were got up on the order of religious revivals, complete with itinerant speakers, public singing, and "a perfect tumult of enthusiasm." Spirits that were harder than cider often enhanced the enthusiasm, and "booze" gained its name from the fact that a Philadelphia distiller, E. C. Booz, marketed his wares in small containers shaped like log cabins. Much larger log cabins, meanwhile, were raised at many gatherings, thus providing an emotional climax to the whole affair. The aristocratic New Yorker Philip Hone reported a "cheering and enthusiastic" crowd at Broadway and Prince streets, where a cabin 50 by 100 feet was raised.[2]

While many old Whigs such as Hone welcomed the prospect of victory, they also worried about the new political tactics. Preferring an eagle to a cider barrel—or a ship to a log cabin—as the true symbol of Union, Hone also feared that personal "huzzas" to the candidate might drown out huzzas to the Constitution. "Behold," he observed, "old things are passed away, and all things have become new." In like fashion, John Quincy Adams condemned such means of popular appeal as the itinerant habits of leading statesmen, who held forth "like Methodists preachers" before hysterical masses under "the broad canopy of heaven." A revolution, he sadly supposed, was taking place in the manners of the people.[3]

What Hone and Adams observed with such mixed feelings was the coming of age of the "party system," which was thenceforth to order political life in America. If Van Buren and the Democratics had begun the process of permanent party organization and warfare, the Whigs now brought it to maturity. There was great truth in the complaint of the *Democratic Review*: "We have taught them how to conquer us." The choice of William Henry Harrison and the adoption of the log-cabin symbol clearly paralleled the Democrats' use of Jackson and hickory poles during earlier contests. The Whigs also developed a "stupendous system of party organization." A group in Washington, headed by Congressmen Rice Garland of Louisiana and John Clark of New York, served in many ways as a national committee. At the local level, a Democratic senator in New Jersey marveled at the Whigs' success in turning out a mass of voters who had escaped the careful canvass of his own party. Thurlow Weed at the *Albany Evening Journal* and Horace Greeley, as editor of a campaign special, the *Log Cabin*, skillfully used the power of the press in what has been called the "image campaign."[4]

Because of the wide circulation of his paper, Greeley exerted an especially large influence, for he had already gained experience in adapting Whig policies to democratic aspirations. The Whigs also provided a convincing ideological alternative. By branding executive usurpation and spoilsman politics as the chief threats to liberty, they made the campaign a crusade for restoring true republicanism. Against the background of depression, finally, the Whigs effectively linked economic interests to the fate of republican ideals.

The first task of the Whig party, which was now coming under the control of young and pragmatic leaders, was to turn from familiar old spokesmen to a man who could more easily be identified with new democratic forces. In a letter to Governor William H. Seward of New York in behalf of "the most available candidate," Harrison's manager bluntly invoked the overriding priority of victory: "It is our common purpose to effect a redress of grievances by a change of rulers." Abraham Lincoln came out early for Harrison on the same grounds and eased his conscience with regard to the claims of Daniel Webster and Henry Clay by the reflection that "their fame is already immortal."[5]

While both desired more fame, Webster was the first to drop out. As early as 1836 he had begun to recast his Whiggery in democratic terms, but his own Federalist past and his aristocratic bearing were not the kind of things that even a new democratic rhetoric could overcome. A series of critical editorials in the *Boston Atlas* in late 1838 took a heavy toll on his chances; and though Massachusetts Whigs dutifully put his name forward, he saw fit to withdraw in June of the following year. By contrast, Clay entertained high hopes for the nomination until the very end. Early in the field against Jackson, he had been one rallying point for southern defectors, and in a strong speech against abolitionism in the Senate in February 1839, he consolidated the support of southern Whigs. By means of a trip to New York during the summer, he sought the added strength that would be needed for the nomination of the convention, which was scheduled to meet in Harrisburg on December 5, 1839. A warm reception at public gatherings in the state and the hospitality of friends at Saratoga bouyed his hopes.

But the new party managers looked elsewhere for a candidate. In New York, Weed and Seward were forging a powerful coalition of old-line Whigs, mainly from New York City; antislavery elements; western Anti-Masons; and Conservative Democrats who had defected from Van Buren. For such a combination, Clay would not do; and Weed bluntly warned Clay at Saratoga that a Masonic slaveholder who was identified with the national bank could not carry the state. Under Weed's influence a majority of New York's delegates went to Harrisburg pledged to support Gen. Winfield Scott, who had gained popularity in the state because of his role in the border crises with Canada. Thaddeus Stevens of Pennsylvania played an even larger role in stopping Clay. Stevens had also won credentials as a pragmatic party manager, fusing his Anti-Mason forces with old-line Whigs in order to elect his man, Joseph Ritner, as governor in 1835 and to push through the state legislature a charter for Biddle's bank. Biddle's wry tribute to him must have been gratifying: "You are a magician greater than Van Buren & with all your professions against Masonry, you are an absolute right worshipful Grandmaster."[6] Difficulties in state politics by 1839 had for a time rent the coalition, and competing delegations of Whigs and Anti-Masons came to the convention. But Stevens's influence with Anti-Masons everywhere and with Harrison delegates from Indiana, Ohio, and New England was especially strong, for his state had hosted the national convention in November 1838 that had given Harrison the Anti-Mason nomination.

The assembling of the Whig convention upon the call of a congressional caucus in May 1838 was itself a measure of party maturity. Back in 1836 the Whigs had used an antiparty rhetoric to condemn the Democratic practice of holding a party convention. The outcome of the convention likewise confirmed its new style of leadership. Two early rulings, arranged by the new party managers, spelled trouble for Clay. The first seated the competing delegations from Pennsylvania and thereby gave Stevens greater leverage; the second adopted a unit rule for voting. This meant that the substantial minorities for Clay in some of the northern states would go for naught. But even under this rule, the first ballot went in his favor—Clay, 103; Harrison, 90; Scott, 57—and subsequent ballots promised no significant shifts.

The turning point came with a move by Stevens, which had the effect of making Virginia, which was solid for Clay, switch its second choice from Scott to Harrison. Moving near the Virginia delegation, Stevens dropped on the floor a copy of the letter that Scott had written to Francis Granger, in which Scott rather clumsily appealed for the antislavery vote in New York. Virginia's switch then precipitated other changes, including the scramble by the New York delegation from Scott to Harrison. On the final ballot the vote then stood 148 for Harrison, 90 for Clay, and 16 for Scott. Embittered friends of Clay, including John Clayton of Delaware and Benjamin W. Leigh of Virginia, refused the nomination for vice-president, which then went to John Tyler. Reflecting somewhat later on the euphony of "Tippecanoe and Tyler Too," a Clay supporter sardonically observed that there was rhyme but no reason in the whole matter.[7]

Having chosen the candidates, the party faced the next task of securing unity. For a brief time the bitter feelings expressed by Clay's friends in Harrisburg posed the prospect of southern defection. Clay's first response to the work of the convention pointed the same way. He exploded: "My friends are not worth the powder and shot it would take to kill them. I am the most unfortunate man in the history of parties: always run by my friends when sure to be defeated, and now betrayed for a nomination when I, or any one, would be sure of an election." But a desire for party victory, good sportsmanship, and reflection upon his earlier views brought a quick recovery. He had, after all, approved the caucus call for the convention, and he had addressed a letter to it, pledging support for its nominee. A dinner in his honor at Washington on December 11 brought reconciliation and exerted a soothing influence on his friends everywhere. Hone could soon report that the nomination was working "like a charm" among Whigs of all backgrounds, who were ready to consign Clay to a "higher eminence" and "to forget that any other candidate than General Harrison has ever been thought of."[8]

Whigs also secured a degree of unity with the decision not to write any platform and not to prepare any party proclamation. Most delegates clearly sensed that degree of diversity within the party which Millard Fillmore stated so well in a private letter: "Into what crucible can we throw this heterogeneous mass of old national republicans, and revolting Jackson men; Masons and anti-Masons; Abolitionists and pro-Slavery men; Bank men & anti-Bank men with all the lesser fragments that have been, from time to time, thrown off from the great political wheel in its violent revolutions, so as to melt them down into one mass of pure Whigs of undoubted good metal?"[9] Exhortations in the convention for the nominations to carry their own weight were followed by one formal resolution, which called upon "our constituents to redeem the solemn pledges here given, and to consummate the *union* of the Whigs for the good of the Union." Amplifying this theme on April 28, 1840, the *Albany Evening Journal* noted that a genuine "people's party" was necessarily divided on many specific issues but was always united "in opposition to misrule." When good men governed, it was assumed, the general good was bound to follow:

> Without a why or wherefore
> We'll go for Harrison therefore.

Another means of unity, which has most often been stressed by historians, was the conscious appeal that party managers made to the passions, rather than to the reason, of the people. For this purpose an article in the Democratic *Baltimore Republican* on December 11, 1839, unwittingly supplied a central theme for Harrison: "Give him a barrel of hard cider, and settle a pension of two thousand a year on him, and my word for it, he will sit the remainder of his days in his log cabin by the side of a 'sea coal' fire, and study moral philosophy." Use of the log cabin as a symbol was apparently first made in Harrisburg on January 20, 1840, at a local gathering of Whigs to ratify the work of the national convention. The great effect it produced upon the feelings of the people invited widespread adoption; and along with many others, Weed was soon traveling throughout New York State "urging the erection of log cabins." Such skillful use of a weapon supplied by the enemy, Hone slyly admitted, was "understood by every man in our ranks."[10]

It was also understood that certain liberties were being taken with the facts in casting the image of Harrison as a newborn Cincinnatus. There was an old log cabin beside his present residence, to be sure, but he had never used it for living quarters. Even more clearly, he had not been born in a log cabin, nor had he been disciplined in youth by the plow. Scion of an old aristocratic Virginia family and son of a signer of the Declaration of Independence, he had attended Hampden-Sydney College, had studied medicine for a time with Benjamin Rush, and had then used family connections to secure a military commission for service in the Northwest, where, in time, he commanded forces at two significant if not entirely heroic battles—Tippecanoe and Thames. In the political arena he had served with competence as governor of the Northwest Territory from 1800 to 1812 and, during the next decade, as a congressman and senator from Ohio. To these duties he had brought modest abilities and, in the judgment of President John Quincy Adams, "a lively and active, but shallow mind." After a year as minister to Colombia, Harrison had settled down as clerk in the Hamilton County Court of Common Pleas, a position of relative obscurity if not of poverty, which the young Abraham Lincoln took to be another recommendation for the presidency.[11]

Great liberties were also being taken by Whigs in casting the counter image of Van Buren as "a democrat by profession and an aristocrat in principle." To earlier portrayals of him as a courtier of effete tastes and foppish habits was now added the masterpiece of Congressman Charles Ogle, an apt scholar in Stevens's school of Pennsylvania Anti-Masonry. Seizing upon a budget item of $3,665 for White House improvements, Ogle spoke for three days—April 14, 15, and 16—on "The Regal Splendor of the Presidential Palace." It was a mansion in which Van Buren preened like a peacock before mirrors larger than barn doors; walked on British carpets at a time when textile workers were unemployed; slept in a fancy French bedstead; drank expensive imported wines; ate with golden spoons; and surrounded himself in all rooms with the most extravagant of furnishings. On the White House grounds, luxurious landscaping, which featured a pair of knolls resembling Amazon bosoms, added to the picture of an indolent and sensual aristocrat. All this contrasted so starkly with the honest farmer, living in a log cabin with the latchstring always out. The *Washington Globe* angrily condemned Ogle's speech as an "omnibus of lies," and conservative Whig Congressman Levi Lincoln took issue with Ogle's facts by showing that other presidents had spent more money on the White House than Van Buren had. The omnibus easily outran such protests, however, as Whig editors gave wide circulation to the speech. Van Buren was so enraged by it, a Louisville editor mischievously added, that "he actually *burst his corset.*"[12]

With all its misrepresentations and excesses, however, the Whig campaign did possess reason as well as rhyme. Giving form and meaning to the mass appeals was a Whig persuasion that, a recent study has shown, made convincing claims on a generation that was anxious for the republican experiment to succeed. In this regard the greatest threat to liberty was Democratic Caesarism—that is, the encroachment of executive power, supported by a drilled and disciplined party that was bent on spoils rather than on the pubic good. At the national convention, with "the great problem of the capacity of man for self-government" in mind, James Barbour of Virginia sounded the keynote that Clay had earlier struck in the bank war: "We are indeed in the midst of a revolution. . . . The forms of the Constitution are retained, but its spirit is gone—your President is a monarch almost absolute."[13]

In person, Van Buren was not a very impressive Caesar, to be sure, yet since he was following in Jackson's footsteps, Whig imagination supposed that Van Buren's divorce proposal would, in connection with a standing army as disguised in Poinsett's militia plan, fatally combine purse and sword in executive hands. Moreover, the political activity of officeholders, whose number was greatly enlarged by a new swarm involved in taking the 1840 census, threatened to perpetuate the regime; and Amos Kendall was using the thirteen thousand postmasters across the country as subscription agents for the party's new campaign sheet, the *Extra Globe.* For several years, Whig Congressman John Bell had tried in vain to pass legislation assuring "the freedom of elections" from the political action of officeholders. Whig campaign tactics, in this light, effectively symbolized the desire to purge the enemies of freedom and to "restore this Government to its original purity." A mass rally was a true "gathering of the people," and the raising of a log cabin was a solemn ritual of regeneration, "an emblem of the simplicity that should characterize Republican institutions.''[14] If religious revival served to restore a sense of community in proper relation to God, political revival similarly brought the nation back to the wholeness of its beginnings.

Holding this persuasion, Harrison had defined the conditions for accepting the Anti-Mason nomination in 1838, and his letter of acceptance became an important Whig campaign document two years later. In it he repudiated executive control over the Treasury, disclaimed all official actions of a ''purely party character,'' and promised to serve only one term, to limit severely the power of veto, and to impose restraint more generally upon executive involvement in the legislative process. He also carried this message in person to the voters, thus becoming the first candidate in the nation's history to campaign directly for the presidency and illustrating, in the process, yet another contribution of Whiggery to the party system. Before a vast throng at Dayton, Ohio, he evoked thunderous applause with the declaration that ''the Government is now a practical monarchy.'' The true issue was not democracy versus aristocracy—the people against a privileged few—as the Democrats claimed, but democracy versus monarchy.[15]

The absence of a platform on specific economic issues was not solely the product of cynical manipulation. For one thing, no major party had ever written a platform up to the time of the Whig convention in 1839. For another thing, the Whig charge of executive usurpation was closely linked to the criticism of Democratic policies, and the presumption was clear that a fundamental change needed to be made. ''We are contending not only for the preservation of our free institutions,'' one central figure in the campaign observed, ''but for the bread with which to feed our wives and children.'' Ascribing all economic evils to ''the original sin of Executive encroachment upon the Legislative authority,'' the National Intelligencer looked to Congress for relief. Webster, in like spirit, wrote to a committee at the Tippecanoe battlefield, pledging Congress to ''a prudential exercise of all its power.''[16]

Wide circulation for Whig speeches during the current session of Congress also invoked the aid of ''parental government.'' For all the virtues of his work on the ''log cabin campaign,'' Robert Gunderson was wrong in concluding that Ogle's speech had a greater effect than did the debates in Congress on the issues of currency, state debts, bankruptcy, and related economic matters. Though the Whigs ''went to the woods,'' they kept coming back to the market place. It was very fitting that one of the biggest log cabins had been erected in Manhattan, at Broadway and Prince streets. Although the Whigs nurtured the self-image of being the ''country'' party opposed to ''corruption'' in Washington, they found their greatest support in the cities and towns.

Finally, the absence of a platform was easily consistent with the Whig view that the will of the people found its true expression in Congress, not in a presidential contest. In this sense, many specific issues were in fact discussed during the congressional races and then were enacted by a victorious Whig Congress. James Barbour voiced the wishes of the older part of the Union for distributing land revenues. On that same issue the *Albany Evening Journal* welcomed federal funds to relieve state debts, to resume projects of internal improvement, and to stimulate new employment. A higher tariff found favor in many quarters, as did the idea of an insolvency law for debtors.

Meanwhile, the call for some degree of currency inflation was universal. Few were more adept than Weed in the art of "log cabin" politics, yet he clearly recognized the issue of currency as being the "real element of strength in that presidential canvass." A new national bank was widely considered as the best means for enlarging the currency, and Abraham Lincoln in Illinois made it the central theme in his campaign speeches. A Van Buren supporter in North Carolina likewise reported the great appeal of the issue: "I am free to say that all the Federal arts would have failed if the people of this state were not in favor of a *National Bank.*" In a widely publicized exchange in the Senate with James Buchanan, John Davis of Massachusetts closely linked the divorce proposal to a deflated currency and low wages for American workers. Similarly, the historian Richard Hildreth made explicit the strong appeal that an expanded currency had for farmers. No longer the self-sufficient agrarian "described by the poets," the farmer now "must have a *market* for his produce."[17] It was significant, in this connection, that the seven states that voted for Van Buren were relatively less integrated into the market economy than the ones that voted for Harrison.

With all his equivocations, Harrison likewise isolated currency as a central issue. Responding to the question of whether he was in favor of paper money, he answered, to the thunderous applause of the Dayton crowd, "I AM." He favored a "correct bank system" to supply paper, moreover, precisely because he was "a democrat," one who was vitally concerned with efforts to raise prices and wages. "But for all this," he seemed to be wavering, "I am not a Bank man"—apparently meaning a national bank—unless the people wanted one! While holding that the Constitution delegated no specific power to Congress to charter a bank, he believed that Congress might create one if it was deemed necessary for carrying out other of its duties. Pledged, in such a case, not to interpose a veto, Harrison vowed, in a true republican spirit, to obey the will of the people as expressed by their representatives.[18] Strict limits on the use of the executive veto here went with a looser interpretation of congressional power.

A revealing question might be raised at this point: How different might the campaign of 1840 look to historians had Harrison not died after only one month in office? It seems highly probable that he would have gone along with the legislative program that Clay pushed through Congress, including the bill for a new national bank. Success for Clay's program might then have had the retroactive effect of giving greater clarity to the issues in the campaign of 1840. Instead, the disruptive veto of "His Accidency" John Tyler has made it easier to stress the divisiveness of the party and thus to find more rhyme than reason in the logcabin campaign. Many southern Whigs voted for Clay's program of economic nationalism and helped him to read Tyler out of the Whig party.[19] While promising the regeneration of republican freedom in 1840, Whigs also tried to deal with economic problems in a positive way. The campaign was not only one of mindless motion and huzzas; it also skillfully blended a concern for republican ideals with the economic self-interests of the voters. In an effective way it brought into sharp focus the opposition to Van Buren's administration that had grown over the last three years.

It was in dealing with sectional issues, far more than economic ones, that Whigs made themselves liable to charges of manipulation and misrepresentation. In the South they pushed especially hard the charge that Poinsett's militia plan would supply the president with a standing army of two hundred thousand men; and by July, Van Buren saw fit to withdraw his support even though the plan was, in the context of depression and foreign crisis, a very statesmanlike one. Crude racist appeals were also made in the case of a navy lieutenant, George M. Hooe. A court martial in Pensacola, at which two Negro seamen had given testimony, convicted Hooe of having used excessive flogging. When President Van Buren refused to overturn the conviction, he was pilloried as being an enemy of the South, even though it was shown that the testimony of the Negroes had not been decisive and that the longstanding precedent for such testimony could only be undone by positive congressional enactment. Southern Whigs also renewed charges made in 1836 that Van Buren was hostile to slavery.

Most blatant of all was the way in which Whigs outflanked their party rivals on the issue of abolitionist petitions. During Van Buren's administration the Democrats simply reaffirmed at each session the principle of the Pinckney resolution, which had been adopted in 1836. By this resolution the House agreed to admit the petitions into the chamber but then to table them without printing or referring them.

Southern Whigs now took the lead to make the "gag" on abolitionist petitions complete, by pushing through a resolution forbidding petitions even to be admitted into the House or to be formally recognized in any way. With most southern members in both parties supporting and with northern Whigs opposing the new "gag," it passed on January 28, 1840, by the narrow margin of 6 votes, 114 to 108, a margin made possible by the affirmative vote of 26 northern Democratic supporters of Van Buren. Southern Whigs now boasted a superior merit in guarding the interests of their section; while Weed, among northern Whigs, invoked the antislavery feelings of his section against "the baseness, the servility, the inconceivable treason of northern Van Burenism."[20] As a "northern man with southern principles," Van Buren was here pictured by Whigs as being too northern for the South and too southern for the North.

To counter these Whig initiatives, Democrats in 1840 assumed a somewhat more prosouthern position than they had taken before. In response to a flood of inquiries from anxious southerners, Van Buren reaffirmed his inaugural pledge to veto any measure against slavery in the District of Columbia that might pass Congress without the assent of the slaveholding states. Now he took a further step, pledging to veto any restriction that Congress might place on the admission of Florida into the Union as a Slave State, or on any other new state that might be formed out of territory belonging to the United States at the time. The party platform and address likewise took strong ground, opposing not only direct intervention by the federal government but also any "incipient steps" against the "domestic institutions" of the South. The party pledge of "undying attachment to our glorious Union" was also accompanied by a recognition that the Union ultimately reposed on the "great compromises of interests" between planters and plain republicans.[21] Unaccountably for many Democrats, however, the more prosouthern their pronouncements, the more the southern Whigs seemed to prosper.

It would be a mistake, however, to stress overmuch the importance of sectional issues in the campaign of 1840. The way in which Democrats dealt with the vice-presidential question is a case in point. In 1836 many southerners had opposed Col. Richard M. Johnson because he had lived with a Negro mistress and claimed two daughters from that union. By 1840 this kind of opposition revived, with rumors of a relapse by Johnson, who, according to the report of an outraged Amos Kendall, was again living openly with "a buxom young *Negro*." Partly for this reason, Jackson urged Van Buren to dump Johnson in favor of James K. Polk; and Georgians pushed the claims of their favorite son, John

Forsyth. But Johnson continued to enjoy strong support in other places: many in the West retained their enthusiasm, and eastern Locofocos considered him a special friend.

Caught between conflicting interests within the party, Van Buren assumed a position of "rigid neutrality."[22] Conformably with this position, his leading spokesman, Silas Wright, soon reached agreement with southerners that the party convention would name no candidate at all for vice-president, leaving the matter to the choice of each state. As it turned out, both Polk and Forsyth withdrew from the running, and Johnson at last claimed the support of the party in most parts of the country. Despite his personal habits, Johnson did provide a Democratic answer of sorts to the military pretensions of Harrison. Johnson had fought with distinction at the Battle of Thames, and he claimed credit for having killed Tecumseh, a leader of Britain's allies and the foe of Harrison at the earlier Battle of Tippecanoe. "Rumpsey dumpsey, Colonel Johnson shot Tecumseh" gave the Democrats at least one catchy slogan of their own.

With regard to issues other than sectional ones, Democrats faced difficult problems, whether on the defensive or on the attack. Much of the predicament was illustrated at Baltimore, where, on May 5, 1840, the party assembled for its national convention. There they encountered the distracting presence of members of the Young Whigs, who had seen fit, entirely by design, to assemble at the same time for the purpose of ratifying the work of the Harrisburg convention. While Democratic delegates were deliberating inside on a platform—the first ever written by a national party—the Whigs were out in the streets, parading, singing, rolling giant campaign balls, and shouting huzzas to Harrison. Clearly on the defensive within the assembly hall, delegates of the incumbent party had only to look out the window to see the problem of mounting an attack, for the foe had been in the field early, arousing an excitement among the people. The coverage given the two groups by the prestigious *Niles' Register* showed the Democratic problem another way: their party proceedings received only fourteen columns, while twenty-three columns were devoted to the antics of the Young Whigs.

On the defensive side of their strategy, Democrats stressed the continuity of Van Buren's administration with that of Jackson. Felix Grundy gave the keynote speech at the convention; another Tennessee protégé, former governor William Carroll, was chosen president; and an early Jacksonian, Isaac Hill, prepared the party's address. The specific parts of the platform likewise evoked the heritage, for they summarized the policies that had been adopted by the party over the last twelve years. During this period the party had taken decisive ground against several measures—a system of internal improvements, a national bank, a tariff favoring special interests, the assumption of state debts, and any further connection between government finance and bank corporations. In this context the address noted the Independent Treasury as Van Buren's distinctive and highly praiseworthy contribution. Along with the principle of States' rights, which underlay all policies, the party also emphasized "equal rights"—as Grundy told the convention, an "open field" for all citizens and "exclusive privileges" for none.[23]

Regarding the issue of the currency, which the Whigs were bringing into sharp focus, the Democratic party reaffirmed the ultimate goal of stability and order. While upholding the "sacred standard" of specie, Van Buren's policy of divorce also constituted the true alternative to a national bank and "the most effectual regulator" of paper currency. Effective regulation in turn would bring stable prices and a steadier pace to enterprise, free from the excesses of a credit system of banking, which ever tended, under English influence, toward violent cycles of expansion and contraction. The *Washington Globe* drew the lines very clearly: "The issue, then, is Martin Van Buren a sound currency, and independence of the honest producing classes, against a spurious and fictitious bank currency, dependency, venality, and servility to the non-producers and aristocrats, the representatives of their available, G. Harrison." A special paper set up in Albany during the campaign, the *Rough Hewer*, followed the same line. Against the "great evil" of violent fluctuations in business it spoke for a currency that would promote the "regular progress of industry," steady employment, and "uniform wages."[24]

But the defense of sound currency, no matter how pure in principle, caused problems during a period of severe deflation. Although the principle of a sound currency served well in explaining past fluctuations and in promising future stability, it clearly did not deal very well with the present realities of currency contraction and low prices. In a somewhat shrill defense of old republican ideals, the *Richmond Enquirer* unwittingly defined the central difficulty of the party: "What! surrender all your principles, because you cannot command the highest prices for your corn and flour!"[25] The Whigs, by contrast, faced no such problem at all, because their republicanism easily incorporated the call for more currency and higher prices. Huzzas for Harrison, mingling with cries of "Martin Van Ruin," made the point most strongly.

With these shouts ringing in his ears, Amos Kendall urged some party leaders to shift from a defense of Van Buren's policies to an attack upon the opposition. Having resigned from the Post Office Department in May to become editor of the *Extra Globe*, he represented the nearest thing that the Democrats had to a national campaign leader. In this role he criticized the tack, which was being taken by many state leaders, of making banks and currency the issue of the campaign. "No man is a greater enemy than myself of corporations and special privileges," he argued, "but this is not the time to take *specific* issues on the subjects and make the elections turn upon them." Assuming that all "intelligent enemies of corporations" were already in the Democratic party, he thought time and further light were needed in order to swell the ranks. Instead of making the contest in 1840 a showdown between "Gog and Magog," he favored a strategy of making an attack upon the Whigs' candidate and their campaign practices.[26]

This attack should involve several things. One—challenging the credentials of Harrison as an authentic military hero—elicited a public letter from Jackson, which was critical of Harrison's attainments. Wide circulation was also given to the charge that Harrison, unsure of his own claims to fame, had solicited affidavits from junior officers to document his hero status. With what must have been particular relish, the Democratic press likewise damned Harrison for "non committalism." At first they pictured him as "General Mum," or as an animal in an iron cage, for a "conscience keeping" committee banned for a time any new statements by the candidate. After Harrison began his unprecedented speechmaking tour, the press started to focus on his equivocations. Most of all, Democrats condemned the Whigs for their endless parades, rolling balls, mindless slogans, and log-cabin raisings. The *Democratic Review* warned that all of this constituted "nothing short of high treason" to the "whole spirit" of republican institutions. Unmindful of the hickory poles and other devices that had gone into his own election, Jackson deplored the "mummeries to degrade the people." Similarly, the "claptrap" in Clay's speech to a vast gathering in Nashville struck Van Buren as "the silliest affair I have read for some time."[27]

There was, however, considerable risk in this strategy of attack. If large masses of people did in fact respond to Whig appeals and to Harrison as a hero, Democratic critics of these appeals would clearly be running the danger of expressing their own contempt for the people. Private remarks by some of the cabinet members showed, indeed, how closely they were flirting with the very position that they were ascribing to their foes. Joel R. Poinsett confessed that he would "lose all confidence" if the people were to succumb to the "contemptible arts" of Whiggery; Levi Woodbury could not believe that the people favored the "imbecile Harrison" over the "sagacious" Van Buren; and James K. Paulding said that a Whig victory would compel him thenceforth to look for political guidance to the "horse of Darius" rather than to "the instincts of two-legged animals." The public demeanor of most cabinet members also concerned a newcomer, John M. Niles, who had replaced Kendall at the Post Office Department. Niles was shocked at the way his colleagues, wrapping themselves in official dignity and reserve, declined an invitation to celebrate July 4 at an Alexandria gathering. Niles shared Van Buren's view of party as being a sentinel to guard the people from the power of organized selfish interests. But he also thought that the times required the guardians to be less courtly and more democratic in their manners. Some elements of truth in Ogle's extravagant indictment of aristocracy, it would seem, had taken passage on the "omnibus of lies."[28]

Underlying many of the problems of the Democrats, whether on the defense or on the attack, was the way in which their old republican ideology tended to obscure as much as it revealed about the political realities of the day. Many Democrats were apparently unable to perceive the possibility of having more than one genuinely popular party. The party address duly observed: "The identity of the modern Whigs and ancient Federalists is evident and undeniable. It may be distinctly traced through all their changes of name, and seen through all their disguises." The "history of parties" served once more as a central theme in the campaign.[29]

In the case of Van Buren there was particular irony: though he was one of the important figures in the creation of the modern party system, he failed to appreciate its imminent coming of age in 1840. His "Thoughts on the Upcoming Election Contest in New York," a 75-page memorandum in his own handwriting, thus constituted a very revealing document. In great detail the first part urged upon state leaders the need for organization down to the lowest level, important alike for canvassing every possible Democratic voter and for ferreting out enemy frauds. But the longest part of the document, which was clearly designed as a draft for an address to the people of the state, focused on the theme of the "origin, history, and conduct of the two great parties." The basic issue separating the parties never changed, in this view: the one was always seeking favors for the few, and the other was always guarding the rights of the patriotic mass of people. Calling for "associations of men" to counter "associations of wealth," Van Buren pictured the campaign of 1840 in archetypal fashion as a rerun of the party contests under Jefferson and Jackson.[30]

By assuming theirs to be the popular party, Democratic spokesmen also believed that a victory for the Whigs could only come by means of corruption and fraud. "The great point in our estimation is to prevent frauds," Van Buren accordingly wrote to Jackson, "and it is upon that only that I fear Tennessee." In New York, Van Buren's friends sought, on the eve of the election, to alert voters to new frauds by exposing an old fraud that had presumably enabled Whigs to win the state two years earlier. This was to be the "trump card" of the Democratic campaign, and it was calculated to affect the outcome in other states as well as in New York. In presenting the case to a grand jury, Benjamin F. Butler, a former attorney general and now district attorney for southern New York, charged that prominent New Yorkers, including Moses H. Grinnell, had imported a large number of laborers from Philadelphia, ostensibly to work on the Croton aqueduct but in fact to vote in the November 1838 election. While abundant evidence showed that money had been given to the "pipe layers"—a term now coined to designated fraudulent voters—none could prove that the "pipe layers" from Philadelphia had actually voted. Worst of all for the Democrats, the wide circulation that was given to the charges of fraud did not produce the desired effect upon public opinion, either in New York or elsewhere.[31]

Van Buren remained in Washington during the campaign of 1840 and took no active part in it. Until the end of the summer he was reported as being optimistic of the outcome, but the cumulative effect of Whig excitement must have been somewhat unnerving. Even more clearly the adverse returns from Maine, North Carolina, and Indiana, among the states that voted early, took a heavy toll; and before the final balloting in early November, he was so resigned to defeat, he later told Buchanan, that he "scarcely felt the catastrophe when it occurred." It is not known whether this mood of resignation had also been influenced by the forecast that an amateur astrologist had sent him in September. In any event, William Haworth's reading of the horoscopes for both Harrison and Van Buren led to a very interesting prediction: "Neither of the candidates (publicly nominated) for the president . . . will fill that office during the next four years." The death of Harrison one month after the inauguration in 1841 bore out one part of the prophecy; the electoral college took care of the other part.[32]

On the face of the returns, Van Buren had suffered an overwhelming defeat. While Harrison received 234 electoral votes from 19 states, Van Buren won only 60 votes from the other 7 states—Missouri, Illinois, New Hampshire, Virginia, South Carolina, Alabama, and Arkansas. Democratic spokesmen predictably blamed the defeat on deception and fraud, yet the apparent dimensions of the defeat also brought a sense of astonishment, bewilderment, and pain. The *Democratic Review* found the loss "no easy matter to believe or realize," at last an "incomprehensible revulsion of popular sentiment." But Philip Hone was not at all puzzled by the "prodigious magnitude" of Whig victory. It was a political landmark which overthrew a dynasty of forty years and ushered in a new political era. Using present-day language, Hone deemed it a "realigning election."[33]

A closer look at the returns, however, gave Democrats reason for both consolation and hope. Van Buren had actually received about 400,000 more votes in defeat than in his victory four years earlier. In New York alone, Azariah Flagg reported that the party had polled 20,000 more votes than in any previous canvass and that the rank and file had displayed throughout the contest an unprecedented degree of energy and zeal. Old Kinderhook Clubs in New York City, which were known for a time by a cryptic "O.K.," reflected the enthusiasm of party workers and gave a new term, in the process, to the nation's vocabulary. The *Washington Globe* pointed out, moreover, that the total margin of Whig victory in four crucial states—Pennsylvania, New Jersey, New York, Maine—was slightly over 16,000 and that a shift of only 8,088 votes would have given 90 added electors to Van Buren and a victory over Harrison by a count of 150 to 144.[34]

Recent studies confirm the contemporary observations that ascribed the Whig victory to the party's success in luring first-time voters. A summary of these studies shows that the high voter turnout in 1840 was the most distinctive and most decisive feature of the election. While only 55.4 percent of the eligible voters turned out in 1832 and 57.8 four years later, an astonishing 80.2 percent of the voters went to the polls in 1840. Because this high turnout was the result of unique and short-run causes, the contest of 1840 was not a "realigning election," as Hone substantially claimed, and certainly not in the way that the elections of 1800, 1860, 1896, and 1932 proved to be. One other consideration strengthens this conclusion. Even though Whigs had attained permanent party organization by 1840, there still remained in their ranks old antiparty feelings that disposed many of them, except in time of excitement or crisis, to be less active in political life than were their Democratic adversaries.[35]

Van Buren remained hopeful. He had no concept of a "realigning election," either of the term itself or its substance, for he believed that his party represented the permanent majority of the nation. This belief shaped his political career and gave basic form to the history of parties that he wrote late in his life. The defeat of the party in 1840 was therefore a temporary setback, an exceptional event produced by several things: foes had practiced deception and fraud; Clay had not been the opponent he desired; and a great commotion had served for a time to obscure the true issues separating the two parties. He did not see the campaign of

1840 as his last political step, nor did he see himself as a "used up man"; his trust remained in the "second sober thought" of the people. "Time," he wrote to Jackson on the day after the election, "will unravel the reasons by which these results have been produced & the people will then do justice to all."[36]

It was in this light that Van Buren composed his last annual message to Congress, making it at once a recital of his achievements and a reaffirmation of party principles. With justifiable pride he pointed to the relative quiet on the nation's extended frontiers, rightly supposing it to be in part a result of the "peace with honor" that he had fashioned in foreign affairs. At home he claimed that he had faithfully fulfilled all of the nation's obligations; he had also run the shop with efficiency and frugality in spite of a "formidable" opposition and "pecuniary embarrassments" that were unprecedented in time of peace. Individual citizens had suffered derangement in their pursuits, he admitted, yet most means of relief lay outside the powers of a government that was limited by the Constitution to matters of general concern. His currency policies did promise a sound recovery, however, as well as greater economic stability in the future, because the currency would be freer from the influences of the foreign and domestic money power.

Three things about his stewardship gave him particular satisfaction: he had not increased taxes, created a new debt, or turned for help to a new national bank. Here, as elsewhere, he wanted to identify his presidency in archetypal fashion with the primordial truths of his beau ideal, Thomas Jefferson. It had been in Jefferson's struggle against Alexander Hamilton's bank and debt policies, Van Buren supposed, that the original act of political creation had been made which had defined once and for all the differences between the political parties. At work during his term but temporarily obscured in the campaign of 1840, these same basic issues would continue to face the nation—in the upcoming session of Congress and in successive presidential contests. "The choice is an important one," he concluded, "and I sincerely hope that it will be made wisely." In this spirit, Benjamin F. Butler deemed the message a "worthy conclusion" to Van Buren's presidency, and a North Carolina partisan thought it had defined for all time the "true political creed of the republican party."[37]

What the message omitted was perhaps as significant as what it said, for his silence on the matter of abolitionism and slavery spoke loudly of an important achievement. Because abolitionism loomed so large at the time of his election in 1836, he made it the only specific issue raised in his Inaugural Address. His last presidential pronouncement, by contrast, made no mention of it at all. Many things had helped to diffuse the urgency of the issue, including the diversionary effect of economic problems and the way in which a maturing party system had worked to contain it. Van Buren nonetheless deserved credit for balancing abolitionist petitions and sectional interests on Texas, among other things, and for assimilating these actions into his economic and political principles. Friends and foes imputed different meanings to the view of Van Buren as a "northern man with southern principles," but he saw himself as a man of national principles who was seeking to preserve the Union as he thought the fathers had made it. The tribute that Thomas Hart Benton made to Van Buren's statesmanship in this regard was especially noteworthy, for it was written in the 1850s, at a time when growing sectional controversy was threatening to destroy the kind of Union that Van Buren had wanted to save: "His administration was auspicious to the general harmony, and presents a period of remarkable exemption from the sectional bitterness which so much afflicted the Union for some time before—and so much more sorely since."[38]

At the end of his presidency, as throughout his earlier career, Van Buren remained a champion of the Union as being the highest good. He contributed more perhaps than any other public figure in his age to the political formula that secured the Union throughout the decade of the 1850s. By grafting new party organization onto the older Jeffersonian ideology, he helped to provide a means for holding together a nation of such diverse elements. If the economic aspect of the formula, with its increasingly doctrinaire emphasis on a negative role for the government, seemed to be out of step with the facts of depression and the regnant spirit of enterprise, it reflected in large part the way in which dynamic forces of economic and social change had begun to strain the bonds of Union that had been fashioned by the fathers in an earlier and more stable age. It sheds further light on Van Buren's achievement to realize that the new Republican party of the 1850s, which was to reshape the Union, incorporated much of the Whiggish spirit of enterprise that had opposed Van Buren during his presidency.

Van Buren's gracious behavior as a defeated incumbent reaffirmed another aspect of his presidency, indeed of his entire career. In a letter to Jackson on the morrow of defeat, Van Buren expressed pride in his course yet vowed to give foes "abundant evidence" that he was leaving in good spirit. The ever-present Philip Hone found the president "fat and jolly," easy and elegant as usual in his hosting duties at the White House, presenting in no way the picture of a man who was about to relinquish the first office of the land.[39] In like spirit, Van Buren personally greeted the president-elect, William Henry Harrison, at the latter's hotel in Washington and soon invited him over to the White House as guest of honor at one of his celebrated dinner parties. Van Buren even offered to vacate the presidential mansion early so that Harrison and his family could move in before inauguration day. Had he received an invitation, Van Buren was also disposed to attend the inauguration ceremony of his successor and thereby to break the precedent against attendance by a defeated incumbent, which had been set by John Adams and followed by his son, John Quincy.

Events after Van Buren left the White House throw further light on the meaning of his presidency. Although victorious Whigs repealed the Independent Treasury in 1841, they were unable to replace it with a national bank. Revived in 1846 by a new Democratic administration, the Independent Treasury remained in operation until the Federal Reserve System was created in 1913. Thus, Van Buren's central domestic measure, which had been put forth in order to save the Jacksonian heritage, survived his defeat for reelection. The companion hope of promoting a stable currency and the growth of enterprise at a sober pace was not as clearly realized. The panics of 1857, 1873, and 1893 showed, instead, a persisting pattern of expansion and contraction. But the charge that the destruction of the national bank by Jackson and Van Buren had lifted all restraints during the nineteenth century must be qualified. By its management of the public debt and by its recurring use of treasury notes, the Independent Treasury did exercise a measure of control and did serve some of the functions of a central bank.[40] Nor is it an indisputable point that a national bank would have made much difference. The ''spirit of enterprise,'' which attained full self-consciousness in the politics of the Van Buren presidency, instead suggests the operation of forces that transcend in some degree particular policies or party programs.

Finally, circumstances in the wake of Van Buren's failure to gain the nomination of his party in 1844 served to underscore his success as president in giving the nation a period of repose. Because he was opposed to the annexation of Texas at the time, the Democratic National Convention denied him the opportunity to vindicate his defeat in 1840. With Jackson's blessing, the party turned instead to James K. Polk and a platform of expansionism that looked to the fulfillment of the nation's ''manifest destiny'' westward to the Pacific. Fatefully, however, the Mexican War, which was to realize this destiny, also raised the issue of the expansion of slavery and defined a sectional controversy that was to end with the Civil War. Van Buren reluctantly defected from the Democratic party in 1848 and stood as the nominee of the Free Soil party. Whatever his reasons for this defection, which another study might explore, he returned to the Democratic party during the 1850s in the belief that it offered the best means for holding the Union together. By the time of his death in 1862, however, the Civil War was transforming the kind of Union that he had sought, as president, to preserve.

NOTES

CHAPTER 1
A RESTLESS NATION

1. Alexis de Tocqueville, *Democracy in America*, 2 vols. (New York: Vintage Books, 1954); John William Ward, *Andrew Jackson: Symbol for an Age* (New York: Oxford University Press, 1962).

2. David Grimstead, "Rioting in Its Jacksonian Setting," *American Historical Review* 77 (1972): 361–397.

3. George Rogers Taylor, *The Transportation Revolution, 1815–1860* (New York: Harper & Row, 1968).

4. Douglass C. North, *The Economic Growth of the United States, 1790–1860* (New York: W. W. Norton, 1966).

5. Peter Temin, *The Jacksonian Economy* (New York: W. W. Norton, 1969).

6. Terms used in Michael A. Lebowitz, "The Jacksonians: Paradox Lost?" in *Towards a New Past*, ed. Barton J. Bernstein (New York: Vintage Books, 1969), pp. 65–89.

7. John R. Commons, *History of Labor in the United States*, 4 vols. (New York: Macmillan, 1918), 1:335–465.

8. Rowland Berthoff, *An Unsettled People: Social Order and Disorder in American History* (New York: Harper & Row, 1971).

9. William G. McLoughlin, *Modern Revivalism: Charles Grandison Finney to Billy Graham* (New York: Ronald Press, 1959).

10. Clifford S. Griffin, *Their Brothers' Keepers: Moral Stewardship in the United States, 1800–1865* (New Brunswick, N.J.: Rutgers University Press, 1960).

11. Emerson is cited in Alice Felt Tyler, *Freedom's Ferment: Phases of American Social History from the Colonial Period to the Outbreak of the Civil War* (New York: Harper & Row, 1962), p. 166.

12. Roy F. Nichols, *The Invention of the American Political Parties* (New York: Macmillan, 1967); Michael Wallace, "Changing Concepts of Party in the United States: New York, 1815–1828," *American Historical Review* 74 (1968): 453–491.

13. Robert V. Remini, *Martin Van Buren and the Making of the Democratic Party* (New York: W. W. Norton, 1970).

14. Robert V. Remini, *The Election of Andrew Jackson* (Philadelphia: J. B. Lippincott, 1963).

15. Amos Kendall, *Autobiography of Amos Kendall,* ed. William Stickney (Boston: Lee & Shepard, 1872), p. 453.

16. Alfred Balch to William Polk, December 3, 1828, cited in Charles G. Sellers, Jr., *James K. Polk: Jacksonian, 1795–1843* (Princeton, N.J.: Princeton University Press, 1957), p. 138.

17. Cited in Richard B. Latner, *The Presidency of Andrew Jackson: White House Politics, 1829–1837* (Athens: University of Georgia Press, 1979), p. 136.

18. David C. Martin, "Metallism, Small Notes, and Jackson's War on the B.U.S.," *Explorations in Economic History* 11 (1974): 227–247.

19. Stanley I. Kutler, *Privilege and Creative Destruction: The Charles River Bridge Case* (Philadelphia: J. B. Lippincott, 1971), pp. 117–132.

20. Latner, *Presidency of Jackson,* pp. 31–57.

21. Churchill C. Cambreling, cited in Major L. Wilson, " 'Liberty and Union': An Analysis of Three Concepts Involved in the Nullification Controversy," *Journal of Southern History* 33 (1967): 349.

22. *Annals of Congress,* 18th Cong., 1st sess., p. 1308; *Memoirs of John Quincy Adams,* ed. Charles Francis Adams, 12 vols. (Philadelphia: J. B. Lippincott, 1874–1877), 8:503.

23. An excellent accounting of the make-up of the Whig coalition is in John Vollmer Mering, *The Whig Party in Missouri* (Columbia: University of Missouri Press, 1967).

24. John M. McFaul, *The Politics of Jacksonian Finance* (Ithaca, N.Y.: Cornell University Press, 1972).

25. Fitzwilliam Byrdsall, *The History of the Loco Focos or Equal Rights Party* (New York: Burt Franklin, 1967).

26. Joel H. Silbey, "The Election of 1836," in *History of American Presidential Elections, 1789–1968,* ed. Arthur M. Schlesinger, Jr., 4 vols. (New York: Chelsea House, 1971), 1:575–640.

27. David Crockett, *The Life of Martin Van Buren* (Philadelphia: Robert White, 1835).

28. William J. Cooper, *The South and the Politics of Slavery, 1828–1856* (Baton Rouge: Louisiana State University Press, 1978), pp. 81–97.

29. Van Buren to Sherrod Williams, August 8, 1836, *Niles' Weekly Register,* September 10, 1836.

30. Van Buren to Junius Amis and others, March 4, 1836, and Richard E. Parker to Van Buren, June 29, 1836, in Papers of Martin Van Buren, Manuscripts Division, Library of Congress.

31. Silbey, "Election of 1836," pp. 639–640.

CHAPTER 2
THE ROAD TO THE WHITE HOUSE

1. Thomas Hart Benton, *Thirty Years' View*, 2 vols. (Westport, Conn.: Greenwood Press, 1968), 1:735.
2. Martin Van Buren, *The Autobiography of Martin Van Buren*, ed. John C. Fitzpatrick (New York: Augustus M. Kelley, 1969), pp. 9–12.
3. Ibid., p. 448.
4. John Forsyth is cited in *Albany Argus*, February 11, 1832.
5. Van Buren, *Autobiography*, p. 199.
6. Van Buren to Gorham Worth, April 22, 1819, Van Buren Papers.
7. Robert V. Remini, *Martin Van Buren and the Making of the Democratic Party* (New York: W. W. Norton, 1970), pp. 12–29.
8. Van Buren to Thomas Ritchie, January 13, 1827, Van Buren Papers.
9. Ibid.
10. J. G. A. Pocock, "Virtue and Commerce in the Eighteenth Century," *Journal of Interdisciplinary History* 3 (1972): 119–134; Lance Banning, *The Jeffersonian Persuasion: Evolution of a Party Ideology* (Ithaca, N.Y.: Cornell University Press, 1978), pp. 126–178.
11. Merrill D. Peterson, *The Jefferson Image in the American Mind* (New York: Oxford University Press, 1960), pp. 20–29.
12. Van Buren to Jesse Hoyt, November 8, 1828, cited in William Lyon MacKenzie, *The Life and Times of Martin Van Buren* (Boston: Cooke & Co., 1846), p. 204.
13. Kendall to Francis Blair, April 25, 1830, cited in Charles G. Sellers, Jr., *James K. Polk: Jacksonian, 1795–1843* (Princeton, N.J.: Princeton University Press, 1957), p. 148.
14. Marvin Meyers, *The Jacksonian Persuasion: Politics and Belief* (Stanford, Calif.: Stanford University Press, 1957), p. 112; Van Buren, *Autobiography*, p. 232; Van Buren to A. J. Donelson, August 26, 1832, Van Buren Papers.
15. Jackson to John Overton, December 31, 1829, *Correspondence of Andrew Jackson*, ed. John Spencer Bassett, 7 vols. (Washington, D.C.: Carnegie Institution, 1926–1935), 4:108; Van Buren to Jackson, August 19, 1833, ibid., 5:160; Van Buren to Jackson, September 11, 1833, Van Buren Papers.
16. Jackson to Van Buren, September 5 and December 17, 1831, *Correspondence*, 4:347, 385; Jackson to R. G. Dunlap, July 18, 1831, cited in John Spencer Bassett, *The Life of Andrew Jackson* (New York: Archon, 1967), p. 531; Jackson to John Overton, December 31, 1829, *Correspondence*, 4:108.
17. Van Buren, *Autobiography*, p. 171; Silas Wright to Azariah Flagg, February 2, 1833, cited in John Arthur Garraty, *Silas Wright* (New York: Columbia University Press, 1949), p. 102.
18. Frank Otto Gatell, "Second Sober Thoughts on Van Buren, the Albany Regency, and the Wall Street Conspiracy," *Journal of American History* 53 (1966): 19–40.
19. Van Buren, *Autobiography*, p. 679; Sydney Nathans, *Daniel Webster and*

Jacksonian Democracy (Baltimore, Md.: Johns Hopkins University Press, 1973), pp. 61–73.

20. Bedford Brown to Van Buren, September 24, 1834, Van Buren Papers.

21. Van Buren to Levi Woodbury, January 29, 1834, Papers of Levi Woodbury, Manuscripts Division, Library of Congress; Van Buren to William L. Marcy, March 31, 1834, Van Buren Papers.

22. Van Buren to Jackson, July 22, 1834, *Correspondence*, 5:274.

23. James A. Hamilton, *Reminiscences of James A. Hamilton* (New York: Charles Scribner, 1869), p. 94; Richard B. Latner, *The Presidency of Andrew Jackson: White House Politics, 1829–1837* (Athens: University of Georgia Press, 1979).

24. Latner, *Presidency of Jackson*, p. 127; Jackson to Joseph Guild, April 24, 1835, *Correspondence*, 5:339.

25. *Washington Globe*, June 12, 1835.

26. Philip Hone, *The Diary of Philip Hone, 1828–1851*, ed. Bayard Tuckerman, 2 pts. (New York: Dodd, Mead, 1910), 1:246; Lewis Linn to Silas Wright, April 8, 1837, Van Buren Papers.

27. Buchanan to Van Buren, February 16, 1837, Van Buren Papers; Niles to Gideon Welles, February 17, 1837, Papers of Gideon Welles, Manuscripts Division, Library of Congress; Van Buren to John Van Buren, December 30, 1836, Van Buren Papers.

28. James D. Richardson, comp., *A Compilation of the Messages and Papers of the Presidents*, 20 vols. (New York: Bureau of National Literature, 1897), 4:1530–1539.

29. Edward Pessen, "The Modest Role of Martin Van Buren," in *Six Presidents from the Empire State*, ed. Harry J. Sievers (Tarrytown, N.Y.: Sleepy Hollow Restoration, 1974), pp. 16–25; Rush Welter, *The Mind of America, 1820–1860* (New York: Columbia University Press, 1975), pp. 276–293.

30. David Grimstead, "Rioting in Its Jacksonian Setting," *American Historical Review* 77 (1972): 361–397.

CHAPTER 3
THE PANIC OF 1837

1. Douglass C. North, *The Economic Growth of the United States, 1790–1860* (New York: W. W. Norton, 1966), pp. 189–203; Albert Gallatin, *The Writings of Albert Gallatin*, ed. Henry Adams, 3 vols. (New York: Antiquarian Press, 1960), 3:388.

2. Bray Hammond, "Long and Short Term Credit in Early American Banking," *Quarterly Journal of Economics* 49 (1934): 79–103; *Congressional Globe*, 24th Cong., 1st sess., app., p. 470.

3. Peter Temin, *The Jacksonian Economy* (New York: W. W. Norton, 1969), pp. 59–82; Treasury Report, December 6, 1836, *Congressional Globe*, 24th Cong., 2d sess., p. 15.

4. Richard H. Timberlake, Jr., "The Specie Circular and Distribution of the Surplus," *Journal of Political Economy* 68 (1980): 109–117; Gallatin, *Writings*, 3:394.

5. *Congressional Globe*, 24th Cong., 2d sess., pp. 36–37.

6. Thomas Hart Benton, *Thirty Years' View*, 2 vols. (Westport, Conn.: Greenwood Press, 1968), 2:10.

7. Van Buren to Jackson, March 1837, Wright to Van Buren, March 21, 1837, Rives to Van Buren, April 7, 1837, Gorham Worth to Van Buren, March 12, 1837, and Thomas Cooper to Van Buren, April 14, 1837—all in Van Buren Papers.

8. Campbell White to Van Buren, March 14, 1837, Van Buren Papers.

9. Roger B. Taney to Van Buren, April 1, 1837, Van Buren Papers.

10. Jackson to Van Buren, March 30, 1837, *Correspondence of Andrew Jackson*, ed. John Spencer Bassett, 7 vols. (Washington, D.C.: Carnegie Institution, 1926–1935), 5:474–475.

11. Azariah Flagg to Van Buren, April 10, 1837, Van Buren Papers.

12. Gouge memo, March 19, 1837, and Jackson to Van Buren, March 30, 1837, Van Buren Papers.

13. Van Buren memo, March 24, 1837, Van Buren Papers; James C. Curtis, *The Fox at Bay: Martin Van Buren and the Presidency, 1837–1841* (Lexington: University Press of Kentucky, 1970), pp. 60–62.

14. Jackson to Van Buren, March 30, 1837, and Van Buren to Jackson, April 24, 1837, Van Buren Papers; Woodbury to Campbell White, April 3, 1837, and Woodbury to John A. King, April 29, 1837, Woodbury Papers.

15. Van Buren to Isaac Hone and others, May 4, 1837, Van Buren Papers.

16. John M. McFaul, *The Politics of Jacksonian Finance* (Ithaca, N.Y.: Cornell University Press, 1972), p. 186.

17. Nathaniel Niles to Rives, June 13, 1837, William C. Rives Papers, Manuscripts Division, Library of Congress.

18. Tallmadge to Rives, May 1, 1837, and Niles to Rives, May 6, 1837, Rives Papers.

19. Arthur M. Schlesinger, Jr., *The Age of Jackson* (Boston: Little, Brown & Co., 1945), p. 222; Nathaniel Niles to Rives, April 22, 1837, Rives Papers.

20. Van Buren to Rives, April 8, 1837, Van Buren Papers.

21. Temin, *Jacksonian Economy*, pp. 139–141; Reginald C. McGrane, *The Panic of 1837* (New York: Russell & Russell, 1965), pp. 91–99.

22. Curtis, *Fox at Bay*, p. 72.

23. North, *Economic Growth*, p. 201.

24. *National Intelligencer*, May 13, 1837; Public Informer to Van Buren, May 17, 1837, Van Buren Papers.

25. Adams to William Foster, July 1, 1837, in *Washington Globe*, August 1, 1837; John Arthur Garraty, *Silas Wright* (New York: Columbia University Press, 1949), pp. 141, 133.

26. Woodbury to Jackson, June 4, 1837, *Correspondence*, 5:485–486.

27. McFaul, *Jacksonian Finance*, does not even mention the efforts; James C. Curtis, *Fox at Bay*, p. 73, devotes less than a paragraph to them.

CHAPTER 4
A PROPOSAL OF DIVORCE

1. Niles to Welles, September 5, 1837, Welles Papers; *Congressional Globe,* 25th Cong., 1st sess., p. 103.

2. Campbell White to Woodbury, July 17, 1837, Woodbury Papers; Buchanan to Jackson, July 28, 1837, *Correspondence of Andrew Jackson,* ed. John Spencer Bassett, 7 vols. (Washington, D.C.: Carnegie Institution, 1926–1935), 5:501, 505.

3. Buchanan to Van Buren, June 5, 1837, Van Buren Papers; Grundy to Woodbury, June 1, 1837, Woodbury Papers; Van Buren to Rives, May 25, 1837, Rives Papers.

4. Throop to Van Buren, May 13, 1837, and Wright to Van Buren, June 4, 1837, Van Buren Papers.

5. Niles to Van Buren, July 1, 1837, Van Buren Papers.

6. Van Buren to Ritchie, August 11, 1837, Van Buren Papers.

7. Tallmadge to Rives, May 21 and 31, June 5 and 28, 1837, Allen to Rives, August 5, 1837, and Whitney to Rives, July 20, August 12, 1837, Rives Papers.

8. Jackson to Blair, July 9, 1837, *Correspondence,* 5:495–496; Raymond to Van Buren, July 26, 1837, Van Buren Papers.

9. William Gouge, *An Inquiry into the Expediency of Dispensing with Bank Currency in the Fiscal Concerns of the United States* (Philadelphia: William Stavely, 1837).

10. Brockenbrough to Rives, May 20, 1837, copy enclosed with Brockenbrough to Van Buren, May 22, 1837, Van Buren Papers; Arthur M. Schlesinger, Jr., *The Age of Jackson* (Boston: Little, Brown & Co., 1945), p. 227.

11. Niles to Van Buren, July 1, 1837, Van Buren Papers; Treasury Report, September 5, 1837, *Congressional Globe,* 25th Cong., 1st sess., app., pp. 1–8.

12. Thomas P. Govan, "Fundamental Issues of the Bank War," *Pennsylvania Magazine of History and Biography* 72 (1958): 305–315.

13. Buchanan to Van Buren, June 5, 1837, Van Buren Papers.

14. James Walker to James K. Polk, August 19, 1837, *Correspondence of James K. Polk,* ed. Herbert Weaver, 4 vols. (Nashville, Tenn.: Vanderbilt University Press, 1969–), 4:213.

15. Butler to Van Buren, August 4, 1837, Van Buren Papers.

16. Joseph H. Harrison, Jr., "Oligarchs and Democrats: The Richmond Junto," *Virginia Magazine of History and Biography* 78 (1970): 184–198.

17. Ritchie to Rives, August 2, 1837, Rives Papers.

18. Marcy to Prosper Wetmore, July 20, August 18, 1837, in Papers of William L. Marcy, Manuscripts Division, Library of Congress; Marcy to Van Buren, May 25, 1837, Van Buren Papers.

19. Welles to Van Buren, August 26, 1837, Welles Papers.

20. Niles to Welles, September 5, 1837, Welles Papers; Levi Reynolds to Woodbury, September 12, 1837, Woodbury Papers; Elam Tilden to Van Buren,

September 8, 1837, Van Buren Papers; Romulus Saunders to Woodbury, September 22, 1837, Woodbury Papers.

21. Special Session Message, September 5, 1837, James D. Richardson, comp., *A Compilation of the Messages and Papers of the Presidents*, 20 vols. (New York: Bureau of National Literature, 1897), 4:1541–1563.

22. Marcy to Albert Gallup, September 23, 1837, Marcy Papers.

23. *Congressional Globe*, 25th Cong., 1st sess., app., p. 4.

24. James C. Curtis, *The Fox at Bay: Martin Van Buren and the Presidency, 1837–1841* (Lexington: University Press of Kentucky, 1970), pp. 89–90.

25. Charles G. Sellers, Jr., *James K. Polk: Jacksonian, 1795–1843* (Princeton, N.J.: Princeton University Press, 1957), pp. 326–328.

26. Niles to Welles, September 15, 1837, Welles Papers.

27. *Congressional Globe*, 25th Cong., 1st sess., app., pp. 32, 156–164.

28. Niles to Welles, September 15, 1837, Welles Papers; *Senate Journal*, 25th Cong., 1st sess. (U.S. serial set no. 308), pp. 51–55.

29. *House Journal*, 25th Cong., 1st sess. (U.S. serial set no. 310), pp. 195–197.

30. *Congressional Globe*, 25th Cong., 1st sess., app., pp. 20, 111–113.

31. Rives to his wife, October 14, 1837, Rives Papers; Niles to Welles, October 3, 1837, Welles Papers.

32. Henry D. Gilpin is quoted in Major William B. Lewis to Rives, November 3, 1837, Rives Papers; Van Buren to Jackson, October 17, 1837, Van Buren Papers.

33. Van Buren to Jackson, October 17, 1837, Van Buren Papers.

CHAPTER 5
THE MEANING OF DIVORCE

1. John M. Niles to Welles, October 3, 1837, Welles Papers; *Congressional Globe*, 25th Cong., 1st sess., app., p. 195.

2. Ibid., p. 122.

3. Ibid., pp. 36–37; Calhoun to Anna Marie Calhoun, September 30, 1837, *Correspondence of John C. Calhoun*, ed. J. Franklin Jameson, *Annual Report* of the American Historical Association for 1899, 2 vols. (Washington, D.C.: Government Printing Office, 1900), 2:373.

4. *Congressional Globe*, 25th Cong., 1st sess., app., pp. 77, 101.

5. Ibid., pp. 168, 220, 183.

6. Ibid., pp. 184, 182, 200.

7. Ibid., p. 220.

8. Ibid., p. 232.

9. Ibid., pp. 201, 182.

10. Ibid., pp. 293, 182.

11. Ibid., pp. 229–236, 294, 181; Sydney Nathans, *Daniel Webster and Jacksonian Democracy* (Baltimore, Md.: Johns Hopkins University Press, 1973), pp. 109–114.

12. Michael A. Lebowitz, "The Jacksonians: Paradox Lost?" in *Towards a New Past: Dissenting Essays in American History,* ed. Barton J. Bernstein (New York: Random House, 1969), pp. 65–89.

13. Bray Hammond, *Banks and Politics in America From the Revolution to the Civil War* (Princeton, N.J.: Princeton University Press, 1957).

14. James Roger Sharp, *The Jacksonians Versus the Banks: Politics in the States after the Panic of 1837* (New York: Columbia University Press, 1970); William G. Carleton, "Political Aspects of the Van Buren Era," *South Atlantic Quarterly* 50 (1951): 167–185.

15. *Congressional Globe,* 25th Cong., 1st sess., app., p. 151; Walter T. K. Nugent, *Money and American Society, 1865–1880* (New York: Free Press, 1968), pp. 3–5; Clifford Geertz, "Ideology as a Cultural System," in *Ideology and Discontent,* ed. David E. Apter (New York: Free Press, 1964), pp. 47–76.

16. "The Moral of the Crisis," *Democratic Review* 1 (October 1837): 108.

17. *Congressional Globe,* 25th Cong., 1st sess., app., pp. 48, 94–95, 123; Parker to Ritchie, May 27, 1837, Van Buren Papers; Henry Adams, *The Life of Albert Gallatin* (New York: Peter Smith, 1943), p. 653.

18. Paulding to Van Buren, September 10, 1837, Van Buren Papers; Adams, *Gallatin,* p. 644; *Congressional Globe,* 25th Cong., 1st sess., app., pp. 103, 64. J. G. A. Pocock deals fully with this concept of republicanism in *Politics, Language, and Time: Essays on Political Thought and History* (New York: Atheneum, 1971), pp. 80–103.

19. *Congressional Globe,* 25th Cong., 1st sess., app., pp. 55, 50, 63; Charles Butler to Van Buren, September 6, 1837, Van Buren Papers.

20. John M. McFaul, *The Politics of Jacksonian Finance* (Ithaca, N.Y.: Cornell University Press, 1972), pp. 313–315; Robert Kelley, *The Cultural Pattern in American Politics: The First Century* (New York: Alfred A. Knopf, 1979), pp. 160–184; *Democratic Review* 1 (October 1837): 119.

21. *Congressional Globe,* 25th Cong., 1st sess., app., p. 55.

22. Wright to Van Buren, June 22, 1837, Van Buren Papers; *Congressional Globe,* 25th Cong., 1st sess., app., p. 100.

23. Marvin Meyers, *The Jacksonian Persuasion: Politics and Belief* (Stanford, Calif.: Stanford University Press, 1957); *Congressional Globe,* 25th Cong., 1st sess., app., pp. 296, 236.

24. *Congressional Globe,* 25th Cong., 1st sess., app., pp. 236, 181.

25. Gabor S. Boritt, *Lincoln and the Economics of the American Dream* (Memphis: Memphis State University Press, 1978).

26. Gerald Stourzh, *Alexander Hamilton and the Idea of Republican Government* (Stanford, Calif.: Stanford University Press, 1970); Lance Banning, *The Jeffersonian Persuasion: Evolution of a Party Ideology* (Ithaca, N.Y.: Cornell University Press, 1978); Daniel Walker Howe, *The Political Culture of the American Whigs* (Chicago: University of Chicago Press, 1979).

27. Jean V. Matthews, *Rufus Choate: The Law and Civic Virtue* (Philadelphia: Temple University Press, 1980), pp. 198–199; Major L. Wilson, "Paradox Lost: Order and Progress in Evangelical Thought of Mid-Nineteenth Century Amer-

ica," *Church History* 44 (1975): 352–366; *Congressional Globe*, 25th Cong., 1st sess., app., p. 200.

28. M. J. Heale, *The Making of American Politics, 1750–1850* (London: Longmans, 1977), pp. 178–190.

29. Ronald P. Formisano, "Political Character, Anti-Partyism and the Second Party System," *American Quarterly* 21 (1969): 683–709.

30. Robert Shalhope, "Toward a Republican Synthesis: The Emergence of an Understanding of Republicanism in American Historiography," *William and Mary Quarterly*, 3d ser., 29 (1972): 72, 49–80.

31. Otis to Van Buren, June 6, 1837, Van Buren Papers; *Congressional Globe*, 25th Cong., 1st sess., app., pp. 168, 181.

32. *Congressional Globe*, 25th Cong., 1st sess., app., pp. 164, 229, 192; Tallmadge to Rives, June 5, 1837, Rives Papers; Jean E. Friedman, "The Revolt of Conservative Democrats: An Essay in American Political Culture and Development, 1837–1844" (Ph.D. diss., Lehigh University, 1976).

33. *Congressional Globe*, 25th Cong., 1st sess., app., p. 182.

34. Charles A. Davis to Nicholas Biddle, September 27, 1837, *The Correspondence of Nicholas Biddle*, ed. Reginald C. McGrane (Boston: Houghton Mifflin, 1919), p. 293.

35. Eliot R. Barkan, "The Emergence of a Whig Persuasion: Conservatism, Democratism, and the New York State Whigs," *New York History* 52 (1971): 367–395.

36. Marcy to Albert Gallup, September 23, 1837, Marcy Papers.

37. Peter Wendell to Van Buren, November 13, 1837, Kearney ——— to Van Buren, November 12, 1837, and Charles Rond to Van Buren, November 25, 1837, Van Buren Papers.

38. Hammond to Van Buren, November 7, 1837, Azariah Flagg to Van Buren, November 9, 1837, and Paulding to Van Buren, November 14, 1837, Van Buren Papers; *National Intelligencer*, November 14, 1837.

CHAPTER 6
A SEPARATION WITHOUT DIVORCE

1. Van Buren to Jackson, November 18, 1837, Van Buren Papers.

2. Cambreleng to Van Buren, November 15, 1837, and M. Fourney to Van Buren, December 28, 1837, Van Buren Papers.

3. Throop to Van Buren, November 23, December 4 and 6, 1837, Van Buren Papers; Woodbury to J. D. Beers, November 17, 1837, Woodbury Papers; Kendall Memo, 1837, Van Buren Papers.

4. James D. Richardson, comp., *A Compilation of the Messages and Papers of the Presidents*, 20 vols. (New York: Bureau of National Literature, 1897), 4:1596–1605; Treasury Report, December 5, 1837, *Congressional Globe*, 25th Cong., 2d sess., pp. 9–14; *Washington Globe*, December 5, 1837.

5. *Congressional Globe*, 25th Cong., 2d sess., app., pp. 82-93.

6. Ibid., pp. 21–22, 62; Charles Maurice Wiltse, *John C. Calhoun: Nullifier, 1829–1839* (New York: Russell & Russell, 1968), pp. 369–376.

7. Niles to Welles, January 4, 1838, Welles Papers.

8. *Congressional Globe*, 25th Cong., 2d sess., app., pp. 618–619.

9. Ibid., pp. 176–181.

10. Ibid., pp. 632–641.

11. Van Buren to Jackson, March 2 and 17, 1838, Van Buren Papers.

12. *Congressional Globe*, 25th Cong., 2d sess., p. 250.

13. Niles to Welles, March 26, 1838, Welles Papers.

14. Biddle to Adams, April 5, 1838, in *National Intelligencer*, April 11, 1838; Reginald C. McGrane, *The Panic of 1837* (New York: Russell & Russell, 1965), pp. 192–196.

15. Throop to Van Buren, April 9, 1838, Van Buren Papers.

16. Woodbury to J. D. Beers, March 18, 1838, and to George Newbold, April 9, 1838, in *National Intelligencer*, April 13, 1838; *Congressional Globe*, 25th Cong., 2d sess., app., pp. 299–304.

17. Woodbury to Campbell White, April 19, 1838, Woodbury Papers; Van Buren to Jackson, April 17, 1838, Van Buren Papers.

18. *Congressional Globe*, 25th Cong., 2d sess., pp. 396–397; Clay to Biddle, May 30, 1838, *The Correspondence of Nicholas Biddle*, ed. Reginald C. McGrane (Boston: Houghton Mifflin, 1919), p. 309.

19. Van Buren to Jackson, March 2, 1837, Van Buren Papers.

20. Charles G. Sellers, Jr., *James K. Polk: Jacksonian, 1795–1843* (Princeton, N.J.: Princeton University Press, 1957), pp. 331–335.

21. *National Intelligencer*, June 27, 1838.

22. *Congressional Globe*, 25th Cong., 2d sess., pp. 495–496; *Washington Globe*, July 5, 1838.

23. Van Buren to Jackson, July 22, 1838, Van Buren Papers; Peter Temin, *The Jacksonian Economy* (New York: W. W. Norton, 1969), pp. 148–152.

24. Marcy to Prosper Wetmore, March 26, 1838, Marcy Papers; *Albany Argus*, June 30, 1838.

25. Charles Henry Ambler, *Thomas Ritchie: A Study in Virginia Politics* (Richmond: Bell Book & Stationery Co., 1913), pp. 201–206.

26. Ibid., pp. 204–205; Peter V. Daniel to Van Buren, August 8, 1838, Van Buren Papers; Rives to David Campbell, August 26, 1838, in Howard Braverman, "The Economic and Political Background of the Conservative Revolt in Virginia," *Virginia Magazine of History and Biography* 60 (1952): 283.

27. John Arthur Garraty, *Silas Wright* (New York: Columbia University Press, 1949), pp. 161–162.

28. Tallmadge to Richard Riker, March 28, 1838, *National Intelligencer*, April 6, 1838; *Washington Globe*, July 5, 1838.

29. Niles to Welles, June 1, 1838, Welles Papers; Tilden to Van Buren, February 28, 1838, Van Buren Papers; Jabez D. Hammond, *The History of Political Parties in the State of New York*, 3 vols. (Syracuse, N.Y.: Hall, Miles, 1852), 2:530.

30. *Albany Evening Journal,* July 9, 1838; Niles to Welles, May 27, 1838, Welles Papers; Parker to Van Buren, April 10, 1838, Van Buren Papers.

31. Joseph H. Parks, *Felix Grundy: Champion of Democracy* (University: Louisiana State University Press, 1940), pp. 323–327; Van Buren to Irving, April 23, 1838, and to Jackson, June 17, 1838, Van Buren Papers.

32. Biddle to Samuel Jaudon, August 3, 1838, *Correspondence,* pp. 318–321.

33. Van Buren memo, January 1839 (internal evidence suggests 1838), Van Buren Papers; Fritz Redlich, *The Molding of American Banking: Men and Ideas,* 2 pts. (New York: Johnson Reprint, 1968), 1:88–95.

34. *Congressional Globe,* 25th Cong., 2d sess., app., pp. 312–316, 330–331; *Democratic Review* 2 (May 1838): 113–128.

35. Redlich, *American Banking,* 1:187–204; Bray Hammond, "Long and Short Term Credit in Early American Banking," *Quarterly Journal of Economics* 49 (1934): 79–103.

36. *Plaindealer,* May 20, 1837; *Democratic Review* 5 (February 1839): 237–239.

37. Throop to Van Buren, April 26, 1838, Van Buren Papers; Albert Gallatin, *The Writings of Albert Gallatin,* ed. Henry Adams, 3 vols. (New York: Antiquarian Press, 1960), 3:428–446.

38. James Roger Sharp, *The Jacksonians versus the Banks: Politics in the States after the Panic of 1837* (New York: Columbia University Press, 1970), pp. 25–34, 328–329; Redlich, *American Banking,* 1:67–87.

39. *Albany Evening Journal,* May 11, 1838.

40. Bray Hammond, *Banks and Politics in America from the Revolution to the Civil War* (Princeton, N.J.: Princeton University Press, 1957), p. 598.

41. Van Buren to Jackson, July 22, 1838, Van Buren Papers.

CHAPTER 7

THE SECOND DECLARATION OF INDEPENDENCE

1. Kendall is cited in John Bach MacMaster, *A History of the People of the United States,* 8 vols. (New York: D. Appleton & Co., 1927–1929), 6:548–549.

2. Kendall to Van Buren, November 6, 1838, Van Buren Papers.

3. Van Buren to Jackson, November 16, 1838, Cambreleng to Van Buren, November 12, 1838, and Dix to Van Buren, November 15, 1838, Van Buren Papers; Marcy to Prosper Wetmore, December 11, 1838, Marcy Papers.

4. *Albany Evening Journal,* January 1, 1839.

5. Cambreleng to Van Buren, November 3, 1838, Van Buren Papers.

6. Van Buren to Jackson, November 16, 1838, Van Buren Papers; James D. Richardson, comp., *A Compilation of the Messages and Papers of the Presidents,* 20 vols. (New York: Bureau of National Literature, 1897), 4:1700–1702.

7. *Congressional Globe,* 25th Cong., 3d sess., p. 197.

8. Van Buren to Jackson, February 17, 1839, Van Buren Papers; 25th Cong., 3d sess., *House Report* 313 (U.S. serial set no. 352); Leonard D. White, *The*

Jacksonians: A Study in Administrative History, 1829–1861 (New York: Free Press, 1965), pp. 424-430.

9. *Congressional Globe,* 25th Cong., 3d sess., app., pp. 404-407, 113-123, 81-88; Van Buren to Jackson, January 8, 1839, Van Buren Papers.

10. *Congressional Globe,* 25th Cong., 3d sess., pp. 21-22; Niles to Welles, December 12, 1838, Welles Papers.

11. *Congressional Globe,* 25th Cong., 3d sess., pp. 354-359; William J. Cooper, *The South and the Politics of Slavery, 1828–1856* (Baton Rouge: Louisiana State University Press, 1978).

12. Wright to Woodbury, March 23, 1839, Cambreleng to Van Buren, April 30, 1839, Gouge to Van Buren, April 20, 1839, Woodbury Papers.

13. *Albany Evening Journal,* December 7, 1838; 25th Cong., 3d sess., *Senate Document* 113 (U.S. serial set no. 339).

14. Van Buren to Jackson, February 17, 1839, Van Buren Papers.

15. J. W. Worthington to Van Buren, February 28, 1839, Van Buren Papers; Jackson to Lewis, October 19, August 13, 1839, *Correspondence of Andrew Jackson,* ed. John Spencer Bassett, 7 vols. (Washington, D.C.: Carnegie Institution, 1926-1935), 6:33-36, 18-25; White, *Jacksonians,* p. 309.

16. *Albany Argus,* July 3 and 6, 1839.

17. Seward to Thomas G. Talmadge, June 30, 1839, Van Buren Papers; Philip Hone, *The Diary of Philip Hone, 1828–1851,* ed. Bayard Tuckerman, 2 pts. (New York: Dodd, Mead, 1910), 1:366.

18. *Albany Argus,* July 6 and 23, 1839; *Albany Evening Journal,* July 8, 11, 16, and 19, 1839; Van Buren to Schenectady Committee, August 1, 1839, Van Buren Papers.

19. Kendall to Van Buren, July 26, 1839, C. J. Ingersoll to Van Buren, July 11, 1839, Van Buren to Jackson, July 30, 1839, and Remarks at Castle Garden, July 2, 1839, Van Buren Papers.

20. Van Buren to Wright, September 21, 1839, and Woodbury to Van Buren, August 8, 1839, Van Buren Papers.

21. Peter Temin, *The Jacksonian Economy* (New York: W. W. Norton, 1969), pp. 148-155; Douglass C. North, *The Economic Growth of the United States, 1790–1860* (New York: W. W. Norton, 1966), pp. 201-203, 232-246.

22. Richardson, *Messages,* 4:1746-1772.

23. Marcy to Van Buren, December 31, 1839, Niles to Van Buren, December 28, 1839, and Lewis Yule to Van Buren, January 13, 1840, Van Buren Papers.

24. *Congressional Globe,* 26th Cong., 1st sess., app., pp. 460-464, 218-220.

25. *Washington Globe,* February 1, 1840; *Congressional Globe,* 26th Cong., 1st sess., app., pp. 93, 110-111.

26. *Senate Journal,* 26th Cong., 1st sess. (U.S. serial set no. 353), pp. 77, 131; *Congressional Globe,* 26th Cong., 1st sess., pp. 139-141.

27. *Washington Globe,* December 2, 1839; James C. Curtis, *The Fox at Bay: Martin Van Buren and the Presidency, 1837–1841* (Lexington: University Press of Kentucky, 1970), pp. 145-146.

28. Van Buren to Jackson, February 2, 1840, Van Buren Papers; *Congressional Globe*, 26th Cong., 1st sess., pp. 477, 495.

29. *Congressional Globe*, 26th Cong., 1st sess., app., pp. 116–123.

30. Calhoun to James Edward Calhoun, February 1, 1840, *Correspondence of John C. Calhoun*, ed. J. Franklin Jameson, *Annual Report* of the American Historical Association for 1899, 2 vols. (Washington, D.C.: Government Printing Office, 1900), 2:445.

31. Glyndon G. Van Deusen, *The Jacksonian Era, 1828–1848* (New York: Harper & Row, 1959), p. 114.

32. *House Journal*, 25th Cong., 2d sess. (U.S. serial set no. 320), pp. 1157–1159; *House Journal*, 26th Cong., 1st sess. (U.S. serial set no. 362), pp. 1175–1177.

33. Charles G. Sellers, Jr., *James K. Polk: Jacksonian, 1795–1843* (Princeton, N.J.: Princeton University Press, 1957), p. 373; William G. Shade, *Banks or No Banks: The Money Issue in Western Politics, 1832–1865* (Detroit, Mich.: Wayne State University Press, 1972), pp. 86–111; James Roger Sharp, *The Jacksonians versus the Banks: Politics in the States After the Panic of 1837* (New York: Columbia University Press, 1970), pp. 190–210.

34. *Congressional Globe*, 26th Cong., 1st sess., app., pp. 129–137.

35. Ibid., pp. 344–347, 617–621, 568.

36. Ibid., p. 726.

37. Ibid., pp. 838–840, 816–818, 797.

38. Ibid., pp. 777–784, 157–159, 495.

39. Ibid., pp. 725–730, 783.

40. Jackson to Van Buren, July 13, 1840, Van Buren Papers.

41. George Sullivan to Woodbury, March 4, 1840, Van Buren Papers.

CHAPTER 8

PEACE WITH HONOR

1. Justin H. Smith, *The War with Mexico*, 2 vols. (New York: Macmillan, 1919), 1:58–66; Samuel Flagg Bemis, *John Quincy Adams and the Union* (New York: Alfred A. Knopf, 1956), pp. 355–358; Alvin Laroy Duckett, *John Forsyth: Political Tactician* (Athens: University of Georgia Press, 1962), p. 199.

2. James D. Richardson, comp., *A Compilation of the Messages and Papers of the Presidents*, 20 vols. (New York: Bureau of National Literature, 1897), 4:1457, 1487.

3. Van Buren to John Van Buren, December 22, 1836, Van Buren Papers; John Spencer Bassett, *The Life of Andrew Jackson* (New York: Archon Books, 1967), pp. 682–683.

4. Richardson, *Messages*, 4:1496–1498; *Congressional Globe*, 24th Cong., 2d sess., pp. 218–219.

5. Hunt to Robert A. Irion, July 1, August 10 and 4, 1837, and Irion to Hunt, June 26, 1837, in George P. Garrison, ed., *Diplomatic Correspondence of the*

Republic of Texas, Annual Report of the American Historical Association for 1907, 2 vols. (Washington, D.C.: Government Printing Office, 1908), 2:237, 253, 245–247, 232–234.

6. Hunt to Forsyth, August 4, 1837, and Forsyth to Hunt, August 25, 1837, *House Executive Documents* 40, 25th Cong., 1st sess. (U.S. serial set no. 311), pp. 2–18.

7. Hunt to Irion, August 10, 1837, and P. W. Grayson to Houston, October 21, 1837, in Garrison, *Diplomatic Correspondence of Texas,* 2:253, 265; J. Fred Rippy, *Joel R. Poinsett: Versatile American* (Durham, N.C.: Duke University Press, 1935), pp. 114, 170.

8. Duckett, *Forsyth,* p. 211.

9. Richardson, *Messages,* 4:1595–1596; Bemis, *Adams,* pp. 361–363.

10. Smith, *War with Mexico,* 1:79–81.

11. Francis Fry Wayland, *Andrew Stevenson: Democrat and Diplomat, 1785–1857* (Philadelphia: University of Pennsylvania Press, 1949), pp. 115–118.

12. Charles Maurice Wiltse, *John C. Calhoun: Sectionalist, 1840–1850* (New York: Russell & Russell, 1968), p. 63; Thomas Hart Benton, *Thirty Years' View,* 2 vols. (Westport, Conn.: Greenwood Press, 1968), 2:183.

13. Duckett, *Forsyth,* pp. 185–186.

14. Bemis, *Adams,* pp. 384–410; *The United States* v. *The Amistad,* 15 Peters (January 1841 term), pp. 594, 518–598.

15. Bemis, *Adams,* pp. 384, 389; Woodbury to Van Buren, September 22, 1839, Van Buren Papers.

16. Albert B. Corey, *The Crisis of 1830–1842 in Canadian-American Relations* (New York: Russell & Russell, 1970), pp. 7–36.

17. Howard Jones, *To the Webster-Ashburton Treaty: A Study in Anglo-American Relations, 1783–1843* (Chapel Hill: University of North Carolina Press, 1977), pp. 23–27.

18. Poinsett to Scott, January 5, 1838, *Congressional Globe,* 25th Cong., 2d sess., p. 82.

19. Charles Winslow Elliott, *Winfield Scott: The Soldier and the Man* (New York: Macmillan, 1937), pp. 335–344; Winfield Scott, *Memoirs of Lieut. General Scott,* 2 vols. (Freeport, N.Y.: Books for Libraries Press, 1970), 1:312.

20. Fox to Forsyth, January 4, 1838, and Forsyth to Fox, January 5, 1838, in William R. Manning, ed., *Diplomatic Correspondence of the United States: Canadian Relations, 1784–1860,* 4 vols. (Washington, D.C.: Carnegie Endowment, 1943), 3:407–408, 31–32; Richardson, *Messages,* 4:1698.

21. Forsyth to Fox, January 5, 1838, Manning, *Diplomatic Correspondence of the U.S.,* 3:31–32; Richardson, *Messages,* 4:1618; *Statutes at Large,* 5:212–214.

22. Corey, *Crisis,* pp. 115–123.

23. Van Buren to James Hamilton, January 23, 1838, and Van Buren to Palmerston, May 16, 1838, Van Buren Papers; Palmerston is cited in Jones, *Webster-Ashburton Treaty,* p. 32; Rice is cited in Jacob Harvey to Van Buren, March 1, 1839, Van Buren Papers; Martin Van Buren, *The Autobiography of Martin*

Van Buren, ed. John C. Fitzpatrick (New York: Augustus M. Kelley, 1969), pp. 480–500.

24. Fox to Forsyth, December 13 and 29, 1840, Manning, *Diplomatic Correspondence of the U.S.*, 3:604, 606.

25. Forsyth to Fox, December 26 and 31, 1840, ibid., 3:127–129.

26. Howard Jones, "Anglophobia and the Aroostook War," *New England Quarterly* 48 (1975): 519.

27. Jones, *Webster-Ashburton Treaty*, pp. 3–8.

28. Fox to Forsyth, January 10, 1838, and Forsyth to Fox, April 27, 1838, Manning, *Diplomatic Correspondence of the U.S.*, 3:410–414, 53–54; Forsyth to Kent, May 8, 1838, Richardson, *Messages*, 4:1691–1692.

29. Fairfield to Van Buren, February 22, 1839, and Jackson to Van Buren, April 4, 1839, Van Buren Papers; David Lowenthal, "The Maine Press and the Aroostook War," *Canadian Historical Review* 27 (1951): 327, 315–336.

30. Richardson, *Messages*, 4:1733–1737, 1743; Forsyth to Fox, February 25, 1839, and Palmerston to Stevenson, April 3, 1839, Manning, *Diplomatic Correspondence of the U.S.*, 3:61–64, 494.

31. *Congressional Globe*, 25th Cong., 3d sess., app., pp. 308–331; Fox is cited in James C. Curtis, *The Fox at Bay: Martin Van Buren and the Presidency, 1837–1841* (Lexington: University Press of Kentucky, 1970), p. 186.

32. Elliott, *Winfield Scott*, pp. 358–366; Lowenthal, "Maine Press," pp. 331–333.

33. Butler to Van Buren, March 28, 1839, Van Buren Papers.

34. Draft of Negotiating Points, March 7, 1839, and Van Buren to Forsyth, June 6, 1839, Van Buren Papers.

35. Forsyth to Fox, July 29, 1839, Manning, *Diplomatic Correspondence of the U.S.*, 3:85–88.

36. Duckett, *Forsyth*, pp. 208–209.

CHAPTER 9
RUNNING THE SHOP

1. Gerald Cullinan, *The Post Office Department* (New York: Frederick A. Praeger, 1968), p. 51.

2. *Democratic Review* 1 (March 1838): 40; Amos Kendall, *Autobiography of Amos Kendall*, ed. William Stickney (New York: Peter Smith, 1949), p. 341.

3. Report, December 4, 1837, *Congressional Globe*, 25th Cong., 2d sess., app., pp. 11–12; James D. Richardson, comp., *A Compilation of the Messages and Papers of the Presidents*, 20 vols. (New York: Bureau of National Literature, 1897), 4:1756.

4. Wayne E. Fuller, *The American Mail: Enlarger of the Common Life* (Chicago: University of Chicago Press, 1972), pp. 111–113; Report, December 7, 1840, *Congressional Globe*, 26th Cong., 2d sess., app., pp. 14–18.

5. Kendall, *Autobiography*, pp. 348–354.

6. Kendall is cited in Richard P. Longaker, "Andrew Jackson and the Judiciary," *Political Science Review* 71 (1956): 354–355.

7. *Kendall v. the United States,* 12 Peters (January 1838 term), pp. 564–626.

8. Richardson, *Messages,* 4:1720–1722.

9. Daniel C. Haskell, *The United States Exploring Expedition, 1838–1842* (Westport, Conn.: Greenwood Press, 1968), pp. 1–5; William Stanton, *The Great United States Exploring Expedition of 1838–1842* (Berkeley: University of California Press, 1975), pp. 33–40.

10. *Washington Globe,* August 1 and 2, 1838; Paulding to Irving, September 10, 1838, *The Letters of James Kirke Paulding,* ed. Ralph M. Aderman (Madison: University of Wisconsin Press, 1962), p. 235.

11. Report, November 30, 1839, *Congressional Globe,* 26th Cong., 1st sess., app., pp. 26–28; Charles O. Paullin, *Paullin's History of Naval Administration, 1775–1911* (Annapolis, Md.: U.S. Naval Institute, 1968), pp. 188–189; Leonard D. White, *The Jacksonians: A Study in Administrative History, 1829–1861* (New York: Free Press, 1965), pp. 232–250.

12. Paulding to George Storer, November 10, 1840, to Hull, November 30, 1838, June 24, 1840, and to Kemble, March 25, 1839, Paulding, *Letters,* pp. 286, 239, 278, 252; Paullin, *Naval Administration,* p. 191.

13. *Decatur v. Paulding,* 14 Peters (January 1840 term), pp. 497–523.

14. Paulding to Kemble, June 16, 1839, Paulding, *Letters,* p. 258.

15. Haskell, *U.S. Exploring Expedition,* pp. 5–6; Richardson, *Messages,* 5:1835.

16. Paulding to Charles Stewart, February 4, 1841, Paulding, *Letters,* p. 294; J. Fred Rippy, *Joel R. Poinsett: Versatile American* (Durham, N.C.: Duke University Press, 1935), pp. 209–214.

17. Poinsett to James B. Campbell, April 20 and November 17, 1837, "The Poinsett-Campbell Correspondence," ed. Samuel G. Stoney, *South Carolina Historical and Genealogical Magazine* 42 (1941): 160, 168; White, *Jacksonians,* pp. 187–212.

18. Rippy, *Poinsett,* pp. 3–166.

19. Poinsett to Campbell, May 11, 1837, "Poinsett-Campbell Correspondence," p. 159.

20. Edwin C. McReynolds, *The Seminoles* (Norman: University of Oklahoma Press, 1957), p. 151; Daniel F. Littlefield, *Africans and Seminoles: From Removal to Emancipation* (Westport, Conn.: Greenwood Press, 1977), pp. 8–31.

21. *House Documents* 267, 24th Cong., 1st sess. (U.S. serial set no. 291), pp. 2–10.

22. Jesup to Adj. General Jones, June 5, 1837, in John T. Sprague, *The Origin, Purposes, and Conclusion of the Florida War* (New York: D. Appleton, 1848), p. 180.

23. John K. Mahon, *History of the Second Seminole War, 1835–1842* (Gainesville: University of Florida Press, 1967), pp. 201–218.

24. Jesup to Poinsett, February 11, 1838, and Poinsett to Jesup, March 1, 1838, in Sprague, *Origin,* pp. 199–201; Jackson to Poinsett, December 3, 1837,

Correspondence of Andrew Jackson, ed. John Spencer Bassett, 7 vols. (Washington, D.C.: Carnegie Institution, 1926–1935), 5:522; Richardson, *Messages,* 4:1719.

25. Littlefield, *Africans and Seminoles,* pp. 42–57.

26. Francis Paul Prucha, *The Sword of the Republic: The United States Army on the Frontier, 1783–1846* (New York: Macmillan, 1969), p. 269.

27. Poinsett to Campbell, October 17, 1837, "Poinsett-Campbell Correspondence," pp. 166, 165.

28. Winfield Scott, *Memoirs of Lieut. General Scott,* 2 vols. (Freeport, N.Y.: Books for Libraries Press, 1970), 1:317.

29. Grant Foreman, *Indian Removal: The Emigration of the Five Civilized Tribes of Indians* (Norman: University of Oklahoma Press, 1952), p. 8.

30. Richardson, *Messages,* 4:1714–1718.

31. *American State Papers: Military Affairs,* 7 vols. (Washington, D.C.: Gales Seaton, 1832–1861), 7:149–155.

32. Report, November 28, 1838, *Congressional Globe,* 25th Cong., 3d sess., app., pp. 1–5.

33. *Statutes at Large,* 5:256–260, 264–267.

34. Report, April 12, 1839, Van Buren Papers.

35. Report, November 30, 1839, *Congressional Globe,* 26th Cong., 1st sess., app., pp. 23–24; Report, March 20, 1840, *House Documents* 153, 26th Cong., 1st sess. (U.S. serial set no. 366), pp. 1–13.

36. Ritchie to Van Buren, June 1, 1840, Van Buren Papers.

37. Van Buren to Citizens of Elizabeth City, Virginia, July 31, 1840, *Richmond Enquirer,* August 7, 1840.

38. Report, December 5, 1840, *Congressional Globe,* 26th Cong., 2d sess., app., pp. 10–13; Poinsett to Van Buren, March 2, 1841, *Washington Globe,* May 3, 1841.

CHAPTER 10

THE LAST STEP

1. Van Buren to Jackson, February 17, 1839, Van Buren Papers.

2. Daniel to Van Buren, September 28, 1840, Van Buren Papers; Philip Hone, *The Diary of Philip Hone,* ed. Bayard Tuckerman, 2 pts. (New York: Dodd, Mead, 1910), 2:33.

3. Hone, *Diary,* 2:22; John Quincy Adams, *Memoirs of John Quincy Adams,* ed. Charles Francis Adams, 12 vols. (Philadelphia: J. B. Lippincott, 1874–1877), 10:355–356.

4. *Democratic Review* 7 (June 1840): 486, and 7 (November 1840): 395; Garrett Wall to Van Buren, November 5, 1840, Van Buren Papers; William Nisbet Chambers, "Election of 1840," in *History of American Presidential Elections, 1789–1968,* ed. Arthur M. Schlesinger, Jr., 4 vols. (New York: Chelsea House, 1971), 1:674.

5. Charles S. Todd to Seward, February 8, 1839, in Robert Gray Gunder-

son, *The Log Cabin Campaign* (Lexington: University Press of Kentucky, 1957), p. 51; *Sangamo Journal*, November 3, 1838, cited in Chambers, "Election of 1840," p. 694.

6. Biddle to Stevens, July 3, 1838, *The Correspondence of Nicholas Biddle*, ed. Reginald C. McGrane (Boston: Houghton Mifflin, 1919), p. 315.

7. Chambers, "Election of 1840," pp. 700-713; Gunderson, *Log Cabin*, pp. 57-66.

8. Hone, *Diary*, 1:398, 394.

9. Fillmore to G. W. Patterson, February 6, 1839, in Chambers, "Election of 1840," p. 651.

10. Thurlow Weed, *Autobiography of Thurlow Weed*, ed. Harriet A. Weed (Boston: Houghton Mifflin, 1884), p. 491; Hone, *Diary*, 2:22.

11. Adams, *Memoirs*, 7:530.

12. *Albany Evening Journal*, July 2, 1840; Gunderson, *Log Cabin*, pp. 101-107.

13. M. J. Heale, *The Making of American Politics, 1750-1850* (London: Longman, 1977), pp. 178-190; Chambers, "Election of 1840," pp. 702-703.

14. *National Intelligencer*, October 2, 1839; *Albany Evening Journal*, May 8, 1840.

15. Harrison to Harmar Denney, December 2, 1838, and speech at Dayton, September 10, 1840, in Chambers, "Election of 1840," pp. 695-699, 737-744.

16. *Albany Evening Journal*, February 14, 1840; *National Intelligencer*, January 14 and June 20, 1840.

17. Weed, *Autobiography*, p. 492; William Haywood to Van Buren, August 15, 1840, Van Buren Papers; *Hunt's Merchants' Magazine* 3 (October 1840): 307.

18. Chambers, "Election of 1840," pp. 741-742.

19. Charles G. Sellers, Jr., "Who Were the Southern Whigs?" *American Historical Review* 59 (1954): 335-346.

20. *Albany Evening Journal*, February 3, 1840.

21. Van Buren to Robert Steele, August 7, 1840, Van Buren Papers; Chambers, "Election of 1840," p. 691.

22. Kendall to Van Buren, August 22, 1839, Van Buren Papers; Van Buren to Jackson, April 1840, *Correspondence of Andrew Jackson*, ed. John Spencer Bassett, 7 vols. (Washington, D.C.: Carnegie Institution, 1926-1935), 6:55.

23. Chambers, "Election of 1840," pp. 691-692.

24. *Washington Globe*, May 14, 25, and 5, 1840; *Rough Hewer*, April 2, 1840.

25. *Richmond Enquirer*, May 8, 1840.

26. Kendall to Niles, August 9, 1840, Welles Papers.

27. *Democratic Review* 8 (September 1840): 198; Jackson to Blair, September 26, 1840, and Van Buren to Jackson, September 5, 1840, *Correspondence*, 6:76, 73.

28. Niles to Welles, July 4, 1840, Welles Papers.

29. *Washington Globe*, May 14, 1840.

30. Thoughts, March 1840, Van Buren Papers.

31. Van Buren to Jackson, September 5, 1840, *Correspondence*, 6:74.

32. Niles to Welles, August 12, 1840, Welles Papers; Van Buren to Buchanan, November 24, 1840, in James C. Curtis, *The Fox at Bay: Martin Van Buren*

and the Presidency, 1837–1841 (Lexington: University Press of Kentucky, 1970), p. 205; William Haworth to Van Buren, September 6, 1840, Van Buren Papers.

33. *Democratic Review* 8 (November 1840): 385; Hone, *Diary*, 2:52–53.

34. Flagg to Van Buren, November 15, 1840, Van Buren Papers; *Washington Globe*, December 28, 1840.

35. Chambers, "Election of 1840," pp. 690, 683.

36. Van Buren to Jackson, November 10, 1840, Van Buren Papers.

37. James D. Richardson, comp., *A Compilation of the Messages and Papers of the Presidents*, 20 vols. (New York: Bureau of National Literature, 1897), 5:1819–1837; Butler to Van Buren, December 11, 1840, and Bedford Brown to Van Buren, February 17, 1841, Van Buren Papers.

38. Thomas Hart Benton, *Thirty Years' View*, 2 vols. (Westport, Conn.: Greenwood Press, 1968), 2:207–208.

39. Van Buren to Jackson, November 10, 1840, Van Buren Papers; Hone, *Diary*, 2:59–61.

40. David Kinley, *The Independent Treasury of the United States and Its Relations to the Banks of the Country* (New York: Augustus M. Kelley, 1970); Ester Rogoff Taus, *Central Banking Functions of the United States Treasury, 1789–1941* (New York: Russell & Russell, 1943); Richard H. Timberlake, Jr., "The Independent Treasury and Monetary Policy before the Civil War," *Southern Economic Journal* 27 (1960): 92–103.

BIBLIOGRAPHICAL ESSAY

It is not the purpose of this essay to deal extensively with the scholarship of the Jacksonian period. A work that was first published in 1935 by W. Harvey Wise, Jr., and John W. Cronin, comps., *A Bibliography of Andrew Jackson and Martin Van Buren* (New York: Burt Franklin, 1970), still has value and supplements the more-extensive listings compiled by Robert V. Remini and Edwin A. Miles in *The Era of Good Feelings and the Age of Jackson, 1816–1841* (Arlington Heights, Ill.: AHM Publishing Corp., 1979). A remarkably well packed bibliographical essay appears in Edward Pessen, *Jacksonian America: Society, Personality, and Politics* (Homewood, Ill.: Dorsey Press, 1969); and three historiographical essays are especially useful: Charles Grier Sellers, Jr., "Andrew Jackson versus the Historians," *Mississippi Valley Historical Review* 44 (1958): 615–634; Alfred A. Cave, *Jacksonian Democracy and the Historians* (Gainesville: University of Florida Press, 1964); and Ronald P. Formisano, "Toward a Reorientation of Jacksonian Politics: A Review of the Literature, 1959–1975," *Journal of American History* 63 (1976): 42–65.

Despite a great body of Jacksonian scholarship, comparatively little has been done on the presidency of Martin Van Buren. Three older biographies—Edward M. Shepard's *Martin Van Buren* (Boston and New York: Houghton, Mifflin, & Co., 1889), Denis Tilden Lynch's *An Epoch and a Man: Martin Van Buren and His Times* (New York: Horace Liveright, 1929), and Holmes Alexander's *The American Talleyrand: The Career and Contemporaries of Martin Van Buren, Eighth President* (New York: Harper & Brothers, 1935)—are dated in many ways and devote relatively little space to the years in the White House. A new biography—John Niven's *Martin Van Buren: The Romantic Age of American Politics* (New York: Oxford University Press, 1983)—is rich in materials for Van Buren's whole career; but it covers the White House years very rapidly, devoting only three of the thirty-two chapters to Van Buren's presidency. Dated but richer in coverage and detail are such older standard works as Hermann Eduard Von Holst's *The Constitutional and Political History of the United States,* 8 vols. (Chicago: Callaghan & Co., 1881–1892); James Schouler's *History of the United States of America, under the Constitution,* 7 vols. (New York: Dodd, Mead, 1885–1913); John Bach MacMaster's *A History of the People of the United States, from the Revolution to the Civil War,* 8 vols. (New York: D. Appleton & Co., 1927–1929). One older and one more recent work do a good job with the relationship between Van Buren and Jackson: Marquis James, *Andrew Jackson: Portrait of a President* (Indianapolis: Bobbs-Merrill, 1937), and Richard B. Latner, *The Presidency of Andrew Jackson: White House Politics, 1829–1837* (Athens: University of Georgia Press, 1979). Three other works deal sympathetically with Van Buren, but their interpretations ultimately focus on his presidency as being the "third term" of Jackson: Frederick Jackson Turner, *The United States, 1830–1850: The Nation and Its Sections* (New York: Henry Holt & Co., 1935); Arthur M. Schlesinger, Jr., *The Age of Jackson* (Boston: Little, Brown & Co., 1945); Glyndon G. Van Deusen, *The Jacksonian Era, 1828–1848* (New York: Harper & Row, 1959).

The only volume that is devoted exclusively to the subject is James C. Curtis, *The Fox at Bay: Martin Van Buren and the Presidency, 1837–1841* (Lexington: University Press of Kentucky, 1970). Joel H. Silbey, among that book's early critics (*American Historical Review* 76 [1971]: 1602–1603), rightly pointed to a relative neglect of economic factors, too much focus on the intraparty problems of Van Buren, and too little attention to the increasingly ideological and national dimension of party debate. Along with its weaknesses, however, there are much greater strengths. It reposes upon an impressive body of sources, utilizes relevant secondary studies, and constitutes, in fact, the point of departure for further study of Van Buren.

A number of other works should be consulted. There are biographies for three cabinet members: Joseph H. Parks, in *Felix Grundy: Champion of Democracy* (University: Louisiana State University Press, 1940), throws light on the politics of the South and the Southwest; while J. Fred Rippy, in *Joel R. Poinsett: Versatile American* (Durham, N.C.: Duke University Press, 1935), and Alvin Laroy Duckett, in *John Forsyth: Political Tactician* (Athens: University of Georgia Press, 1962), are best when dealing with departmental matters. Two books about long-time political associates—John Arthur Garraty's *Silas Wright* (New York: Columbia University Press, 1949) and Ivor Debenham Spencer's *The Victor and the Spoils: A Life of William L. Marcy* (Providence, R.I.: Brown University Press, 1959)—do a better job with the New York than with the Washington side of Van Buren's presidency; and the same is true of a work about his other power base in Virginia: Charles Henry Ambler's *Thomas Ritchie: A Study in Virginia Politics* (Richmond, Va.: Bell Book & Stationery Co., 1913). The following are especially good on politics in other states: Donald B. Cole, *Jacksonian Democracy in New Hampshire, 1800–1851* (Cambridge: Harvard University Press, 1970); John Niven, *Gideon Welles: Lincoln's Secretary of the Navy* (New York: Oxford University Press, 1973); Charles McCool Snyder, *The Jacksonian Heritage: Pennsylvania Politics,*

1833–1848 (Harrisburg: Pennsylvania Historical and Museum Commission, 1958). Among other works on men who were close to the president are: William Nisbet Chambers, *Old Bullion Benton: Senator from the New West: Thomas Hart Benton, 1782–1858* (Boston: Little, Brown, 1956); William Ernest Smith, *The Francis Preston Blair Family in Politics*, 2 vols. (New York: Macmillan, 1933); Philip S. Klein, *President James Buchanan: A Biography* (University Park: Pennsylvania State University Press, 1962).

Biographies of two prominent figures provide the best general coverage of the Van Buren years: Charles Maurice Wiltse, *John C. Calhoun*, 3 vols. (Indianapolis: Bobbs-Merrill, 1944–1951, and Russell & Russell, 1968), vols. 2 and 3; and Charles G. Sellers, Jr., *James K. Polk: Jacksonian, 1795–1843* (Princeton, N.J.: Princeton University Press, 1957). Works on leading Whig spokesmen are also very helpful: Glyndon G. Van Deusen, *The Life of Henry Clay* (Boston: Little, Brown & Co., 1937), *William Henry Seward* (New York: Oxford University Press, 1967), and *Thurlow Weed: Wizard of the Lobby* (Boston: Little, Brown & Co., 1947); Sydney Nathans, *Daniel Webster and Jacksonian Democracy* (Baltimore, Md.: Johns Hopkins University Press, 1973); Thomas Payne Govan, *Nicholas Biddle: Nationalist and Public Banker, 1786–1844* (Chicago: University of Chicago Press, 1959). Samuel Flagg Bemis, *John Quincy Adams and the Union* (New York: Alfred A. Knopf, 1956), is good on Texas and slavery issues; Charles Winslow Elliott, *Winfield Scott: The Soldier and the Man* (New York: Macmillan, 1937), devotes a good deal of space to the foreign crises and the problem of Indian removal; Francis Fry Wayland, *Andrew Stevenson: Democrat and Diplomat, 1785–1857* (Philadelphia: University of Pennsylvania Press, 1949), is very pertinent for Anglo-American relations; and two books by Justin H. Smith provide valuable background for Van Buren's relations with Mexico and Texas: *The War with Mexico*, 2 vols. (New York: Macmillan, 1919), and *The Annexation of Texas* (New York: Barnes & Noble, 1941).

The fact that Van Buren came between the more-dramatic presidencies of Jackson and Polk explains some of the neglect that his administration has suffered. But there is also a problem of sources, and Van Buren was partly responsible. Students will always regret his failure to carry the account of his career beyond 1834. However self-serving, *The Autobiography of Martin Van Buren*, edited by John C. Fitzpatrick, the *Annual Report* of the American Historical Association for 1918, 2 vols. (Washington, D.C.: Government Printing Office, 1920; reprint, New York: Augustus M. Kelley, 1969), volume 2, has been of great use in studying his earlier career and, had it been carried forward, would have been of enormous value in reconstructing the course of his presidency. The most basic source remains his papers, assembled largely by himself in preparing the autobiography in the 1850s and turned over to the Library of Congress in 1904 and 1905 by a daughter-in-law, Mrs. Smith Thompson Van Buren. Elizabeth Howard West, *Calendar of the Papers of Martin Van Buren* (Washington, D.C.: Government Printing Office, 1910), is a very reliable guide. Although letters written by Van Buren comprise only a small portion of this voluminous material, they are obviously indispensable. Many of the incoming letters are of particular value as well, because they were responses to his own. Much of the other correspondence also yields special insights when read in close conjunction with his messages, for these latter often reflected rather closely the varied perceptions and pressures bearing in upon him. Of great use also are the exchanges between Van Buren and Jackson that are found in *Correspondence of Andrew Jackson,* edited by John Spencer Bassett, 7 vols. (Washington, D.C.: Carnegie Institution of Washington, 1926–1935).

Other sources available for the study of Van Buren's presidency are also uneven. The extensive researches of James C. Curtis (*Fox at Bay,* pp. 211–212) turned up very little material on most of the cabinet members. *The Letters of James Kirke Paulding,* edited by Ralph M. Aderman (Madison: University of Wisconsin Press, 1962), and "The Poinsett-Campbell Correspondence," edited by Samuel G. Stoney, *South Carolina Historical and Genealogical Magazine* 42 (1941): 31–52, 149–168, and 43 (1942): 27–34, are not very extensive and deal mainly with matters in the Navy and War departments. In two cases the lack of material is especially critical, for Benjamin F. Butler was closest to Van Buren; and Amos Kendall, though not personally as close, did exert great political influence. Nor is the *Autobiography of Amos Kendall,* edited by William Stickney (New York: Peter Smith, 1949), of much use, for it pertains chiefly to his earlier career and to personal matters in the Post Office Department. The Papers of Levi Woodbury, Manuscripts Division, Library of Congress, are an exception, for they richly document Van Buren's dealings with the "Specie Circular" issue, responses to the panic of 1837, and formulation of fiscal policy. Numerous letters from Francis P. Blair to Jackson, in *Correspondence of Jackson,* also yield insights on the course of the administration.

One lamentable gap in the sources was due to the failure of Van Buren's most-trusted associates, Senator Silas Wright and Congressman Churchill C. Cambreleng, to leave significant traces of the maneuvers in Congress. Nor, unfortunately, does *Correspondence of James K. Polk,* edited by Herbert Weaver, 4 vols. (Nashville, Tenn.: Vanderbilt University Press, 1969–), provide much help; it is important chiefly for politics and the outlook of Polk's friends in Tennessee and the Southwest. The best source for the actions of Congress is the correspondence between Senator John M. Niles and Gideon Welles, found in the Papers of Gideon Welles, Manuscripts Division, Library of Congress. Volume 2 of the *Correspondence of John C. Calhoun,* edited by J. Franklin Jamison, the *Annual Report* of the American Historical Association for 1899, 2 vols. (Washington, D.C.: Government Printing Office, 1900), is important but less extensive. *The Papers of Willie P. Mangum,* edited by Henry T. Shanks, 4 vols. (Raleigh, N.C.: State Department of Archives and History, 1952), and the *Memoirs of John Quincy Adams,* edited by Charles Francis Adams, 2 vols. (Philadelphia: J. B. Lippincott, 1874–1877), are also helpful. Thomas Hart Benton, *Thirty Years' View,* 2 vols. (Westport, Conn.: Greenwood Press, 1968), is valuable, though it was written during the 1850s and is further distorted by the senator's sense of self-importance.

A great number of studies on the office of the presidency, done mainly by political scientists, have come out in recent years; but they are relevant to the modern presidency more than to the office during the early part of the nineteenth century. One notable exception is Richard E. Neustadt, *Presidential Power: The Politics of Leadership* (New York: John Wiley & Sons, 1961). A good sampling of these studies appears in an anthology compiled by Stanley Bach and George T. Sulzner, *Perspectives on the Presidency* (Lexington, Mass.: D. C. Heath, 1974). Of much greater value are a number of works that deal with the decline of the presidency after Jefferson and its dramatic revival under Jackson. Among these are Wilfred E. Binkley, *The Man in the White House: His Powers and Duties* (Baltimore, Md.: Johns Hopkins University Press, 1958); Edward S. Corwin, *The President: Office and Powers, 1787–1957* (New York: New York University Press, 1957); William M. Goldsmith, ed., *The Growth of Presidential Power: A Documented History*, 3 vols. (New York: Chelsea House, 1974); James Sterling Young, *The Washington Community, 1800–1828* (New York: Columbia University Press, 1966); Robert V. Remini, *Andrew Jackson and the Bank War: A Study in the Growth of Presidential Power* (New York: W. W. Norton, 1967). Though Van Buren was not a powerful figure like Jackson, two things illustrated the enhanced power of the office: Van Buren's threat to veto measures of Congress dealing with slavery or a national bank and the expectation placed on him to provide leadership after the panic of 1837. The magisterial work of Leonard D. White, *The Jacksonians: A Study in Administrative History, 1829–1861* (New York: Macmillan, 1954), is good for an overall perspective, but it devotes relatively little space to administrative matters during the Van Buren presidency.

Two works provide a broad economic background for understanding the Van Buren years: Paul Wallace Gates, *The Farmer's Age: Agriculture, 1815–1860* (New York: Harper & Row, 1960), and George Rogers Taylor, *The Transportation Revolution, 1815–1860* (New York: Rinehart, 1951). With regard to the central economic event of Van Buren's presidency, a book first published in 1924, Reginald C. McGrane's *The Panic of 1837: Some Financial Problems of the Jacksonian Era* (New York: Russell & Russell, 1965), contains rich descriptive material but is weak on analysis of economic forces. A number of studies meet this need by placing the economy of the United States in the perspective of a debtor nation in relation to creditor England: R. C. O. Matthews, *A Study of Trade-Cycle History: Economic Fluctuations in Great Britain, 1833–1842* (Cambridge: Cambridge University Press, 1954); William B. Smith and Arthur H. Cole, *Fluctuations in American Business, 1790–1860* (Cambridge: Harvard University Press, 1935); J. G. Williamson, "International Trade and United States Economic Development, 1827–1843," *Journal of Economic History* 21 (1961): 372–383. In this connection, Douglass C. North, *The Economic Growth of the United States, 1790–1860* (New York: W. W. Norton, 1966), shows that "king cotton" was central in the relations between England and the United States and that cotton was the "carrier industry" for dynamic economic development within the United States. Peter Temin, *The Jacksonian Economy* (New York: W. W. Norton, 1969), clearly distinguishes the panic of 1837 from the more profound downturn two years later and demonstrates that the extraordinary influx of specie after 1834 was one important cause of currency inflation preceding the panic.

Two articles give focus to the debate over the relative impact of Jackson's policies on the panic of 1837: Richard H. Timberlake, Jr., "The Specie Circular and Distribution of the Surplus," *Journal of Political Economy* 68 (1960): 109–117; Harry N. Schieber, "The Pet Banks in Jacksonian Politics and Finance, 1833–1841," *Journal of Economic History* 23 (1963): 196–214. An older work, first published in 1885, Edward G. Bourne, *The History of the Surplus Revenue of 1837* (New York: Burt Franklin, 1968), covers all aspects of the distribution problem. Walter B. Smith, *Economic Aspects of the Second Bank of the United States* (Cambridge: Harvard University Press, 1953), and Bray Hammond, *Banks and Politics in America from the Revolution to the Civil War* (Princeton, N.J.: Princeton University Press, 1957), deal fully with the cotton speculations of Nicholas Biddle and the suspension in 1839. For an impressionistic account of other aspects of economic dislocation see Samuel Rezneck, "Social History of an American Depression, 1837–1843," *American Historical Review* 40 (1935): 662–687.

An understanding of Van Buren's central domestic measure, the Independent Treasury, can be deepened by a close reading of works on banking and currency at the time. Among the more important are: Albert Gallatin, *Considerations on the Currency and Banking System of the United States* (Westport, Conn.: Greenwood Press, 1968); William Gouge, *A Short History of Paper Money and Banking in the United States* (New York: Augustus M. Kelley, 1968); Condy Raguet, *A Treatise on Currency and Banking* (New York: Augustus M. Kelley, 1967); Charles Francis Adams, *Reflections upon the Present State of Currency in the United States* (Boston: Ezra Lincoln, 1837); Richard Hildreth, *Banks, Banking, and Paper Currencies* (Westport, Conn.: Greenwood Press, 1968). Sister M. Grace Madeleine, *Monetary and Banking Theories of Jacksonian Democracy* (New York: Kennikat Press, 1970); Harry E. Miller, *Banking Theories in the United States before 1860* (New York: Augustus M. Kelley, 1962); and Fritz Redlich, *The Molding of American Banking: Men and Ideas* (New York: Johnson Reprint, 1968), are among recent works of great value. For all its virtues, the magisterial work of Bray Hammond, *Banks and Politics,* sorely neglects the Van Buren administration and misconceives of the divorce proposal as being a measure for liberating banks from government control. Politically, Van Buren proposed divorce of the Treasury from banks as an alternative to the old national bank; economically, he saw it as being in line with the Jacksonian quest for a way to control currency that would replace the old national bank. Two works are very good on this quest for a new form of control: David A. Martin, "Metallism, Small Notes, and Jackson's War with the B.U.S.," *Explorations in Economic History* 11 (1974): 227–247; and John M. McFaul, *The Politics of Jacksonian Finance* (Ithaca, N.Y.: Cornell University Press, 1972).

In this connection, a special effort has been made in the present volume to analyze at some length the enormously important distinction between the deposit and the funds-receivable aspects of the divorce proposal. Three works dealing with the later operation of the Independent Treasury clearly show the elements of currency control: David Kinley, *The Independent Treasury of the United States and Its Relations to the Banks of the Country* (New York: Augustus M. Kelley, 1970); Ester Rogoff Taus, *Central Banking Functions of the United States Treasury, 1789–1941* (New York: Russell & Russell, 1943); and Richard H. Timberlake, Jr., "The Independent Treasury and Monetary Policy before the Civil War," *Southern Economic Journal* 27 (1960): 92–103.

The growing unity among Whigs and an effective party organization together constituted a central political development of Van Buren's presidency and brought to maturity the two-party system. Building on certain emphases in Lee Benson, *The Concept of Jacksonian Democracy: New York as a Test Case* (New York: Atheneum, 1966), many studies place primary stress on "ethnocultural" factors in the formation of parties and in the voting behavior of the masses. Of particular prominence are Ronald P. Formisano, *The Birth of Mass Parties: Michigan, 1827–1861* (Princeton, N.J.: Princeton University Press, 1971), and William G. Shade, *Banks or No Banks: The Money Issue in Western Politics, 1832–1865* (Detroit, Mich.: Wayne State University Press, 1972). Two review articles strongly challenge the extended claims of the ethnocultural explanation: Richard P. McCormick, "Ethnocultural Interpretations of Nineteenth-Century American Voting Behavior," *Political Science Quarterly* 89 (1974): 351–377; and Richard B. Latner and Peter Levine, "Perspectives on Antebellum Pietistic Politics," *Reviews in American History* 4 (1976): 15–23. A book by William J. Cooper, *The South and the Politics of Slavery, 1828–1856* (Baton Rouge: Louisiana State University Press, 1978), argues at length for the primacy of the slavery issue; but a larger number of recent studies tend to agree with the thesis in Charles G. Sellers, Jr., "Who Were the Southern Whigs?" *American Historical Review* 62 (1957): 537–551—namely, that economic concerns were most important and that southern Whigs moved toward the economic nationalism of their northern colleagues: Norman D. Brown, *Edward Stanly: Whiggery's Tarheel "Conqueror"* (University: University of Alabama Press, 1974); Burton W. Folsom II, "Party Formation and Development in Jacksonian America: The Old South," *Journal of American Studies* 7 (1973): 217–229; John Vollmer Mering, *The Whig Party in Missouri* (Columbia: University of Missouri Press, 1967).

Debate over economic issues, particularly the currency, gave increasing coherence to the lines of party division. Yet the debate was not as sharply drawn as Schlesinger supposed in the *Age of Jackson*, that is, one between the business community and the rest of the people. Walter Hugins, *Jacksonian Democracy and the Working Class: A Study of the New York Workingmen's Movement, 1829–1837* (Stanford, Calif.: Stanford University Press, 1960), shows that most eastern radicals did not question the rights of capital, private property, and enterprise. The debate, as suggested earlier by William G. Carleton in "Political Aspects of the Van Buren Era," *South Atlantic Quarterly* 50 (1951): 167–185, was over the proper pace of enterprise and the role of the government in the process. James Roger Sharp, *The Jacksonians versus the Banks: Politics in the States after the Panic of 1837* (New York: Columbia University Press, 1970), demonstrates that in most parts of the country, Whig constituencies were more fully integrated into the market economy than were Democratic ones and that Democrats most often placed themselves on the restrictive side of economic issues in the state legislatures. Other studies confirm this finding: Shade, *Banks or No Banks;* Herbert Ershkowitz and William G. Shade, "Consensus or Conflict? Political Behavior in the State Legislatures during the Jacksonian Era," *Journal of American History* 58 (1971): 591–621; Peter D. Levine, *The Behavior of State Legislative Parties in the Jackson Era: New Jersey, 1829–1844* (Rutherford, N.J.: Fairleigh Dickinson University Press, 1977). Frank Otto Gatell, "Second Sober Thoughts on Van Buren, the Albany Regency, and the Wall Street Conspiracy," *Journal of American History* 53 (1966): 19–40, also finds that Van Buren and his political associates in New York were on the restrictive side.

Studies on the ideology of "republicanism" serve to refine and deepen an understanding of the party contests. To match Marvin Meyers, *The Jacksonian Persuasion: Politics and Belief* (Stanford, Calif.: Stanford University Press, 1957), are a number of studies on the outlook of Whigs: Elliot R. Barkan, "The Emergence of a Whig Persuasion: Conservatism, Democratism, and the New York State Whigs," *New York History* 52 (1971): 367–395; Jean V. Matthews, *Rufus Choate: The Law and Civic Virtue* (Philadelphia: Temple University Press, 1980); Daniel Walker Howe, *The Political Culture of the American Whigs* (Chicago: University of Chicago Press, 1979). Another work, M. J. Heale, *The Making of American Politics, 1750–1850* (London: Longman, 1977), fruitfully suggests that Democrats and Whigs divided the old republican heritage—the one was conservative on the economic side, the other on the social and political side—and that both had great appeal during a period of wrenching change. Jean E. Friedman, "The Revolt of the Conservative Democrats: An Essay on American Political Culture and Political Development, 1837–1844" (Ph.D. diss., Lehigh University, 1976), contends that the ideology of republicanism played a large part in the defection of Conservatives from Van Buren's party. Two books by Robert Kelley attempt to synthesize the economic, political, and ethnocultural elements: *The Transatlantic Persuasion: The Liberal-Democratic Mind in the Age of Gladstone* (New York: Alfred A. Knopf, 1969) and *The Cultural Pattern in American Politics: The First Century* (New York: Alfred A. Knopf, 1979). When read in this context, Van Buren's *Inquiry into the Origin and Course of Political Parties in the United States* (New York: Augustus M. Kelley, 1967) takes on greater significance for the study of his presidency.

In the perspective of party contests during Van Buren's presidency, the election of 1840 was anything but a confirmation of political consensus as presented by Louis Hartz in *The Liberal Tradition in America: An Interpretation of American Political Thought since the Revolution* (New York: Harcourt, Brace, 1955). The only book-length account of the campaign—Robert Gray Gunderson's *The Log Cabin Campaign* (Lexington: University of Kentucky Press, 1957)—does provide considerable support for Hartz's view; but a much sounder assessment can be found in William Nisbet Chambers, "Election of 1840," in *History of American Presidential Elections, 1789–1968*, edited by Arthur M. Schesinger, Jr., 4 vols. (New York: Chelsea House, 1971), 1:643–744. For all the excitement and emotion of the campaign, there were deeper concerns that divided the parties and appealed to the voters. In a more general way, two important articles provide a critique of the consensus view: J. G. A. Pocock, "Virtue and Commerce in the Eighteenth Century," *Journal of Interdisciplinary History* 3 (1972): 119–134; and Frank Otto Gatell, "Beyond Jacksonian Consensus," in *The State of American History*, edited by Herbert J. Bass (Chicago: Quadrangle Books, 1970), pp. 350–359.

INDEX

Abolitionism: in context of other reforms, 5; and mob in Charleston, 14; and petitions to Congress, 14; Van Buren's pledge against, 19, 41; Slade's speech on, 109–110. *See also* Gag rule

Adams, John Quincy: and election of 1824, 7–8, 27, 29; and election of 1828, 8–9; on Jacksonian democracy, 14; opposes Texas annexation, 14; and outrage over suspension, 56; on resumption, 107; and organization of House, 139; on Texas, 148; on crisis with Mexico, 152; on *Amistad*, 156; on Indians, 185; and log cabin campaign, 192

Albany (N.Y.) *Argus:* supports Regency, 6; on "Specie Circular," 49; on divorce, 69, 112; on Locofocos, 97; on Van Buren's trip to New York, 131–132

Albany (N.Y.) *Evening Journal,* 96, 132, 192, 195, 199

Albany Regency, 6, 96, 97

Allen, Thomas, 64

American System: policies of, 8; Adams on, 8, 29; undone by Jackson, 10–12; in relation to slavery, 14

Amistad: crisis with Spain over, 154–157

Anti-Mason party, 10, 14, 30; and Whig coalition in New York, 96, 193; nominates Harrison, 198

Aroostook War: background of, 165; precipitated by Maine, 166; response of Congress to, 167–168; and truce, 168. *See also* Northeastern boundary dispute

Atherton, Charles, 128

Augusta (Maine) *Journal,* 168

Baldwin, Roger, 156

Baltimore (Md.) *Republican:* coins "log cabin and cider" phrase, 195–196

Banking. *See* Credit system; Currency; Free banking; State banks

Bank of the United States: Clay's recharter of, 11; Jackson's war on, 11–12, 34–35; defeat of, 62; and paper medium for exchange, 66; as a check on state banks, 67; Van Buren's view of, 71; under Pennsylvania Charter, 102; and "resurrection notes," 102, 108; and bond deal with Treasury, 116; and suspension, 133–134

Bankruptcy measure: Butler's advice on, 67–68; Van Buren's proposal of, 73; defeat of, 77, 137; opposed by Calhoun, 81; opposed by Whigs, 83, 143; and insolvency measure as alternative to, 143

Barbour, James, 197, 199

Barbour, Philip P., 27

Bayard, Richard H., 82, 83

Bell, John, 15, 16, 74, 110, 139, 197

Bemis, Samuel Flagg: on *Amistad* case, 156

Benton, Thomas Hart: hard-money views of, 15; on "Specie Circular," 15, 47; on Van Buren's inauguration, 21; warns of crisis, 49; supports bankruptcy measure, 77, 137; on republicanism, 88; on Clay-Calhoun encounter, 104; on state banks,

117; opposes assuming state debts, 138; on passage of divorce bill, 138; on the meaning of divorce, 139–140; and censure of Jackson, 192; praises Van Buren presidency, 209

Biddle, Nicholas: and "resurrection notes," 102; opposes resumption, 107; for repeal of "Specie Circular," 107; and bond deal with Treasury, 116, 128; and suspension, 133–134

Black, Edward, 139

Blair, Francis: as editor of *Washington* (D.C.) *Globe*, 10; and Van Buren, 68

Booz, E. C.: and "booze" in campaign of 1840, 192

Brockenbrough, John: and moderate interpretation of divorce, 65; and Richmond Junto, 68

Buchanan, James: criticizes Van Buren's appointments, 39; on divorce proposal, 62; on Van Buren's "committalism," 62; on government paper, 66; and check on state banks, 67, 81, 137; on republicanism, 87, 90, 142; is instructed against divorce, 106; chairs Foreign Relations Committee, 152; for peace with Mexico, 152; his role in Aroostook crisis, 167

"Bucktails," 6, 8, 18, 25, 27

Burke, Edmund, 142

Butler, Benjamin F.: as Van Buren's law partner, 23; retained as attorney general, 38; on bankruptcy measure, 67–68; leaves cabinet, 115; on Stockton and Stokes case, 174–175; charges Whig fraud, 206; praises Van Buren's last message, 208

Cabinet: Van Buren's selection of, 38–39; later appointments to, 115–116, 156, 205

Caesarism, xii, 13, 17, 21

Calderón de la Barca, Angel: as Spain's minister to U.S., 155; in *Amistad* case, 155, 157

Calhoun, John C.: and election of 1824, 7; and election of 1828, 8–9; and alienation from Jackson, 9–10; in nullification crisis, 11; and Whig party, 15; as rival of Van Buren, 30; on tariff, 32; and specie amendment, 76; and radical interpretation of divorce, 80; and sectional interpretation of divorce, 80–81; and defection from Whig party, 81, 105; opposes bankruptcy measure, 81; on republicanism, 87–88, 91; and role in 1837/1838 session, 103–106; proslavery resolutions of, 103–104, 152; administration's view of, 103–

104; and confrontation with Clay, 104–105; and personal relations with Van Buren, 105; opposes Cuthbert amendment, 106; opposes divorce bill in 1838/1839 session, 127; on Clay's antiabolitionist speech, 128; opposes small-note amendment, 137; on the meaning of divorce, 140; on slave brigs, 154; as political ally of Poinsett, 181

Cambreleng, Churchill C.: as administration spokesman in House, 76; on divorce bill, 76–77; on ideology of divorce, 86; in 1837/1838 session, 110; on New York elections, 125; on Swartwout defalcation, 126; in 1838/1839 session, 126; opposes compromise on divorce, 129–130

Campaigning, techniques of: Democratic contributions to, 6, 30; and "log cabin and cider," 191–192; and "image campaign," 192; and "Tippecanoe and Tyler Too," 194

Canadian crisis, 157–163; Navy Island occupied in, 158; and *Caroline* affair, 158; and retaliation for *Caroline*, 160; raids at Prescott and Windsor during, 160; and Durham Report, 161; and McLeod case, 162–163

Caroline affair: British actions in, 158; congressional response to, 160; diplomatic handling of, 162; and McLeod case, 162–163

Carroll, William, 202

Cass, Lewis, 32

Catlin, George, 183

Channing, William Ellery, 149

Choate, Rufus, 92

Cilley, Jonathan: killed in duel, 110

Cinque: in *Amistad* case, 155

Clark, John, 77, 192

Clay, Henry: and election of 1824, 7; and compromise tariff, 11; on censure of Jackson, 13, 35; and Whig party, 14–15; and bank issue in 1832, 34; his encounter with Van Buren, 35; on defeat of divorce bill, 77; on a national bank, 82; on state-bank notes, 83–84; on currency, 84, 85; on republicanism, 91; and party spirit, 94; on divorce and Caesarism, 95; and confrontation with Calhoun, 104–105; defends Biddle, 109; and repeal of "Specie Circular," 109; and Cilley duel, 110; and speech against abolitionism, 128; as likely Whig nominee, 128, 130; on credit system and enterprise, 143, 144; on bankruptcy measure, 143; and defeat on the nomination, 193–195

Clayton, John, 143, 194
Clinton, De Witt: as political foe of Van Buren, 6, 18, 25; as governor, 26; memory of, invoked by Seward, 132; widow of, snubs Van Buren, 132
Conservative Democrats: oppose "Specie Circular," 54; led by Tallmadge and Rives, 61; and defection from Van Buren, 63–64; cooperate with Whigs, 75, 83; antiparty views of, 94–95; vote against divorce, 111; Van Buren's estimate of, 112–113; dismissal of, by Van Buren, 131; coalesce with New York Whigs, 193
Cooper, John, 144
Cooper, Mark, 139
Cranch, William, 174
Crawford, William: and election of 1824, 7; Van Buren and, 8
Credit system: nature of, 15, 45; praised by Tallmadge, 45; as foil of hard money, 83; and support of enterprise, 83–85; as substitute for capital, 84; and ties to English credit, 136, 142; defended by Whigs, 143. See also State banks; Enterprise, spirit of
Croswell, Edwin, 97
Currency: bank-note component of, 44–45; specie component of, 45–46; expansion and contraction of, 45–46; effect of Deposit Act on, 47; hard-money views on, 50–51; effect of suspension on, 55; Whig views of, 84–85; Democratic views of, 85. See also Credit system; State banks
Currency Resolution (1816): and divorce proposal, 75–76, 126; and divorce bill, 106, 112, 114
Cuthbert, Alfred, 106, 107

Dade, Francis, 182
Daniel, Peter V., 191
Davis, John, 144, 199
Democratic party: differences within, over currency, 15–16; and convention in 1835, 16; differences within, over "Specie Circular," 49–51; and response to suspension, 56; greater unity in, 85–86; on enterprise, 85, 90; constituencies of, 86, 89; and concept of republicanism, 87–90, 205–206; and views on party organization, 89, 92–93; and strategy in final divorce debate, 141–142; differences within, over Texas, 151–152; southern strategy of, 201–202; on the vice-presidency, 201–202; and strategy in campaign of 1840, 202–205
Democratic Republican party, 8–9, 27

Democratic Review: on panic of 1837, 87; on party ideology, 89; on bank reform, 117, 119; on log cabin campaign, 192, 204; and election results, 206
Deposit Act (1836): connects Treasury to state banks, 15; distributes surplus, 15; inflationary intent of, 46–47; deflationary effect of, 47; impact of suspension on, 61; and efforts to amend, 111–112
Deposit banks: number of, increased by Deposit Act, 47; effect of "Specie Circular" on, 50; Van Buren's criticism of, 71
Dickerson, Mahlon: retained as secretary of the navy, 38; favors national bank, 70; leaves cabinet, 115, 175; on the exploring expedition, 176; and naval discipline, 177
Divorce bills: in special session, 75–76; in 1837/1838 session, 102–103; as amended by Cuthbert, 106; impact of, on resumption, 107; in 1838/1839 session, 126–127; in 1839/1840 session, 138–139; meaning of House vote on, 141
Divorce proposal: political reasons for, 63; deposit side of, 64, 71; funds-receivable side of, 64–65, 71–72; radical interpretation of, 64–65; moderate interpretation of, 65–67; made at special session, 71–72; republicanism in, 73–74, 86–87; and focus on funds-receivable side, 79–80, 84; and charge of Caesarism, 95, 114, 121; renewed by Van Buren, 101, 126, 135–136; and pragmatism of Van Buren's course on, 140–141
Dix, John, 125
Durfee, Amos, 158

Eaton, John, 10
Economic cycle: of 1830s, 3, 44–55, 133–134; role of "king cotton" in, 3, 54, 133; and spirit of enterprise, 3; and impact on labor, 4; panic of 1837 as interruption in, 43, 55; impact of English credit on, 44, 46, 134; effect of Jackson's policies on, 45–46; and end of, in 1839, 133–134
Ellis, Powhatan, 148
Emerson, Ralph Waldo, 5, 179
Enterprise, spirit of: Tocqueville on, 1; and economic cycle, 3; and credit system, 45, 84–85; Democrats on, 85, 90; Whigs on, 86, 91–92; and republican virtue, 91–92; in triumph of free banking, 120; invoked against Independent Treasury, 143; and military discipline, 177, 180; in campaign of 1840, 199–200, 203; in later nineteenth century, 210. See also Credit system

Erie Canal, 2, 26, 32

Exploring Expedition, South Seas: launched by Van Buren, 113; originated by Adams, 176; delays in, 176; itinerary of, 179; and discovery of Antarctica, 179; other achievements of, 179–180

Fairfield, John: his role in Aroostook War, 166–168

Federalist party, 7

Fillmore, Millard, 195

Finney, Charles G., 4

Flagg, Azariah, 207

Forsyth, John: retained as secretary of state, 38; on Texas, 148, 151; on Mexico, 150; as a party man, 151–152; his style as secretary of state, 151; on *Amistad* case, 155, 156; on Canadian crisis, 159, 160, 162; on McLeod case, 162–163; on northeastern boundary crisis, 168–169; mentioned for vice-president, 201, 202

Fox, Henry: as England's minister to U.S., 158; in Canadian crisis, 158, 160, 162; on McLeod case, 162–163; on Aroostook crisis, 166–167

Free Banking: Van Buren objects to, 117; New York bill on, 117–118; principle of, 118; radical criticism of, 118–119; conservative criticism of, 119; later triumph of, 119–120; as a Whig coup, 120

Gag rule: passed in 1836, 14; renewed, 110, 128; strengthened in 1840, 201

Gallatin, Albert: on economic cycle, 44, 49; on Deposit Act, 47; on republicanism, 87, 88; on resumption, 107; criticizes free banking, 119

Garland, Rice, 192

Garrison, William Lloyd, 5, 14

Geertz, Clifford, 86

Giddings, Joshua R., 185

Gilpin, Henry D.: as attorney general, 156; on *Amistad* case, 156

Gouge, William: supports "Specie Circular," 51; hard-money views of, 51; and radical interpretation of divorce, 65; advises Van Buren on divorce, 130

Government land: rise in revenue from, 3; Jackson opposes sale of, 11; Clay's bill distributing revenues of, 33; decline in revenue from, 58; preemption of, 102; graduating price of, 102

Granger, Francis, 194

Graves, William, 110

Greeley, Horace: edits *Log Cabin* in 1840, 192–193

Green, Duff, 18

Greenhow, Robert, 150

Grinnell, Moses, 206

Grundy, Felix: on coalition with Webster, 34–35; fears national bank, 62; opposes bankruptcy measure, 77; instructed against divorce bill, 106; and bill against "resurrection notes," 108; becomes attorney general, 115; opposes assuming state debts, 138; on *Amistad* case, 155; in campaign of 1840, 202–203

Gunderson, Robert, 198

Hamer, Thomas, 108

Hamilton, Alexander: policies of, 7, 28; and republicanism, 88, 92

Hamilton, James, 30

Hammond, Bray: on Jackson's bank war, 85; on free banking, 120

Hammond, Jabez, 97, 115

Hard money: Jackson on, 11–12; and "Specie Circular," 15, 47, 50–51; Gouge as high priest of, 51; in relation to divorce proposal, 64–65. *See also* Currency; Enterprise, spirit of

Harrison, William Henry: as Whig candidate in 1836, 17, 19; nominated over Clay in 1840, 144; praised for "availability," 193; early career of, 196; cast as Cincinnatus, 196; on issues in campaign, 198, 199–200; is criticized for "non committalism," 204; election of, 206–207; is invited to White House, 209–210

Harvey, William: as governor of New Brunswick, 165; his involvement in Aroostook War, 166–168

Head, Francis Bond: as governor of Upper Canada, 157; and the Canadian crisis, 157, 158

Hildreth, Richard, 199

Hill, Isaac, 202

Holabird, William S., 155

Hone, Philip: on Van Buren's presidency, 38; on Van Buren's trip to New York, 132; on log cabin campaign, 192, 196; on Harrison, 195; on election results, 206–207; on Van Buren, 209

Hooe, George M., 200

Hull, Isaac, 178

Hunt, Memucan: as minister from Texas, 150; requests admission of Texas to Union, 150–151

Hunter, Robert M. T., 139

Hunter's Lodge: supports Canadian rebels, 160

Immigration, 2
Independent Treasury: as basic measure of Van Buren, xi; called the second declaration of independence, 123, 142; established in 1840, 123; as alternative to national bank, 191; as issue in campaign of 1840, 203; later operations of, 210. *See also* Divorce bills
Indian removal: Choctaws, Chickasaws, and Creeks, 181; Seminoles, 181–185; Cherokees, 184, 185–187; Sacs, Foxes, Potawatomies, and Winnebagos, 185; Van Buren on, 186–187
Internal improvements: and canals and railroads, 2–3; and American System, 8; and Maysville Road bill, 10, 32; impact of English credit on, 44, 134; state debts for, 138
Irving, Washington, 24, 115

Jackson, Andrew: popular perceptions of, 1–2, 21–22; and mob violence, 2; in election of 1824, 7–8; in election of 1828, 8–9; response of, to nullification, 11; hard-money views of, 11–12; and war on national bank, 11–12, 34; and growth of presidential power, 12–13; censured by Senate, 13; at Van Buren's inauguration, 21–22; and Van Buren, 31–32; policies of, 32–35; on the Union, 33–34; on coalition with Webster, 34; on party organization, 36–37; issues "Specie Circular," 47; vetoes Rives bill, 48–49; pressures Van Buren on "Specie Circular," 52; on suspension, 58; on Van Buren's "committalism," 62; and Blair, 68; vindicated by divorce proposal, 70; on patronage, 131; on political effect of Independent Treasury, 144; and crisis with Mexico, 147, 149; on Texas annexation, 148–149; on Maine dispute, 164; and Aroostook War, 166; on Seminole War, 184; supports Polk, 210
Jefferson, Thomas: and Republican party, 7; on republicanism, 28–29; on party organization, 29
Jesup, Philip S.: in Seminole War, 182–184; on Dade Capitulation, 182; and proposal of truce, 184
Johnson, Richard M.: is nominated for vice-president, 16; is supported by Locofocos, 16, 202; and nomination in 1840, 202; and Tecumseh, 202
Jones, John W., 139
Jones, Thomas ap Catesby, 176
Judson, Andrew P., 156

Kendall Amos: on the Jackson presidency, 9; on the Calhoun–Van Buren rivalry, 31; retained as postmaster general, 38; favors compromise on divorce, 101; on Independent Treasury, 123; on elections of 1838, 124; on Van Buren's trip to New York, 132; on *Amistad* case, 155; early career of, 171–172; and postal reforms, 172; proposes other reforms, 173; his problems with Stockton and Stokes, 174–175; on executive power, 174; in campaign of 1840, 197, 203–204; opposes Johnson for vice-president, 201
Kent, Edward, 165
King, John, 94
King, Rufus, 17, 18

Legaré, Hugh S., 91, 181
Leggett, William, 118
Leigh, Benjamin W., 194
Lewis, Dixon, 139
Lewis, William B., 131
Liberator, 5
Lincoln, Abraham: on spirit of enterprise, 91; in log cabin campaign, 193, 196, 199
Lincoln, Levi, 197
Livingston, Edward, 32
Locofocos: hard-money views of, 15–16; oppose Van Buren in 1836, 18; favor divorce proposal, 69; applaud special-session message, 71–72; as Whig foil in New York, 97; and Van Buren's trip to New York, 132; support Johnson, 202
Lundy, Benjamin, 14, 148

MacKenzie, William Lyon, 158, 161
McLeod, Alexander: arrested in New York, 162; diplomatic crisis over, 162–163
Madison, James: and Republican party, 7; and suspension of 1814–1816, 57; and national bank, 59; and resumption in 1816, 108
Madisonian, 64, 75
Maine: and boundary dispute with New Brunswick, 163–169; and adamant position on boundary, 164; party politics of, in boundary dispute, 165–166

Mangum, Willie P., 19
Marcy, William L.: opposes divorce proposal, 69; on New York elections in 1837, 97; on resumption, 108; reassesses divorce proposal, 112; is passed over for cabinet, 116; loses governor's election, 125; praises Van Buren's message, 137
Martinez, Francisco, 152
Maysville Road bill, 10, 32
Mexico: Jackson and, 148–149; Van Buren and, 150, 152–153. *See also* Texas
Missouri controversy: and party organization, 7, 13, 17, 27, 28
Mobs: as related to Jackson, 2; tabulated in *Niles' Register*, 40–41; Van Buren's views on, 41
Monroe, James, 7, 27, 70
Montez, Pedro, 154, 155, 156
Morris, Thomas, 106

National Gazette, 148
National Institution: founded by Poinsett, 180; succeeded by the Smithsonian Institution, 180
National Intelligencer, 75, 98, 111, 152, 158, 198
National Republican party, 8, 14
Nat Turner insurrection, 14
Navy Department: under Van Buren, 175–180; problems of discipline in, 177–178; regular operations of, 178–179; exploring expedition under, 179
Neutrality: and Neutrality Act of 1818, 157, 159; violations of, on Canadian border, 158, 160; Van Buren's proclamations of, 159, 160; and new legislation, 160
New Jersey: disputed House seats from, 139
New York: as Empire State, 2, 27; party organization in, 5–6; and elections of 1834, 35–36; delegation of merchants from, 51–52; suspension of banks in, 54; and elections in 1837, 96–97; bank convention in, 107; greater Democratic unity in, 112; free-banking law in, 117–118; and elections of 1838, 124; Van Buren's trip to, 131–133
New York Herald, 158
Niles, John M.: criticizes Van Buren's appointments, 39; on "Specie Circular," 53; on divorce proposal, 61, 64, 66, 77; on republican virtue, 88; criticizes Calhoun, 104, 107; on Van Buren's leadership, 115; passed over for cabinet, 116; on state banks, 117; defends Woodbury, 127; on

gag rule, 128; praises Van Buren's message, 137; on Aroostook crisis, 167; is appointed postmaster general, 205; in campaign of 1840, 205
Niles' Register, 40, 202
Northeastern boundary dispute: affecting Maine and New Brunswick, 163–169; arising from Treaty of Paris (1783), 163; and "rivers question," 163, 164, 169; American claims in, 163–164; and Webster-Ashburton Treaty, 163, 169; British claims in, 164; Maine's position on, 165; and Aroostook War, 166
Norvell, John, 103
Nullification: South Carolina on, 11; Jackson's response to, 11; Van Buren on, 33

Ogle, Charles: and caricature of Van Buren, 196–197
Osceola, 182, 183
Otis, Harrison Gray, 94

Palmerston, Lord: on slave brigs, 153–154; on Van Buren, 161; on McLeod case, 163
Panic of 1837. *See* Economic cycle; Resumption; Suspension
Papineau, Louis Joseph, 157
Parker, Richard B., 115
Party organization: and democratic forces, 5–6; and era of good feelings, 7; in New York, 25–26; and politics of conflict, 36; Democratic emphasis on, 89, 94; Whigs ambivalent toward, 92–93; and Whig efforts in New York, 96–97; matures by 1840, 192
Patton, John, 110
Paulding, James K.: on republicanism, 88; on New York elections, 97; appointed secretary of the navy, 115–116; background of, 176–177; on problems of discipline, 177–178; and issue of executive independence, 178; on steam frigates, 179; and exploring expedition, 179–180; in campaign of 1840, 204–205
Pickens, Francis, 77
Poinsett, Joel R.: appointed secretary of war, 39; favors national bank, 70; favors Texas annexation, 151; in Canadian crisis, 159; on the exploring expedition, 176, 179, 180; and National Institution, 180; early career of, 180–181; his marriage, 181; on party politics, 181; rejects truce with Seminoles, 184; and role in Indian removal, 185; on frontier defense, 187; on enlarging army, 188–189; on

reform of militia, 188–189; final reports of, 189; in campaign of 1840, 204

Polk, James K.: presidency of, compared to Van Buren's, xii, 210; chosen Speaker, 74–75; and strategy on divorce bill, 110; runs for governor, 131; is elected governor, 141; is mentioned for vice-president, 201, 202; and election of 1844, 210

Post Office Department: reforms in, 127, 172; operations of, 171–175; grows under Van Buren, 172; its problems with contractors, 172–173; rate strategy of, 173

Presidential elections: of 1824, 7–8; of 1828, 8–9; of 1832, 10; of 1836, 16–19; of 1840, 191–207; outcome of, in 1840, 206–207; of 1844, 210

Presidential messages of Van Buren: Inaugural Address, 39–42; special-session message, 70–74; first annual message, 101–102; second annual message, 126; third annual message, 134–137; fourth annual message, 208–209

Presidential power: growth of, under Jackson, 12–13; and censure of Jackson, 13; Van Buren on, 32, 41; and divorce proposal, 70; and Post Office Department, 174, 175; and Navy Department, 178

Presidential style: in "Specie Circular" decision, 51; and party leadership, 53–54; based on fidelity to party, 59–60; and the divorce proposal, 70; and executive departments, 71

Preston, William, 91, 152

Radicals, 7, 8
Randolph, Ellen, 23
Randolph, John, 14, 23
Raymond, Daniel, 65
Religious revivalism: and democratic forces, 4–5; conservative responses to, 5; and influence on political campaigning, 6, 192

Republicanism: Jefferson on, 28–29; and "history of parties," 28–29, 36; Van Buren on, 29, 40; in divorce proposal, 73–74, 87; Democrats on, 87–90; Whigs on, 91–93; defined, 93–94; Conservative Democrats on, 94–95; stressed in third annual message, 136–137; featured in final debate over divorce, 141–142; and Whigs in 1840, 197–198; and Democrats in 1840, 205–206

Republican party: of Jefferson and Madison, 7; of "planters" and "plain republicans," 7, 27; of 1850s, 209

Resumption: impact of Van Buren's policies on, 107–108; and effect of English credit on, 108

Richmond (Va.) Enquirer: as Democratic paper in Virginia, 28; opposes "Specie Circular," 49; opposes divorce proposal, 69; equivocations of, 113; on currency issue in 1840, 203

Richmond (Va.) Junto, 68

Ritchie, Thomas: as editor of Richmond Enquirer, 27; opposes divorce proposal, 69; reassesses positions, 113; opposes militia plan, 189

Ritner, Joseph, 194

"Rivers question," 163, 164, 169. See also Northeastern boundary dispute

Rives, William C.: vice-presidential nomination eludes, 16; turns down secretary of war post, 38; and bill repealing "Specie Circular," 48; urges Van Buren to rescind "Specie Circular," 49; and Conservative defection, 63–64; Ritchie on, 69; offers amendment to divorce bill, 76; on defeat of divorce bill, 77; supports deposit banks, 83, 106; and Van Buren's trip to Virginia, 113–114; on Biddle bond deal, 127–128; fails to be reelected, 139

Rives bill, 48
Roane, William, 128
Rough Hewer (Albany, N.Y.), 203
Rucker, Edmund, 16
Ruiz, José, 154, 155, 156
Rush, Benjamin, 196
Russell, Lord John, 157

Safety Fund System, 96, 117
St. Lawrence Republican, 69
Scott, Winfield: and foreign crises, 147; on Canadian frontier, 159, 162; his role in northeastern boundary crisis, 167–168; and Unionists in South Carolina, 181; on Cherokee removal, 185–186; as a presidential candidate, 194

Seminole War: background of, 181–182; under Van Buren, 182–185; problem of Negroes in, 182, 183, 184; Jesup's role in, 182–184; and Dade massacre, 182; cost of, 185

Sergeant, John, 82, 83, 92, 144

Seward, William H.: and Whig coalition in New York, 96–97, 193–194; is elected governor, 125; snubs Van Buren, 132; and McLeod case, 163

Shepard, Charles, 142
Silvester, Francis, 22

Singleton, Angelica, 24
Skidmore, Thomas, 97
Slade, William, 109–110
Slave brigs: *Comet, Encomium,* and *Enterprise,* 153; and issue with England, 153–154; settlement for, 154
Smith, Oliver H., 94
Smithsonian Institution, 180
Social reform: and democratic forces, 5; Emerson on, 5. *See also* Abolitionism
Special deposits: nature of, 64; as a compromise feature, 101, 102; with Biddle's bank, 116
Specie: influx of, in 1830s, 45; impact of, on bank notes, 46. *See also* Currency; Hard money
"Specie Circular": hard money intent of, 15, 47, 51; its effect on currency, 47; political debate over, 48–49; its effect on deposit banks, 50; retained by Van Buren, 52; and divorce proposal, 63, 64; repeal of, 109
Spring-Rice, Thomas, 161
State banks: rapid increase in number of, 3, 44; and conservative principles before 1812, 44; change in nature of, 45; and contraction of currency, 46; and suspension, 54; impact of divorce on, 64–67; check on, by national bank, 67; and bankruptcy measure, 67–68; blamed for crisis, 71; and efforts to resume, 107–108; resumption of, 108; legislation on, 116–118; Van Buren's call to regulate, 133, 135–136
State debts: on internal improvements, 44, 138; assumption of, by federal government, 137–138; Democrats oppose assumption of, 137–138; Whigs favor assumption of, 143. *See also* Economic cycle
Stevens, Thaddeus, 194
Stevenson, Andrew: as minister to England, 153; on issue of slave brigs, 153–154; on *Caroline* affair, 162
Stockton and Stokes, 174–175
Story, Joseph, 156
Strange, Robert, 87, 137
Suffolk System, 120
Supreme Court: its decision in *Charles River Bridge* case, 12; and *Briscoe* v. *Kentucky,* 12; on executive power, 174, 175, 178
Surplus, Treasury: causes for, 12, 45; distribution of, 47; and impact on currency, 47; and postponement of distribution, 74
Suspension: in 1837, 54; impact of English credit on, 54; economic effects of, 55; political impact of, 55–56; in 1839, 133; political impact of, 134; discredits Biddle bank, 143

Swartwout, Samuel: and defalcation of Treasury funds, 125–26; Van Buren on, 125

Tallmadge, Nathaniel P.: praises credit system, 15, 45, 83, 84; opposes "Specie Circular," 48, 53; leads Conservative defection, 63–64; and radical reading of divorce, 64; antiparty views of, 94; reelected as a Whig, 138
Taney, Roger B.: in the bank war, 13; at Van Buren's inauguration, 21; favors "Specie Circular," 50; upholds executive power, 178
Taylor, John W., 27
Taylor, Zachary, 183
Tecumseh, 16, 202
Texas: and battle of San Jacinto, 14, 148; and antislavery debate, 14; Van Buren opposes annexation of, 18; Jackson's policies on, 148–149; Van Buren's course on, 149–152; seeks admission to the Union, 150–151. *See also* Mexico
Thomas, Philip, 77
Thompson, Smith, 175
Thompson, Waddy, Jr., 84
Throop, Enos: advises Van Buren on divorce proposal, 62–63; favors compromise on divorce, 100; on resumption, 107–108
Tilden, Elam, 114
Tilden, Samuel, 70
Tocqueville, Alexis de, 1, 4
Treasury: operations of, during suspension, 56–58, 101; operations of, under divorce, 66; report of, 101; and bond deal with Biddle, 116. *See also* Surplus, Treasury
Treasury notes: nature of, 66–67; Van Buren calls for, 74; Calhoun on, 80
Turney, Hopkins L., 110
Tyler, John: and Seminole War, 185; is nominated for vice-president, 194; is read out of the Whig party, 200

Union: Jackson on, 33–34; as a "great experiment," 40–41; Van Buren's concept of, 41–42, 201, 209
United States Telegraph, 8, 10

Van Buren, Abraham (father), 22
Van Buren, Abraham (son): as private secretary to his father, 24
Van Buren, Hannah Hoes (mother), 22
Van Buren, Hannah Hoes (wife), 23

Van Buren, John (son), 161
Van Buren, Martin: and Jackson's presidency, xi–xii; and Polk's presidency, xii, 210; on party organization, 6; and election of 1828, 8–9, 29–30; and rivalry with Calhoun, 10, 30–31; is nominated for vice–president, 10; is nominated for president, 16; and election of 1836, 18–19; opposes abolitionism, 18–19, 41; inauguration of, 21–22; description of, 22; early years of, 22–23; law career of, 23–24; social style of, 24–25; as a "politician by trade," 25; political career of, in New York, 25–26; and ideas about party, 25–28; as a conservative on policies, 26; visits Monticello, 28; on party ideology, 28–29; as secretary of state, 30; as minister to England, 30; and Jackson, 31–32; his influence on Jackson's policies, 32–35; on coalition with Webster, 34–35; in bank war, 35–36; on Jackson's views of party, 35–37; as conservative broker, 37; cabinet selection by, 38–39; on patronage, 39; inaugural address of, 39–42; on "experiment" of Union, 40–41, 93; "Specie Circular" decision of, 49–53; and relations with Rives, 53–54; calls for special session, 57; on Treasury operations after suspension, 57–59; his reasons for divorce proposal, 62–63; and moderate interpretation of divorce, 68; special-session message of, 70–74; as described by friend, 78; reflects on defeat of divorce bill, 78; and political issue of divorce, 95–96; and New York elections in 1837, 96–97; on eve of 1837/1838 session, 95–100; on resumption, 100, 108; first annual message of, 101–102; and relation to Cuthbert, 107; on Biddle, 108; on Cilley duel, 110; and postmortem of 1837/1838 session, 112; visits Virginia, 113; is criticized for his leadership, 114–115; new cabinet appointments of, 116; on state banks, 117, 120; and crisis of his presidency, 120–121; on New York elections in 1838, 125; on Swartwout, 126, 127; wavers on divorce proposal, 129; on Clay as possible foe, 130; reaffirms commitment to divorce, 130, 133; and new patronage policy, 130–131; takes trip to New York, 131–133; third annual message of, 134–137; on English credit, 135, 136; praised for Spartan virtues, 137; his pragmatic course on divorce, 140–141; and paradox of course, 145; and inaugural hope for peace, 147;

on Texas, 148–151; on Mexico, 150, 152–153; on slave brigs, 153–154; on *Amistad* case, 155–157; responds to *Caroline* crisis, 158, 160; issues neutrality proclamations, 159, 160; and Lord Palmerston, 161, 162; on Maine boundary claim, 165; political problems of, with Maine, 165–166; responds to Aroostook crisis, 166–167; and final effort to resolve boundary dispute, 168–169; defends postmaster general, 174, 175; on executive independence, 175; rejects truce with Seminoles, 184; on Indian policy, 186–187; on Poinsett's defense plans, 187, 189; anticipates reelection campaign, 191; as pictured by Whigs in 1840, 196–197; on slavery, 201; on vice–presidential nomination, 202; on log cabin campaign, 204; role of, in campaign of 1840, 205–206; his defeat predicted, 206; assesses election results, 207–208; fourth annual message, 208–209; and personal style after defeat, 209–210
Vanderbilt, Cornelius, 173
Van Rensselaer, Rensselaer, 158, 159
Virginia: on the vice-presidential nomination, 16, 38; as one of Van Buren's power bases, 27; is divided over divorce proposal, 69; Van Buren's trip to, 113–114; Conservatives in, 113; and cabinet appointments, 115

Walker, Robert, 81, 141
Wall, Garrett, 137
War Department: under Van Buren, 180–189; problems of discipline in, 180; and problems of frontier defense, 187; and enlargement of army, 187–188; and Poinsett's militia plan, 188
Washington (D.C.) *Globe:* becomes administration paper, 10; and strategy on divorce proposal, 68; loses election as House printer, 75; on republicanism, 89; and compromise on divorce, 101, 112, 114; elected as House printer, 139; on naval discipline, 177; and "omnibus of lies," 197; on currency issue in campaign of 1840, 203; assesses election results, 207
Webster, Daniel: as candidate in 1836, 16; flirts with Jackson's administration, 34–35; focuses on currency issue, 82; and New York elections, 97; and pro-Union speech against divorce, 105–106; offers amendment to Deposit Act, 111; favors insolvency measure, 143–144; against

annexing Texas, 149; on *Creole* case, 154; is suggested for special mission to England, 168; in campaign of 1840, 193, 198
Webster-Ashburton Treaty, 163, 169
Weed, Thurlow: and Whig coalition in New York, 96–97, 193–194; mocks Van Buren for "non committalism," 130; on Van Buren's New York trip, 132; in campaign of 1840, 192, 195, 196; on currency issue, 199; on gag resolution, 201
Weller, John, 142
Welles, Gideon, 69
Whig party: on party organization, 5–6; constituencies in, 14–15, 86; and strategy in 1836, 16–18; responds to suspension, 55–56; impact of divorce proposal on, 61, 62; and strategy in debate over divorce, 75, 83–85, 142–144; and praise for credit system, 83–85; on republicanism, 91–93; antiparty tendency in, 93–95; and maturity of, in 1840, 192, 198; and Harrisburg convention, 193–194; and efforts for unity, 195–196; and image of Van Buren, 196–197; and economic issues in campaign of 1840, 198–199; southern strategy of, 200–202; on abolitionist petitions, 201–202; and voter fraud in New York, 206; attracts first-time voters, 207
White, Hugh L.: as Whig candidate in 1836, 16, 19

Whitney, Reuben, 64
Wilkes, Charles, 176, 179
Woodbury, Levi: retained as secretary of the Treasury, 38; on currency inflation, 46; on "Specie Circular," 52; and Treasury operations during suspension, 57–58; on funds receivable, 66; on state banks, 67; favors compromise on divorce, 100–101; report of, 101; on resumption, 108; on bond deal with Biddle, 117, 127, 129; and Swartwout's defalcation, 127; assesses Democratic strength in House, 133; on *Amistad* case, 155, 157; in campaign of 1840, 204
Wright, Frances, 97
Wright, Silas: on "Specie Circular," 49; on suspension, 56; and doubts on divorce proposal, 63; on New York politics, 69; on Senate strategy, 75–76; on republican virtue, 90; and divorce bill at 1837/1838 session, 102–103; accepts Cuthbert's amendment, 106; amends Deposit Act, 111–112; and trip to Virginia, 113; grows weary of divorce fight, 114; on divorce bill in 1838/1839 session, 126; opposes retreat on divorce proposal, 129, 130; and divorce bill in 1839/1840 session, 138; in campaign of 1840, 202